Stella Gordon

IN
SEARCH
OF THE
SUN

IN SEARCH OF THE SUN

A Woman's Courageous Victory Over Lupus

HENRIETTA ALADJEM
& PETER H. SCHUR, M.D.

With a Foreword by Arnold S. Relman, M.D.,
Editor of *The New England Journal of Medicine*

Charles Scribner's Sons
NEW YORK

Charles Scribner's Sons

Macmillan Publishing Company

866 Third Avenue, New York, NY 10022

Collier Macmillan Canada, Inc.

Library of Congress Cataloging-in-Publication Data

Aladjem, Henrietta, 1917–

 In search of the sun: a woman's courageous victory over lupus/

 Henrietta Aladjem and Peter H. Schur; with a foreword by Arnold S. Relman.

  p. cm.

 Portions of this book were originally published as: The Sun is my enemy.

 Bibliography: p.

 Includes index.

 ISBN 0-684-18759-0

 1. Aladjem, Henrietta, 1917– —Health. 2. Lupus erythematosus, Systemic—Patients—United
States—Biography. 3. Lupus erythematosus, Systemic—Popular works. I. Schur, Peter H.
II. Aladjem,
Henrietta, 1917– Sun is my enemy. III. Title.

 [DNLM: 1. Aladjem, Henrietta 1917– . 2. Lupus Erythmatosus,
Systemic—personal narratives. WR 152 A316i]

RC924.5.L85A385 1988

362.1'9677—dc19

[B]

DNLM/DLC

for Library of Congress   87-28492

                                CIP

Macmillan books are available at special discounts for bulk purchases
for sales promotions, premiums, fund-raising, or educational use.
For details, contact:

Special Sales Director

Macmillan Publishing Company

866 Third Avenue

New York, NY 10022

10 9 8 7 6 5 4 3 2 1

Printed in the United States of America

To the late Emily Heller,
who fought gallantly against the ravages of lupus.
Her life was an inspiration to me.
—H. A.

Contents

         the Mountains in His Chest: The Patient's Story   142
22 Back in Wellesley: The Patient's Story   149
23 Professor Dr. Liuben Popoff: The Patient's Story   157
24 "Girls Don't Whistle": The Patient's Story   177
25 Peter Bent Brigham Hospital, 1970: The Patient's Story   181
26 Paris, 1968: The Patient's Story   192
27 Emotional Healing: The Physician's Point of View   204
28 A Dialogue: Between the Patient and the Physician   211
29 Questions Asked by Lupus Patients:
         The Physician's Point of View   215

    Glossary   229
    References   239
    Lupus Foundation of America, Inc.   243
         Constituent Chapters   243
         International Associates   253
    Index   257

Foreword

This is a book for general readers about a mysterious disease called systemic lupus erythematosus—a relatively uncommon, but not rare, disorder mainly affecting young women. What makes this book different from others of the same genre is that it is written independently by a patient and a physician, both of whom give their own perspective on the disease.

The patient, Mrs. Henrietta Aladjem, suffered for years before her illness was identified, and for many more until—after numerous therapeutic trials—it finally went into remission. She provides us with an interesting and detailed personal diary of the impact of this disease upon her life. Interspersed through this story are chapters by Dr. Peter H. Schur, an expert on lupus and a wise general physician, who tells us all about the disease and how doctors deal with it. He also provides insight into the way good physicians practice their profession. At the end, doctor and patient talk about doctor-patient relations and what each can contribute to the diagnosis and management of difficult clinical problems.

Like all good books, this one is about much more than its immediate subject. It is about lupus, but it is also about the human spirit under adversity and how doctors and patients can work together to sustain hope and promote recovery. I found it illuminating and engrossing, and I suspect that many other readers will, too.

ARNOLD S. RELMAN, M.D.

Preface

In Search of the Sun is the story of two persons, a patient and a physician. It is the saga of a woman who had (has) systemic lupus erythematosus (SLE), or lupus, as it is commonly known. It is the story of a woman who, despite the illness and its accompanying fatigue, did not succumb to apathy or lose hope. She has enjoyed marriage, motherhood, and social responsibilities by tapping into the inner resolve that is in all of us and has applied her strength and energies to conquer her own disease and to aid other lupus sufferers.

This is also the story of a physician, both scientist and clinician, who has seen and dealt with a large number of lupus patients and has come to recognize the important difference between illness and disease. Illness is what a patient perceives he or she has, and disease is what the physician determines is affecting the patient. The difference is a critical one when dealing with lupus, whose psychological affects are often as debilitating and deserve as much attention as the physical symptoms.

Mrs. Aladjem and I have worked together to understand lupus from both the patient's and physician's point of view. This joint effort has been facilitated by cooperation of the Brigham and Women's Hospital. As a founder of the Lupus Foundation of America and a former SLE patient who has been in remission for twenty-five years, Mrs. Aladjem has been in the ideal position to help the physician understand the difficulties a patient has coping with a chronic illness. We have both found that patients more freely reveal their intimate concerns to each other rather than to their physician no matter how trusting their relationship. When Mrs. Aladjem's publishers asked her to revise, update, and write a sequel to her first book on lupus, *The*

Sun Is My Enemy, she suggested I contribute as coauthor the scientific and humanistic perspective that would further our efforts at improving the knowledge of lupus from both our points of view.

This book is also a medical commentary on Henrietta Aladjem's case history, a commentary that I feel privileged and challenged to provide. This book, then, affords the reader a rare opportunity to explore a case history as seen through the eyes of the patient and the physician. However, it is a book that transcends our individual experiences, for we have seen, talked to, and corresponded with hundreds of lupus patients, whose experiences are also noted in the book. Mrs. Aladjem and I hope that this effort will encourage mutual respect and understanding by both patients and physicians for their roles in dealing with the emotional, physical, and medical manifestations of a chronic illness.

In Search of the Sun is organized to lead the reader through the evolution of a disease, from its early symptoms to diagnosis, treatment, rehabilitation, recovery, and finally remission.

What goes through a physician's mind as he sees a disease unfold and engulf a human being? How does he respond to each symptom, physical manifestation, and emotional reaction? What can he do to reverse the illness, bring it under control, and help effect a remission? What can he do to help the patient accept the illness with all of its manifestations, cope with its frustrations, and channel psychic energy to develop a sense of well-being and regain the confidence to pick up the pieces and resume a normal life? What does it feel like being that patient?

Many years ago I read *The Sun Is My Enemy* and was moved by Mrs. Aladjem's compelling story. I am now rereading it as a case history and find both old and new themes to consider in the analysis and treatment of lupus. Despite the great scientific advances in immunologic and lupus research, what remains constant and unchanging is the psychological response to illness and disease by both patient and physician and the critical need for a good patient-doctor relationship.

This chronicle begins with a description of lupus.

PETER H. SCHUR, M.D.

Acknowledgments

The authors express appreciation to the many people who have lupus for candidly sharing their concerns and hopes with us. We are equally indebted to the many physicians whose combined knowledge and experience added to the medical accuracy of this book.

Peter H. Schur would like to thank his physician-parents, his entire family, and the close friends who have textured his life, enabling him to draw on those relationships and write a book that is compassionate to the human condition. He is also grateful for time given by Naomi Storm for fruitful discussion and keen insight on the humanistic point of view. He also appreciates the excellent typing skills of Joanne Davis, who helped complete this manuscript on schedule.

Henrietta Aladjem is grateful to her two daughters, Ingrid Neresian and Martha Climo, for editing parts of the manuscript and helping her with the English grammar. She is grateful to her entire family, and to Vicki Kroke of the *Boston Globe* for helping to complete the story in its last few moments.

The authors owe a great deal to the enthusiasm of Elizabeth Rapoport, our editor at Charles Scribner's Sons, who undertook the task of organizing this manuscript.

Introduction: What Is Lupus?

Any book dealing with lupus must begin with a basic understanding of the disease—its description, the methods of diagnosis, and its treatment. This book is no exception. I have been treating people with lupus and conducting research on this disease for almost thirty years. What follows is a synthesis of the clinical experience and research conducted by my colleagues and myself.

Medical terms are defined either within the text or in the glossary.

GENERAL CONSIDERATIONS

SLE is a chronic, inflammatory disease of unknown cause that may affect the skin, joints, kidneys, lungs, nervous system, tissue linings (serous membranes), and other organs of the body. Patients with SLE develop distinct immunologic abnormalities, especially antinuclear antibodies (ANAs), and the clinical course of their illness is characterized by periods of remission and relapses that can be acute or chronic.

INCIDENCE AND ETIOLOGY

SLE occurs in approximately 1 per 400–2,000 population and appears more frequently in blacks, Chinese, and some Indian tribes than in whites. It develops nine times more frequently among females than males, although boys and girls up to the age of adolescence are affected almost equally. The majority of patients are first discovered to have SLE while in their twenties or thirties, although

SLE has been diagnosed in patients ranging from two to ninety-seven years old!

Although the cause of SLE remains unknown, we do know that certain factors trigger the disease in those prone to develop it. Ultraviolet B (and occasionally A) radiation from sunlight or fluorescent lights often leads to the prompt appearance of the characteristic facial "butterfly" rash or a rash on other exposed skin. Infections, surgery, certain drugs, and as yet undiscovered factors may also trigger the symptoms of SLE. In addition, procainamide, hydralazine, hydantoins, and other drugs may precipitate a lupuslike illness.

The preponderance of the disease in females suggests that endocrine or hormonal factors may influence the development of SLE. Birth control pills, which inhibit ovulation, may exacerbate SLE, and breakdown products (metabolites) of the female hormone estrogen are found in high levels in SLE patients. Lupus is sometimes seen in men with Klinefelter's syndrome (men who possess an extra X chromosome).

Genetic factors appear to make people prone to develop SLE. Connective-tissue disorders (including SLE), and immune-system abnormalities appear in up to 10 percent of relatives of patients with SLE, although they are observed in less than 1 percent of the general population. There is a 25–67 percent concordance rate of SLE in identical twins. Research has shown an increased frequency of specific genetic markers—identifying sites on the individual's chromosomes —in SLE patients vis à vis their frequency in the general population.

Lupus erythematosus (LE) is characterized particularly by autoimmune phenomena, that is, the presence of antibodies to a patient's own cells, cell constituents, and proteins. Normally the body makes antibodies to foreign substances known as antigens as part of its protective immune response. In an autoimmune syndrome the body perceives its own tissues as foreign and manufactures antibodies against them. Medically we refer to these phenomenon as a loss of self-tolerance. This loss may be due in part to such components of the immune system as overactive B lymphocytes, overactive helper T lymphocytes, and/or a loss of suppressor T lymphocytes. This last defect may reflect the body's manufacture of antibodies to suppressor T lymphocytes. Autoantibodies react with these "self" antigens to form immune complexes, which can build up in the tissue and cause inflammation and injury.

It is possible that SLE may be caused by a virus. Loss of tolerance may be influenced by viral infections. Structures resembling viral particles (nucleocapsids) have been found frequently in tissue lining (endothelial) cells in SLE patients. The levels of antibodies to certain viruses are elevated in SLE sera, but no one virus has been implicated. The presence, in many SLE patients, of antibodies to double-stranded RNA suggests reaction to an RNA virus infection. "C"-type RNA virus particles have been found in lupus mice; other viruses, including DNA and RNA viruses, can provoke the development of autoantibodies and nephritis in mice with lupus. Experiments on dogs with lupus also indicate the possible presence of an SLE virus.

These data suggest that an abnormal immune response in genetically predisposed SLE patients may alter the delicate balance between immunity and tolerance and result in the development of antibodies to the contents of the body's cells released during inflammation or chronic viral infection or to new antigens on those cells that result from viral infection or transformation. The abnormal immune response may be triggered by infections, ultraviolet (UV) light, drugs, pregnancy, stress, or other factors. Variation in the genetic or abnormal immune process may result in different clinical expression of SLE, including arthritis, rash, or nephritis.

MECHANISM OF TISSUE INFLAMMATION, INJURY, AND PATHOLOGY

Some of the manifestations of SLE appear to result from the formation of antigen-antibody immune complexes. Such complexes may develop in the circulatory system or form on cells or tissue surfaces. Patients with SLE may have a defect in clearing such complexes from the circulation, resulting in their deposition in the kidneys, skin, brain, and elsewhere. During immune-complex formation and deposition the complement system—part of the protective immune response—becomes activated and fixed, releasing certain factors that attract phagocytic cells to the immune deposits. The phagocytic cells function to digest and eliminate the immune complexes. The process of phagocytosis results in the release of enzymes that also injure cells and tissue. Complement fixation also results in reduced blood levels of complement. These low levels are an indirect measure of the disease's activity.

These mechanisms appear to cause specific tissue and/or organ injury:

- Biopsies of skin lesions demonstrate changes characteristic either of SLE or discoid LE. Antibodies and complement may be deposited there as well as in blood vessels.
- Lymph nodes in patients with active disease may show nonspecific changes such as an increased number of cells. The thymus often shows atrophy.
- Nonbacterial adhesions may develop on heart valves. The heart may be affected by vasculitis.
- Brain changes are usually minimal and may show white blood cells clustering about small blood vessels or microhemorrhages.
- Renal lesions are highly variable, from mild to severe. The mildest form of renal lesions, called mesangial nephritis, consists of deposits of immune complexes and complement without any other histological abnormality and little if any urinary abnormalities. The most common renal lesion, called focal glomerulonephritis, is characterized by a minimal local increase of white blood cells. Immune complexes and complement are found in the lesions. In contrast, diffuse proliferative glomerulonephritis is characterized by a marked increase in white blood cells infiltrating the kidney and usually some scarring. Immune complexes and complement clumps are found throughout the kidney. Some kidneys are found to have only a membranous glomerulonephritis, with few white blood cells but considerable thickening of the basement membrane of the glomerulus. Fine granules of antibody and complement are noted there.

CLINICAL MANIFESTATIONS

The typical patient with well-advanced lupus is a young woman exhibiting fever (unrelated to infection), weight loss, arthralgia/arthritis, a facial butterfly rash, pleural effusion (fluid accumulation around the lungs) and nephritis. Since this chronic disease is best characterized by periods of remission and activity, these symptoms may wax and wane. With better methods of detection (ANA tests), many more patients with less obvious, fewer, and more varied symptoms and signs are now being diagnosed. The frequencies of various symptoms are listed in table 1, on page xxxiii. At the onset, only one or more organ systems may be involved. However, most patients will have only a few symptoms at the same time or during the course of their illness.

Musculoskeletal System

Most patients complain of pain in their joints at some time. Commonly the fingers, hands, wrists, knees, ankles, and elbows are affected. Arthritis, that is, inflammation, of joints is observed less frequently. Although slight deformities at the knuckles and other finger joints may occur, major joint swelling and deformities are uncommon. X rays of joints rarely demonstrate abnormalities. Muscle pain is a frequent complaint and is occasionally accompanied by muscle atrophy. The bones are rarely affected, but aseptic necrosis of the hip is seen in over 10 percent of patients, especially in those receiving corticosteroid therapy. Infected joints (septic arthritis) have been observed.

Skin (Mucocutaneous) Manifestations

The classic butterfly rash is seen in less than half the patients with SLE. There may be only a blush and swelling or a scaly red (erythematosus), pimply (maculopapular) rash on both cheeks and the bridge of the nose after exposure to the sun. This may clear spontaneously, only to recur. Other skin areas, particularly those exposed to the sun, may react similarly. Discoid lesions differ in that they scale (hyperkeratosis), are associated with follicular plugging, and can result in atrophy, scarring, telangiectasia, hyperpigmentation, or hypopigmentation (vitiligo). Skin problems may also occur on the forehead, earlobes, and scalp, resulting in hair loss (alopecia). Patchy hair loss is frequent in active disease and usually reversible, but discoid lupus with scarring can lead to permanent partial baldness. Subacute cutaneous LE is characterized by either annular or papulosquamous lesions. Periungual erythema (redness at the base of the nails) is found in about 10 percent of patients with SLE. Livedo reticularis of arms and legs is common. Raynaud's phenomenon, an inhibition of circulation, may occur in both fingers and toes. Small ulcerations, signifying an underlying vasculitis, often develop on the fingertips and may progress to gangrene. Painless ulcers can be seen inside the mouth and nose and on the gums. Purpura and ecchymoses (bruises) may reflect an underlying blood platelet and clotting problem, renal insufficiency, the side effects of corticosteroids, or vasculitis. Hives (urticaria) may be present. Lupus profundus (panniculitis) may cause subcutaneous atrophy.

Renal Disease

The deposition of immune complexes in the kidney (defined by electron microscopy or immunofluorescence) is found in most SLE patients, while clinical renal involvement (i.e., abnormal urinalysis or renal function) is found in only about one-half of SLE patients and usually occurs within two years of the onset of symptoms. Acute nephritis or the nephrotic syndrome may be the presenting manifestation of SLE. The most common abnormality is minimal protein in the urine (proteinuria) or red blood cells in the urine (hematuria), or both. This lesion generally responds well to therapy initially but may recur in mild form or as more severe renal involvement. Acute lupus glomerulonephritis occurs less often and is associated with varying degrees of white blood cells in the urine (pyuria), hematuria, proteinuria, fluid retention, edema, hypertension, and elevated levels of BUN (azotemia). The nephrotic syndrome is characterized by proteinuria and fluid retention and is frequently associated with normal serum cholesterol levels. The finding of pyuria with fever in patients with SLE, especially those receiving corticosteroids, may reflect a urinary-tract infection rather than lupus nephritis.

Most patients recover well from attacks of acute nephritis, but usually some proteinuria and decreased kidney function persist. Some patients have recurrences, and some develop chronic glomerulonephritis with hypertension and fixed azotemia and proteinuria.

Cardiovascular Manifestations

The lining of the inside of the heart (endocardium), heart muscle (myocardium), or lining of the outside of the heart (pericardium) is involved in nearly half the patients with SLE. Precordial chest pain may be caused by either pleurisy or pericarditis, or chest-wall tension. Electrocardiographic (EKG) changes are not uncommon. Recurrent thrombophlebitis may be the first manifestation of SLE. Occlusion of major arteries occurs rarely, but coronary artery disease is becoming an increasing problem for the young person on chronic steroids.

Pulmonary Involvement

Pleurisy is common in SLE and is generally detected by the physician hearing a friction rub between the pleura and a variable amount of fluid accumulation in the pleural space. However, some pleural effusions may be painless. Chest X-ray abnormalities may be difficult to distinguish from infections. The involvement can progress to lung collapse but rarely to marked pulmonary insufficiency and cyanosis. Pulmonary-function tests may appear somewhat abnormal even though the patient may be symptom-free. Most pulmonary symptoms related to SLE respond well to intensive corticosteroid therapy. Pulmonary infection should always be excluded as a cause of pulmonary symptoms prior to initiating steroid therapy.

Neurological and Psychological Manifestations

Many patients have heard that lupus is an invariably fatal disease; this understandably leads to great anxiety. Similarily, when a patient learns that he or she has arthritis, ungrounded fears of disabling deformities arise. The natural fears and anxieties that accompany chronic illness should not be confused with organic neurological disturbances. The latter may manifest as behavioral disturbances, including hyperirritability, confusion, hallucinations, obsessional or paranoid reactions, or frank organic psychosis. The psychosis of SLE may also be difficult to differentiate from a steroid-induced psychosis; other symptoms and signs of active SLE usually accompany the organic disease. The electroencephalograph (EEG) is often abnormal in SLE patients with central nervous system (CNS) involvement. Brain scans are usually normal, and examination of cerebrospinal fluid (CSF) is not very diagnostic. Convulsions occur in about 15 percent of patients. Other less frequent neurological findings include peripheral neuropathy, hemiparesis, motor aphasia, ptosis (eyelid droop), diplopia (double vision), nystagmus (rapid movements of the eyeball), chorea (involuntary muscle movement), transverse myelitis, and migraine.

Gastrointestinal Manifestations

Anorexia, nausea, vomiting, or abdominal pain is common. Their cause is obscure, but may be from inflammation of the lining of tissues within the abdomen (peritonitis), enteritis, inflammation of the pancreas (pancreatitis), or an obstruction of the intestine (paralytic ileus). Diarrhea and blood in the stool are uncommon. The liver is sometimes enlarged because of chronic passive congestion, but this is usually transitory. Aspirin therapy may cause abnormalities of liver-function tests, although liver disease is not present. Liver biopsy may be normal or show fatty infiltration and/or fibrosis.

Lymph Nodes and Spleen

Lymph nodes are characteristically enlarged but not tender in patients with active disease. The enlarged nodes have been mistaken for lymphoma. Spleen enlargement is seen in about 15 percent of patients.

Menses and Pregnancy

Menses are frequently irregular or heavy, or both. In patients with circulating anticoagulants (antibodies to clotting factors), bleeding may be very heavy. Although pregnancy carries some increased risk of miscarriage in the first trimester, most SLE patients without renal disease carry to term. However, there is a risk of postpartum exacerbation of the disease. Infants of SLE mothers may have congenital heart block, especially those with anti-Ro antibodies.

Prognosis

Until recently the natural course of untreated SLE was considered to be very bleak. The average patient was considred to have, at best, a few years to live. The development of the LE cell test in 1948 and the ANA test in the 1950s altered this situation dramatically. Patients having mild forms of SLE were more easily diagnosed and benefited from the concurrent development of improved forms of therapy. The disease in most patients is characterized by periods of remissions and relapses, which may be protracted or brief. Individuals usually have recurrent symptoms such as arthritis, pleurisy, nephritis, or rashes. However, variable symptoms and signs may develop years apart. If nephritis develops, it generally does so early in the course of the disease.

The prognosis for patients seems to improve each year. Whereas in 1956 patients were given only a 50 percent chance of surviving four years, today they have a better than 90 percent chance to survive at least ten years. Prognosis still remains somewhat poorer for patients with diffuse proliferative glomerulonephritis and/or with CNS involvement. Patients who only present skin involvement have an excellent prognosis but have a 15 percent chance of eventually developing mild systemic disease—especially if they have ANAs.

LABORATORY FINDINGS (See table 2, p. xxxiv.)

Hematologic

Anemia occurs in many patients with SLE and is generally mild. Anemia may also be due to infection, renal insufficiency, iron deficiency, medications, or bleeding. Many patients have antibodies to red blood cells detected by the Coombs test, which does not necessarily cause (hemolytic) anemia. A low white-blood-cell count (leukopenia) occurs in at least one-half of patients. Lymphocyte-cell counts may be more suppressed than neutrophil counts. Complicating infections generally cause a rise in the white blood cell count either into the normal or elevated range. Corticosteroid therapy also causes an increase in white blood cell count. A low platelet count (thrombocytopenia), with or without purpura, may precede other symptoms of SLE by years or may disappear, leaving other manifestations of the disease. A circulating anticoagulant occurs in as many as 25 percent of patients with SLE but is infrequently associated with clinical bleeding. It may, however, be associated with excessive thromboses.

Joint (synovial) fluid is generally clear; its white blood cell content is generally low. Complement levels tend to be very low. CSF is abnormal in many patients: the total protein and gamma-globulin level may be elevated, and some mononuclear cells may be detected. These abnormalities are more likely with active CNS disease. The EEG and CT scans are commonly abnormal. Brain scans are usually normal.

Renal

Renal dysfunction occurs in over half of SLE patients. Most patients have only some impairment of concentrating ability, a few red and/or white blood cells in their urine, and perhaps some proteinuria (>0.5 gm per day). Active nephritis is defined when there is hematuria ($\geqq 5$ red blood cells per high-powered field [hpf]), pyuria ($\geqq 5$ white blood cells per hpf), red blood cell casts, increasing proteinuria, or a decreasing glomerular filtration rate. Hematuria and pyuria are rarely seen in lupus nephritis in remission.

Plasma Proteins

The erythrocyte sedimentation rate (ESR) is often elevated. Serum albumin levels are low, especially in the nephrotic syndrome. Gamma-globulin levels, elevated in many patients, may be low in nephrotics. Cryoglobulins, consisting of immunoglobulins and complement components, have been noted frequently, especially in patients with active nephritis.

Abnormal Immunologic Reactions

Biologic false-positive (BFP) tests for syphilis are noted in about 15 percent of patients with SLE, especially in those with circulating anticoagulants. The BFP may be the first laboratory clue to the diagnosis of SLE and may precede symptoms by years! Antibodies to clotting factors (circulating anticoagulant) are rarely the cause of overt bleeding. In SLE, rheumatoid factors are nonindicative of rheumatoid arthritis and are found in about 15 percent of patients with SLE, and more often in those with active lupus.

Most characteristic of SLE is the large number of autoantibodies that react with cells (red cells, platelets, polys, monocytes, B and T lymphocytes—including suppressor T lymphocytes) and their nuclear and cytoplasmic constituents. Of historical interest is the LE cell phenomenon. Since only about 25 percent of LE cell tests are positive in SLE patients, more sensitive tests have been developed for the detection of ANAs. Tests employing rodent liver or kidney cells or tissue-culture cell lines as the source of nuclei, detect ANA in over 99 percent of SLE patients. Different patterns of nuclear fluorescence reflect antibodies to different nuclear structures. The "homogeneous" or "diffuse" pattern reflects antibodies to nucleoprotein. The "peripheral," "rim," or "shaggy" pattern reflects primarily antibodies to DNA. The speckled pattern reflects antibodies to a group of RNA proteins, including "Sm," ribonucleoprotein (RNP), Ro and La. Each of these antigens contain unique RNAs. Sm has U1, 2, 4, 5, and 6 and RNP has only U1-RNA. Patients with antibodies to DNA or Sm are more likely to have renal disease; patients with antibodies to RNP are less likely to have renal disease; and patients with antibodies to Ro are likely to be very photosensitive. Antibodies to histones are seen particularly in drug-induced LE, but in SLE, as well.

Antibodies to these nuclear antigens are detected by several methods, including diffusion in agar, complement fixation, agglutination, immunofluorescence, radioimmunoassays, or enzyme immunoassays. The blood levels of antibodies to DNA tend to be higher during periods of clinical activity, especially of active nephritis, than during clinical remissions.

Blood complement levels are low in most patients with SLE at some time during their illness, especially when disease activity is present. Markedly low complement levels are seen primarily in patients with active lupus nephritis. The low levels reflect activation and fixation of complement components by circulating immune complexes. Serial determination of total complement levels (CH50) or of individual complement components (especially C3 and C4) may be useful in following and managing patients with SLE. SLE has also been seen in some patients with genetic deficiency of complement components.

Immune complexes may be detected in plasma and/or serum, particularly during flare-ups of SLE. Numerous tests have been devised for the detection of these complexes, which depend on their ability to react with added complement or rheumatoid factor or to react with cells. Different complexes may have different biologic activities, so one test result may be positive while another is negative. Thus, it is often necessary to follow a number of assays to assess patients critically.

Patients may be anergic, that is, they may fail to respond to antigen. In addition, they often have increased numbers of T helper cells and decreased numbers of T suppressor cells—especially during stages of active disease.

DIAGNOSIS

Lupus usually begins with either unexplained fever, fatigue, weight loss, anemia, photosensitive rash, arthralgia/arthritis, Raynaud's phenomenon, serositis, seizures, psychosis, or nephritis. SLE should also be suspected in individuals—especially in young females—who have unexplained fever, purpura, easy bruising, many enlarged lymph glands, hepatosplenomegaly, peripheral neuropathy, endocarditis, my-ocarditis, interstitial pneumonitis, peritonitis, or aseptic meningitis. On first examination, patients are frequently misdiagnosed as having rheumatoid arthritis, rheumatic fever (especially children), juvenile rheumatoid arthritis, glomerulonephritis, scleroderma, vasculitis, idiopathic thrombocytopenic purpura, lymphoma, anemia, or leukopenia.

The diagnosis of SLE can be made if any of the four or more of the following manifestations are present, serially or simultaneously, during any interval of observation—see table 3, on page xxxv.

The ANA test is the best screening test for SLE, since it is positive in virtually all SLE patients, and should be performed whenever SLE is suspected. However, the test is also positive in 68 percent of patients with Sjögren's syndrome, 40–75 percent of patients with scleroderma—especially those with a speckled pattern ANA—16 percent of patients with juvenile rheumatoid arthritis, and 25–50 percent of patients with rheumatoid arthritis—especially those with a diffuse pattern ANA. ANAs tend to be present in higher levels in patients with SLE than in those with other disorders. Antibodies to double-stranded DNA and to Sm are highly diagnostic of SLE, although found in only about 75 and 25 percent of patients, respectively. Antibodies to single-stranded DNA, nucleoprotein (NP), are found frequently in patients with SLE and rheumatoid arthritis, antibodies to RNP (ribonucleoprotein) are found frequently in patients with SLE and scleroderma. Antibodies to Ro (SS-A) and La (SS-B) are frequently found in patients with SLE or Sjögren's syndrome.

Skin biopsies of both inflamed and normal areas showing immune deposits at the dermal-epidermal junction are often useful in the diagnosis of lupus.

Some patients have clinical features of SLE, scleroderma, and dermatomyositis. The term mixed connective disease (MCTD) has been applied to some of these patients, as they appear to have a combination of clinical and laboratory findings. MCTD is characterized by diffuse polyarthritis and polyarthralgias, Raynaud's phenomenon, swollen hands, abnormal esophageal motility, and decreased pulmonary diffusing capacity. These patients often have severe pulmonary disease, rarely have nephritis or CNS disease, and usually respond to treatment with corticosteroids. The serological abnormalities seen in MCTD include a positive ANA test with a speckled pattern in high titer and a high titer of antibodies to RNP. Patients with MCTD rarely have antibodies to DNA. Some researchers maintain that MCTD represents a subgroup of either SLE or scleroderma.

Table 4 (p. xxxvi) lists some useful questions in detecting SLE and differentiating it from other conditions. If the patient answers only one or two positively, SLE is highly unlikely. If he or she answers three or more positively, SLE is a possibility, and an ANA test is indicated.

Drug-Induced Lupus

Drugs that relate to lupus can be divided into three categories: drugs that induce lupuslike condition (drug-induced lupus), drugs that induce ANA, and drugs associated with exacerbations of SLE. In the first group are hydralazine, procainamide, and possibly hydantoin. In the second group are these same drugs plus isoniazid and chlorpromazine. In the third group are penicillin, sulfonamides, gold salts, and oral contraceptives, which are associated with exacerbations of SLE and rarely cause lupuslike symptoms or ANAs in the general population.

Nearly 75 percent of subjects taking procainamide develop ANAs, including antibodies to RNP and single-stranded DNA; however, only about 25 percent of those developing ANAs develop symptoms and signs of lupus. Therefore, the development of ANAs without lupus symptoms is not a reason to stop administering the drugs. Arthralgia, pleurisy with effusion, fever, and weight loss are common features associated with these drugs, but renal disease, hypocomplementemia, and antibodies to double-stranded DNA are rarely seen. Patients with procainamide drug-induced lupus often have antibodies to histones. Symptoms generally clear in a few weeks after discontinuation of the drug even though ANAs may persist in blood tests for months.

ANAs appear less frequently in subjects taking hydralazine. Patients with hydralazine lupus syndrome may have arthritis, dermatitis, serositis, leukopenia, ANAs, and anti-DNA antibodies but rarely have renal or CNS disease. Symptoms usually stop after cessation of the drug. Patients with hydralazine lupus are usually slow acetylators of the drug who have taken large amounts for a long time. These studies suggest that certain subjects may have a genetic predisposition to developing drug-induced lupus.

Some drugs frequently induce ANA in individuals without causing LE. These drugs include isoniazid and chlorpromazine. The drugs that may exacerbate SLE are penicillin (but not semi-synthetic penicillins) and sulfonamides. However, as infections may also cause exacerbation, this issue remains unclear. In the absence of a history of an allergic reaction to these drugs, they can be used if no other antibiotic is available.

THERAPY AND MANAGEMENT

The goal of treatment is to prevent inflammation, manage it when it occurs, prevent organ damage, and maintain the health and sense of well-being of each patient. Treatment must therefore focus on both intervention of acute relapses and management of chronic problems. To date there are no specific remedies for the treatment of the underlying processes of SLE, so nonspecific, anti-inflammatory drugs are generally prescribed. SLE patients should avoid ultraviolet B radiation, blood transfusions, penicillin, and sulfonamides when possible. They should receive immunization to prevent infection, but probably only with inactivated or killed vaccines. Surgery or infections may trigger a relapse and may require more aggressive concurrent management of the lupus. In the long-term management of this illness, both patient and physician must learn to recognize those symptoms and signs that herald relapses. Although these symptoms may involve fever and arthralgia in some patients, in others they may appear as hair loss, mucosal ulcers, pleurisy, weight loss, rashes, or simply fatigue. Before frank clinical symptoms develop, many patients will develop abnormal laboratory tests such as a reduced level of hemoglobin, serum complement, white blood cells, or platelets; abnormal urinalysis or creatinine clearance; and/or a rising level of anti-DNA antibodies or immune complexes.

Many patients seen in hospitals by physicians or students have severe but not life-threatening disease. By contrast, many of the patients seen in the office have much milder disease characterized by chronic intermittent features. The patient, fearing the unknown or having heard the worst, must be reassured that a majority of patients have mild to moderate disease and that with proper management many of the more serious complications of organ damage can now be prevented and/or controlled.

Active disease should be treated aggressively to prevent permanent tissue injury. General measures should include rest when the disease is active, sunscreens, and physical therapy for muscle weakness and deformities. Drugs used for the treatment of SLE include topical steroids, nonsteroidal anti-inflammatory drugs (NSAIDs) particularly salicylates, antimalarials, corticosteroids, and immunosuppressives. The use of corticosteroids in most patients with SLE has improved their survival; patients on moderate to high dosages of corticosteroids may find that salt restriction, antacids, and diuretics minimize side effects. Dosage should be individualized, taking into account the degree of activity of inflammation, the prognostic implication with regard to which organ is involved, and the possible side effects of treatment. Immunosuppressives are best used in life-threatening or seriously crippling SLE, in the presence of reversible lesions, when the patient fails to respond to conventional therapy or cannot tolerate the side effects of other therapies. Immunosuppressives should only be used where no active infection exists, with no hematologic contraindication, with meticulous follow-up, and with continued objective evaluations. Plasmaphoresis remains controversial: Two controlled studies have demonstrated no efficacy.

The treatment of specific aspects of SLE are outlined in table 5, on page xxxvii. For each facet of the disease treatment is outlined in respect to its severity, that is, the more or less severe the manifestation (viz., mild versus severe skin disease), the more or less aggressive the therapy. An inadequate response to one set of drugs indicates employing more potent medication, again taking into consideration the risks of possible (unacceptable) side effects. When a particular organ may become critically affected by SLE, initial therapy should be more aggressive. It should be remembered that anti-inflammatory and immunosuppressive drugs will only be effective against inflammatory lesions and not yield favorable results in permanently injured (scarred, fibrotic) organs.

The acute erythematous maculopapular rash responds well to local application of corticosteroids and the systemic introduction of antimalarials such as hydroxychloroquine. Systemic corticosteroids are rarely warranted. The chronic lesion, or discoid lupus, responds to these same measures to a variable degree. Severe, extensive lesions have been treated with large doses of antimalarials when all else has failed. However, the patient should be cautioned about the possible risks of retinal damage when taking large doses of antimalarials.

Arthralgia and arthritis respond well to rest, physical therapy, splinting, NSAIDs, and antimalarials. Steroids should not be needed.

Fever often responds to rest and salicylates. Antimalarials may be beneficial. Persistent fever not responsive to these measures usually coincides with other signs of activity and responds to moderate doses of corticosteroids. Infections must be excluded.

Pericarditis and pleurisy respond well to indomethacin or corticosteroids.

Hemolytic anemia and thrombocytopenia need not be treated unless symptomatic. They generally respond well to steroids. If not, immunosuppressives or a splenectomy may be necessary.

Acute inflammatory involvement of the CNS generally responds well to treatment. Organic psychosis due to SLE may be difficult to differentiate from a steroid-induced psychosis. Because of the risk of permanent brain damage, large doses of steroids are recommended until maximal improvement is achieved, at which time the dosage of steroids is gradually tapered. Immunosuppressives may be helpful. The longer that steroids are given in high dosages, the greater the risk for life-threatening infections.

Mild focal glomerulitis with minimal urinary abnormalities may respond on occasion to bed rest. However, these patients usually benefit from systemic corticosteroid therapy, such as prednisone. Those patients with focal or diffuse proliferative glomerulonephritis generally require higher doses, depending on the severity of the renal impairment. Patients unresponsive to these regimens may benefit from immunosuppressives, plasmaphoresis, or corticosteroid pulse therapy. Medication is maintained until hematuria clears and serum complement levels return toward normal; this usually occurs within three weeks. Proteinuria, elevated sedimentation rate, and high levels of ANAs may persist. The prednisone dosage is then tapered slowly. Complete blood counts, urinalyses, serum creatinine levels, and serum complement levels should be checked regularly to detect relapses; relapses usually respond either to maintaining the dosage of prednisone at the current level or increasing it by a dosage of 5–10 mg. Some patients benefit from and/or can tolerate steroids on alternate days; a few patients can discontinue steroids and remain asymptomatic. Continued careful monitoring and early treatment of slight relapses may avoid more severe exacerbations.

Patients with chronic membranous glomerulonephritis and nephrotic syndrome respond less well to corticosteroids or immunosuppressives. Some, usually those with normal complement levels, may have permanent proteinuria.

Patients with SLE generally tolerate all medications well. It is particularly important to control hypertension. Diastolics in younger patients should probably be maintained at about 80–85, using combinations of diuretics, beta blockers, calcium channel antagonists, hydralazine, and methyldopa.

TABLE 1

Clinical Features of Patients with SLE

FEATURES	PERCENTAGE OF PATIENTS WITH THIS FEATURE
Weight loss	62
Fever	83
Myalgia	Common
Arthralgia, arthritis	90
Aseptic necrosis	10
Skin	74
Butterfly rash	42
Photosensitivity	30
Mucous-membrane lesions	12
Alopecia	27
Raynaud's phenomenon	17
Purpura	15
Urticaria	8
Telangiectasia	Common
Renal	53
Nephrosis	18
Gastrointestinal	38
Pulmonary	47
Pleurisy	45
Effusion	24
Pneumonia	29
Cardiac	46
Pericarditis	27
Murmurs	23
EKG changes	39
Libman Sacks endocarditis	Rare
Lymphadenopathy	46
Splenomegaly	15
Hepatomegaly	25

TABLE 2
Laboratory Abnormalities in SLE

GENERAL	PERCENTAGE
Anemia	71
Elevated ESR	Common
Leukopenia	56
Thrombocytopenia	11
Hemolytic anemia	8
Circulating anticoagulant	2
Rheumatoid factor	19
Bilogic false-positive test for syphilis	15
Hypoalbuminemia	50
Hyperglobulinemia	37
Increased serum levels of IgG and/or IgM	often elevated

TABLE 3
Criteria for SLE

1. **Butterfly rash:** fixed erythema, flat or raised, over the malar eminences, tending to spare the nasolabial folds.

2. **Discoid lupus:** erythematous raised patches with adherent keratotic scaling and follicular plugging; atrophic scarring may occur in older lesions.

3. **Photosensitivity:** skin rash as a result of unusual reaction to sunlight; by patient history or physician observation.

4. **Oral ulcers:** oral or nasopharyngeal ulceration, usually painless; observed by a physician.

5. **Arthritis:** nonerosive arthritis involving two or more peripheral joints, characterized by tenderness, swelling, or effusion.

6. **Serositis:** (a) pleuritis—convincing history of pleuritic pain or rub heard by a physician or evidence of pleural effusion; or (b) pericarditis—documented by EKG or rub or evidence of pericardial effusion.

7. **Renal disorder:** (a) persistent proteinuria greater than .5 gm./day or greater than 3+ if quantitation not performed or (b) cellular casts—may be red cell, hemoglobin, granular, tubular, or mixed.

8. **Neurological disorder:** (a) seizures—in the absence of offending drugs or known metabolic derangements; e.g., uremia, ketoacidosis, or electrolyte imbalance or (b) psychosis—in the absence of offending drugs or known metabolic derangements, e.g, uremia, ketoacidosis, or electrolyte imbalance.

9. **Hematologic disorder:** (a) hemolytic anemia—with reticulocytosis; (b) leukopenia—less than 4,000/mm^3 total on two or more occasions; (c) lymphopenia—less than 1,500/mm^3 on two or more occasions; or (d) thrombocytopenia—less than 100,000/mm^3 in the absence of offending drugs.

10. **Immunologic disorder:** (a) positive LE cell preparation; (b) anti-DNA—antibody to native DNA in abnormal titer; (c) anti-Sm: presence of antibody to Sm nuclear antigen; or (d) false-positive STS (serological test for syphilis) known to be positive for at least six months and confirmed by FTA-ABS tests.

11. **Antinuclear antibody (ANA):** an abnormal titer of ANA by immunofluorescence or an equivalent assay at any point in time and in the absence of drugs known to be associated with "drug-induced lupus" syndrome.

TABLE 4

Screening Questionnaire for
SYSTEMIC LUPUS ERYTHEMATOSUS

1. Have you ever had arthritis or rheumatism for more than three months?

2. Do your fingers become pale, numb, or uncomfortable in the cold?

3. Have you had any sores in your mouth for more than two weeks?

4. Have you been told that you have low blood counts (anemia, low white cell count, or low platelet count)?

5. Have you ever had a prominent rash on your cheeks for more than a month?

6. Does your skin break out after you have been in the sun (not sunburn)?

7. Has it ever been painful to take a deep breath for more than a few days (pleurisy)?

8. Have you been told that you have protein in your urine?

9. Have you ever had rapid loss of lots of hair?

10. Have you ever had a seizure, convulsion, or fit?

TABLE 5
Treatment of Specific Problems in Lupus

Fever	ASA → NSAID → antimalarial → steroid
Arthralgia	ASA → NSAID → antimalarial
Arthritis	ASA → NSAID → antimalarial → steroid
Rashes	Hydrocortisone → triamcinolone → fluorinated steroid → antimalarial → injection
Raynaud's phenomenon	Stop smoking → warm clothing → biofeedback → nifedipine
Serositis	Indomethacin → steroids
Pulmonary	Steroids
Hypertension	Diuretic → propranolol → methyldopa → etc.
Thrombocytopenia/ hemolytic anemia	Steroids → immunosuppressives → splenectomy
Renal disease	Steroids → pulse steroids → immunosuppressives ? Plasmaphoresis
CNS	Steroids → immunosuppressives
Migraine	Propanolol

IN
SEARCH
OF THE
SUN

1. Onset of Lupus

The Patient's Story

Primum non nocere
"Above all, do no harm"
—The First Law of Medicine

"YOUR patient doesn't have a chance. Her last LE prep was positive.* Her kidneys have collapsed sixty percent. What more evidence do you need?" The authoritarian voice with a sonorous Harvard accent sounded nightmarish behind the door of my hospital room at Peter Bent Brigham. The narrow metal bed I was lying in reeled in a spinning room. In this fraction of a moment, I reached within for my center of balance and learned more about myself than I had in a lifetime. How could I have known that day that a few years later my rare and little-known disease would be arrested and I would again be able to enjoy an active life; that fifteen years after the onset of my lupus I would be free-lancing and writing stories for the *Boston Globe* from Paris during the Vietnam peace talks in May 1968; that I would be instrumental in founding the National Lupus Foundation of America.

*In 1948 M. Hargraves and his associates reported the presence of an abnormal leukocyte in the bone marrow aspirate from patients with SLE, and its apparent specificity. The cell and its inclusion body were named the "LE cell." The LE cell is of great diagnostic value in systemic lupus erythematosus. The factor responsible for LE cell formation, in the opinion of some researchers, may play a role in the clinical course of the disease. (M. M. Hargraves, H. Richmond, and R. Morton. 1948. Presentation of two bone marrow elements: The "tart" cell and "L.E." cell, *Proc. Staff Meet. Mayo Clin.* 23:25–28.)

I didn't know then that I would write and edit *Lupus News*, a paper with a circulation of over fifty thousand, write four books on the subject, and serve as a member of the National Allergy and Infectious Disease Advisory Council at the National Institutes of Health. I couldn't have guessed that in 1985 I would go to the White House with my granddaughter Ani to receive the Volunteer Action Award for Health, presented by President Ronald Reagan.

My first symptoms of SLE appeared in the second week of June 1953. My husband, a wool merchant, had to go to Holland on business for a few weeks. We combined his business trip with the family's summer vacation. Our children were still too young to enjoy such a trip, but we decided to take them along. Martha, almost one and a half, was in diapers; Ingrid, almost five, was quite mischievous; and Al, six and a half, at the very peak of his exploring curiosity, had to be chased all the time.

I remember vividly the five of us riding in a taxi after we had spent a sleepless night in a stuffy train compartment from Boston to New York. Shortly after we drove through the Holland Tunnel, the S.S. *Nieuw Amsterdam* appeared in full sight. The children's growing excitement infected their parents. For an instant I thought that I felt dizzy but suppressed the feeling.

"It's hot." My husband scanned my face and pointed to a thermometer on a building we were passing—it read eighty-four degrees. Moments later, I started shaking and shivering with chills that seized me with uncontrollable fury. As our taxi stopped, I was violently nauseated. After that I felt better. The date was June 14, 1953. I have never been able to recall how we boarded the ship or how I descended below deck to our two cabins. I do remember the steward's friendly greeting; he recognized us from our previous voyage. The sturdy Dutchman had courtly manners and a sense of humor, as well. He ruffled up the hair of the two older children; then, counting one, two, three, he congratulated us on the new addition to the family. After we were settled in our cabins, I felt much improved. I attributed the whole episode of my upset to the tension, the heat, and my usual discomfort when riding in an automobile for very long.

Under normal circumstances the nine-day sail to Rotterdam would have been a real pleasure, but my nausea persisted. I felt sure it was due to the motion of the boat. I never thought to take my temperature.

I was looking forward to visiting Holland again. We had spent the entire summer there in 1947, right after World War II. Then the city of Rotterdam lay in ruins. The center of town was totally razed, a metropolis without a heart. Odd remnants of walls stood here and there, preserved for future use. The debris had been cleared and the streets cleaned. Now, crossing the city, my husband and I marveled at the changes six years had brought. The city was indeed returning to life, but there was still much to be rebuilt.

Al and Ingrid, who were sitting in the front seat with the driver, repeatedly asked him the same question: "What happened to that house?"

The answer was always the same: "The Germans burned it!"

Ingrid was first to notice a badly bombed cathedral and asked, "What happened to that church?"

The driver replied again, "The Germans burned the church!"

"The Germans must have wanted to burn God," Ingrid said, examining the ruins with big, serious eyes.

"Given a chance, they would," the driver mumbled. As we left Rotterdam and approached Scheveningen, where we were to stay at the Witte-Brug Hotel, it was my turn to speak out when I saw the newly planted woods outside the city. Six years ago, the forests had been burned to the ground.

The moment I entered the hotel, vapors of fresh paint hit my nostrils, giving me an instant headache. That night everyone was restless; Martha, in particular, cried all night. Toward morning I took her temperature. I couldn't believe it read 105 degrees. Red welts covered her body. A month before leaving West Newton, Massachusetts, the children had had chicken pox, which Martha had caught last. I remembered that ten days before the chicken pox appeared she had come down with purpura,* and her condition had become

---

*Purpura: a disease that is characterized by the rupture of blood vessels, with leakage of blood into the tissues.

aggravated by infectious mononucleosis.* The pediatrician had told me that both conditions could cause serious complications with chicken pox. I had never seen a delirious child before, and I nearly lost my mind waiting for the Dutch doctor. He assured us that Martha would be all right in a couple of days. He was right—Martha did get better, but I was completely exhausted.

June, that summer in Holland, was cold and very windy, more like late October or early November in Boston. The headache I got the day I entered the Witte-Brug never left me. Our Dutch friends said that most visitors, unaccustomed to the winds of the lowlands, were so affected. The headache would subside when the wind diminished.†

The wind never diminished. The headache increased. On a Tuesday morning, Mrs. Van Voorhees, the wife of an executive of a large spice concern, called to remind us of the invitation to their cocktail party the following afternoon. As I held the phone, I panicked—I couldn't speak. I could not find breath to utter a sound. Eventually I managed to whisper that something seemed to have happened to my voice.

"Oh, dear! What a time to get ill." Mrs. Van Voorhees sounded heartbroken. She confessed that the party was to be given in our honor and that everyone was so eager to meet us. "Please be well by tomorrow," she pleaded. In the same low tone, I promised to attend the affair. The next day I stayed in bed until I had to dress for the party. As I glanced at myself in the full-length mirror on the bathroom wall, I was glad that in a frivolous moment I had bought the Jacques Fath pink chiffon gown at a sale in Boston. The four layers of sheer petticoats in all the shades of the rainbow renewed my feminine vanity.

The Van Voorhees's large drawing room was crowded and smoky. The air, too thick to breathe, smelled strongly of coarse Dutch tobacco and heavy French perfume. The very instant I stepped into

*Infectious mononucleosis: a self-limited probably infectious disease that presents with fever, upper respiratory symptoms, and swelling of the lymph nodes.
†R. Dubos: 1965. *Man adapting* (New Haven, Conn.: Yale University Press), p. 62.

the room, I felt as if I were riding on a stuffy bus with nothing to hold on to. I looked around for a place to sit down, but all the chairs had been removed for the occasion.

An exotic-looking woman in a mink jacket was leaning against the grand piano at the other side of the room. She watched me with a sympathetic eye; her face was streaked with perspiration, just like my own. I wondered why she should swelter in that fur.

The man who stood beside me reeked of wine and garlic. With busy eyes he followed my gaze and whispered close to my ear that Mrs. So-and-So was half Indonesian. For a split second, my short, red-faced neighbor, the floor, and everything around me seemed to sway before my eyes. "She's charming," I heard him say as I regained my composure.

I looked at him absently, not sure I could get through the party. Only stubborn determination kept me on my feet. I searched in the crowd for my husband, planning my escape. A matron on my right started talking to me faster than I could follow. She was telling me that everyone at the party was dressed according to price and style to show how successfully each husband was managing his directorship. She told me that the woman by the piano had sold an oriental rug, a family heirloom, to buy her mink jacket for this occasion. My new acquaintance, barely pausing, said that my husband and I belonged to the "in" crowd, even though we were not of Dutch origin.

Curious, I couldn't resist asking her to explain. According to her, our two husbands had reached their present position by appointment, in contrast to most of the other husbands in the room, who began their careers right after high school as stock clerks. When my husband appeared, I told him in a voice sounding quite unlike my own that the room was stifling and perhaps we ought to go. He didn't hear my last words but led me over to a Dutch man with whom he had played tennis many years ago—in Bulgaria, my native country, of all places.

The party had started with cocktails and endless trays of hors d'oeuvres, followed by turtle soup and morsels of pheasant and countless Indonesian specialties—a veritable dinner. But the food tasted bitter to me. My throat felt constricted. I could not swallow a bite. As soon as the coffee was passed around, as if on cue, the guests made their excuses and started leaving. By then I could hardly walk. "How do you feel?" my husband asked me in the car.

"Giddy," I said, taking off my shoes with some difficulty. In the few hours I stood through the party, I had started to hate my own feet. The I. Miller "rose-de-bois" satin slippers, so divine when I had tried them on in Boston, pinched me beyond endurance. Now, looking down, I was amazed to find my feet swollen to double their normal size.

"From now on you'll have to learn how to say no when you don't feel well." My husband watched me from the corner of his eye.

"That would be very hard," I found the strength to tease. "Remember, I'm the girl who can't say no."

"I do." He put his arm around me and repeated once more, "You'll have to learn how to say no! That's all there is to it." Later, more than once, I remembered his prophetic warning when I was tempted to overtax my energies. Back in our hotel room, while he showered, I sat at the edge of my bed, too sick even to undress. During the night I experienced a peculiar and frightening sensation in my arms, or rather, no sensation in them at all—they had vanished in the darkness. Seized by fear, I reached for the electric switch; everything felt normal again. I persuaded myself that whatever was wrong with me was similar to whatever Martha had had in the previous few days, and I fell asleep again.

In the morning I awoke with a temperature of 102 degrees. My whole face was swollen; I was bothered by a sharp pain in my nose, which, the children remarked, looked red. Ingrid brought me a small mirror, and I saw a bright red and slightly swollen nose. Briefly, I lost my speech again. Horrified, I succeeded in calling Dr. Vandam. He appeared in the late afternoon. With a solemn expression, he made a diagnosis of erysipelas.*

---

*Erysipelas: a contagious infectious disease of skin and subcutaneous tissue, marked by redness and swelling of affected areas and often accompanied by fever, chills, and general weakness.

"Erysipelas?" My husband struggled with the word. "What does it mean, Doctor? Is it serious?"

"Well, yes and no." The phlegmatic Dr. Vandam took his time. "We used to call it St. Anthony's Fire." His thick lips stretched in a faint smile.

My husband glanced at him impatiently. "It still doesn't mean a thing to me."

"Erysipelas is triggered by an organism of the same origin as that which causes scarlet fever and other infections," the doctor explained, and settled more comfortably into the old-fashioned armchair. With a sigh he unbuttoned his tightly fitted brown tweed jacket, allowing his large stomach to protrude. "It's an old troublemaker well described by Hippocrates, Galen, and Celsus. . . ." He pronounced the last words with obvious satisfaction. I smiled at his last remark and complimented him on his knowledge of the ancient Greeks and Romans.

"She'll be all right," he told my husband, "but keep the children away from her for the next few days."

I read my husband's thoughts. How could one possibly keep three little children away from their mother in two tiny hotel rooms with an adjoining bathroom?

Dr. Vandam thought I might go to a hospital but almost immediately rejected the idea. "They won't take her," he said. "The hospitals still fear the infection getting close to the surgical wards. Your best bet is to take care of your wife for a few days right here in the hotel, then return to the States and have her seen by a doctor there." With that, he wrote a prescription for sulfadiazine* with instructions to take it for eight days and left. Dr. Vandam gave me no clues whatsoever that I was about to embark on a fifteen-year battle for my life.

I had no idea that his prescription for sulfonamide might unmask for the second time the disease I was harboring in my system. I did not dream that all the suffering I was to endure would advance medical research and that doctors would question the sulfonamides

---

*Sulfadiazine: an anti-infective drug—one of the sulfonamides.

as a potential menace for lupus-susceptible persons and urge preventive medicine.

Lying in bed, feverish, I recalled that I'd had erysipelas once before. In 1939, in Sofia, Bulgaria, shortly after my eighteenth birthday, I had gone on a skiing trip. I had fallen and bruised my left ankle, which had become infected, and had spent a month in the hospital. The drugs that Dr. Karamichailov had given me then made me deadly sick. I wondered if sulfadiazine was a derivative of that earlier medication.

My thoughts drifted. The hospital in Sofia came alive for me again, with images of corridors smelling discomfortingly of disease and decay and antiseptic. My first morning out of quarantine I had taken a walk and had seen in the room next to mine a young boy sprawled flat on his back. He was very weak but still had a spark of life in his eyes. His mop of bright red hair gleamed around his emaciated cheeks. He had acknowledged my presence with a heave of his chest. I could tell that he was suffering unbearable pain. My heart was terrified; surely I was witnessing the last spark of life flickering away. A spindly resident took my arm and helped me back to bed. He explained gently that the boy had been in a car accident and the organs in his lower abdomen were smashed. Gangrene had set in. The stench was from his decaying flesh. On his way out, the young doctor mumbled, "In a few days he'll be in a coma."

"But that's inhuman," I cried after him. "You must do something to end his suffering."

"You mean kill him?"

"There must be another word for that . . ."

He shook his head stubbornly. "Not in my language. Nature has her ways, young lady. Who are we to interfere?" As he walked away, he muttered to himself, "One must assert life, even at the edge of death."

That had been so long ago. . . .

Following Dr. Vandam's instructions, we hired a Dutch girl, through the hotel office, to help keep the children away from my room. My husband attended to me, applying cold Epsom-salt compresses to my face and coaxing me to drink liquids. The high fever lasted for four days. I just could not keep the fluids down.

The trip back to New York was trying. On the second day, a terrific storm developed. The waves heaved as high as seventy feet, and for forty-eight hours nobody was allowed on deck for fear that he might be washed overboard. I remember the whole family lying in bed, seasick. With the portholes closed, the air was stuffy and heavy. The children cried constantly, frightened by the rolling motions of the boat. As the storm increased, the ship's physician, followed by a steward, came into our cabin. The steward placed a tray of sliced bread on the dresser.

The doctor smiled at the children. "Try to eat some bread. It will help settle your stomachs. I wish I could offer you something more," he said, turning to my husband and me. He left us saying that all the passengers were sick and that most of the crew were not feeling too well, either.

The steward winked at Al. "Cheer up, fellow—weather predictions are good for tomorrow."

When the door closed, Al, impressed by the doctor's uniform, asked what the captain of the ship had wanted. I told him that he was the doctor, not the captain, and he had promised that we would feel better by tomorrow. "He suggested that we eat some bread," I said, and joked that today was sick day on board ship—everybody was celebrating the same holiday by feeling miserable, even the sailors.

Ingrid sighed. "Who knows, maybe by tomorrow there'll be a different celebration."

"Yeah"—Al made a sour face—"tomorrow might be fun."

Early next morning the storm subsided. The steward came to open the portholes, letting in a rush of fresh air. Sunlight flooded our cabins. My husband and the children eagerly dressed to go on deck. But my own nausea persisted. I remember, at one point, thinking about the rotation of the earth around the sun and fearing that I would feel its motion and feel earth sick for the rest of my days.

During those dreadful hours on board the ship, fears, real and imaginary, were gnawing at my subconscious as the ship plowed toward New York. I felt so ill that I thought to myself, If someone would only throw me overboard—what a relief that would be.

2. Onset of Lupus
The Physician's Point of View

READING the *The Sun Is My Enemy*, I pretend that I am sitting in my office chair listening to Mrs. Aladjem tell me of her trip to Holland. She tells me of the excitement of the transatlantic voyage, the formal receptions, but also of the problems. I read carefully, for she is an excellent historian, and I imagine watching her face for those small mannerisms that convey the emotional implications of what one is saying. Some people avoid eye contact, perhaps because the subject matter is too emotionally charged to relate; others look at you directly and express themselves in a straightforward, factual manner. I am glad that Mrs. Aladjem looks directly at people most of the time. I sense that she was troubled, sincerely trying to understand what happened to her and seeking an explanation.

She described her symptoms in detail: the fever, the chills, the headaches, why some odors bothered her, the loss of sensation at night, her red nose, how she responded to the medication, her exhaustion. I am interested in details; I was to determine how the pieces fit together, what the puzzle will show and how to eliminate her symptoms.

I read on. Mrs. Aladjem was complaining of a headache. Who ever heard of not complaining of a headache, feeling that one's head is going to explode. How aggravating it must be not to feel near instant relief as promised by TV advertisments. In my experience, very few people seek a physician for a headache. Most headaches go away—thank God. But when a patient complains of recurrent headaches, I listen very carefully. I continue to ask lots of questions. I search; I probe. I ask the patient to bear with me even though some of the questions seem irrelevant to the "investigation," for I am determined to find the cause of the symptoms. I explain that headaches can indicate tension, migraine (a specific headache due to blood-vessel spasm), infection, lupus, or any of several conditions. When I finish reading about her headaches, I cannot tell if they were caused by the winds of Holland or if they were marking the beginning of her lupus. How frustrating for her and for her physician. Like my hero Inspector Poirot, I keep searching for clues that will help solve the puzzle of lupus.

Later, I consider what Mrs. Aladjem described as the loss of sensation at night, which she claimed improved when she turned on the light. I recognize that the fear of the unknown is real and acknowledge its effects—disorientation and confusion, until one admits light and can be in control of environment and body again. Many persons put pressure on the nerves or blood vessels of their arms and legs, depending on their sleeping position, and I tell this to my patients to reassure them, explaining that organic disease is unlikely if the symptoms disappear with light. Still, it is frightening to feel that one has suddenly lost a limb, and I again reassure patients that this feeling is normal but if it recurs we will explore it further.

Again and again we will come back to the theme of light and the lupus patient.

What does a red nose mean to me, to a patient, to Mrs. Aladjem? My father used to tell me it came from being out in the cold. I was later taught that alcoholics develop red noses. Then I saw people with sunburns, acne, infections, tumors, and, of course, lupus. I need to differentiate, because the treatment will differ markedly, from standing by a warm fire or having something warm to drink to prescribing an antibiotic or a corticosteroid cream. I want to find out what symptoms accompanied the red nose—was there a pimple there first, did it come from being in the sun, were there bumps, was there redness or a rash elsewhere, how fast did it develop, did it ever happen before? Mrs. Aladjem was told she had erysipelas, a skin infection caused by bacteria that responds well to antibiotic treatment and whose lesions can be confused with the red butterfly facial lesions characteristic of lupus. A history of recent sun exposure will help differentiate them. However, the treatment for the two differ; in fact, certain antibiotics, that is, penicillin and the sulfonamides, both used for the treatment of infections, have been incriminated as causing SLE flares. Therefore, it is important to distinguish between the two types of skin lesions.

I turn back to the book. Mrs. Aladjem, determined to discover the name and nature of her "mystery disease," summoned up her inner strengths and chose to stay in the States and fight her illness.

3. Back in Boston

The Patient's Story

AND so I returned to the States to start a long siege with lupus. Fortunately, I was unaware of how ignorant the medical world was about this devilish disease. For, in truth, I was half dead, and if I'd known that three long years would elapse before any diagnosis was reached, with another seven years of experimenting on top of that, I might have lost my spirit.

We reached our home in West Newton, Massachusetts, on the twelfth of July, five weeks after we had sailed on the S.S. *Nieuw Amsterdam*. The first few days at home I felt better; the redness of my nose subsided, as did my temperature. But getting out of bed in the morning was a torment. I lay under the blanket waiting for someone to bring me two aspirins and a cup of hot tea to resurrect me. Then I could not dress until I soaked in a warm bath to loosen my joints. I was determined to keep going and to do my chores even though after a few hours I was forced to go back to bed and lie down.

Our next-door neighbor, Dr. Antoine Fried, was our family physician. After he had examined me several times, he suggested that I enter Newton-Wellesley Hospital for a thorough checkup. Following four days of hospital tests, I returned home feeling no better. None of the hospital reports contained any diagnostic surprises. The sedimentation rate* of my blood was slightly elevated, and the white count was somewhat low but with a normal differential. Dr. Fried suspected a low-grade infection and didn't see cause for any alarm. "You might benefit from a few vitamin B$_{12}$ injections," he said, and proposed to institute them for a week or two. "In any event," he added sympathetically, "take it easy for a while and don't overexert yourself." He felt confident that the whole thing would blow over. The results of the tests had strengthened his feelings that there was nothing very wrong with me. In case my discomfort persisted, he had plans to send me to a specialist to be tested for arthritis. He ended each visit with a smile of sincere reassurance.

One afternoon Martha ran out of the yard, and as I tried to catch her, I found that I could not run. My legs felt heavy, as though stuffed with cement. I could barely walk. Just to test myself, the following day I tried to run across the yard, but I couldn't. For the first time I feared that my condition might be really serious.

A month later my eyes started feeling peculiar. I had the same feeling—or lack of feeling—I'd experienced in my arms in Holland, as if they had vanished in the dark. Now my right eye felt as though it were an empty socket. Both eyelids were swollen with fluids. The right one was slightly discolored. It turned a ghostly white, but only for a few hours at different times of the day. I made an appointment with an eye specialist in Boston. He examined my eyes patiently but couldn't find anything wrong. He said that I wouldn't need glasses for at least another ten years. As I left his office, he actually congratulated me on my excellent eyesight. Nevertheless, my eyes continued to feel bizarre.

As summer turned into fall, my waning strength could not cope with the housework and the children, so we hired a young Norwegian girl to live with us. Birgitta assumed her duties with a sense of responsibility and eagerly assisted me in every way possible. With her help I somehow managed to keep the household running. Ingrid and Al were in school now, which helped. I could live a semblance of a normal life if I were careful and didn't exert myself.

---

*Sedimentation: the settling of red blood cells to the lower portion of a volume of blood that has been treated to prevent clotting.

When the cold weather set in, my joints became extremely sensitive. One day I noticed a new symptom. If I leaned on my arms just below my elbows, twenty-four hours later tiny pale pink lumps about the size of kernels of corn would appear around the areas of pressure. If I used scissors, similar nodules appeared around my finger joints where the scissors had pressed. If I walked for any length of time, the bottoms of my feet would turn red and hurt terribly. I tried to explain this new development to Dr. Fried, but whenever I made an appointment, the lumps would disappear before I arrived at his office. It was very embarrassing. I couldn't understand it at all. After three such appointments, Dr. Fried joked that he was scaring the lumps away. "I do have such an effect on certain disorders," he said, smiling. That day I left his office feeling more than foolish.

4. Florida

The Patient's Story

SINCE Christmas vacation was approaching and I was still feeling miserable, my husband suggested that I try a warm climate for a couple of weeks. "Take the children and Birgitta to Florida," he said. "There is nothing like a ray of sunshine when one's joints ache." I agreed, and he promised to join us for as much of the time as he could.

We started on this trip on a clear Friday morning in mid-December. When we left the house at seven o'clock in the morning, Commonwealth Avenue was covered with a few inches of fresh snow. The sun gleamed in the icy blue sky.

"The sun looks frozen," said Ingrid.

"It shines like a crystal ball," said Al.

"It's covered by ice cubes," added Ingrid, who had climbed onto my lap. "It must be shivering like Mommy." She snuggled closer.

By the time we reached South Station, more icy shivers ran through my body. The cold clung to me with incredible sharpness, and my blood felt frozen. On the train, the change from snowsuits and boots to light summer clothes delighted the children. Birgitta bubbled in anticipation of seeing semitropical country.

The next day, I got off the train in Miami tired and listless. I could scarcely lift my legs off the ground to enter a taxi. In the bright semitropical sunlight, I developed a prompt pupillary reaction* that forced me to shade my eyes with my hand until I could buy a pair of dark glasses. Birgitta could not believe the brightness of the sky and the intense sunlight. She also seemed bewildered by the artificial garlands of Christmas decorations on Collins Avenue. From every store, songs like "White Christmas" and "Jingle Bells" blared out at us. The sweltering Santa Clauses ringing bells in front of gas stations cut incongruous figures amid the palm trees. This was Birgitta's first Christmas away from home, and she began to cry. When she had controlled her emotions, I could hear her telling the children that in Norway, Christmas was a spiritual experience—not mundane and vulgar as it seemed here. I fully agreed with Birgitta, with whom I felt an affinity at that moment. I, too, was homesick.

Birgitta had grown up in Tromsö, a fishing town in Norway with a population of 40,000. Tromsö is about two hundred miles inside the Arctic Circle, with alternate periods of "Midnight Sun" and continuous darkness. The sun sets in Tromsö in late November and does not appear until Sol-Tag, Sun Day, in late January. Birgitta described those sunless days as sad and depressing. The people, she said, become very irritable and quarrelsome. They are furious not only with others but with themselves, as well. Crime increases, and there are many suicides and divorces. Some drink more than usual, some eat all the time, and very few smile.

Birgitta was twenty-two years old when she came to work for us. She had just graduated from the University of Oslo with a degree in biochemistry. A tall, rather pretty girl, at once childlike and keen, with a large forehead and blue eyes, she had shoulder-length blond hair and looked radiant in the Florida sun.

An emancipated Western European girl, accustomed to speaking her mind, she grew up with five younger brothers and an

---

*Pupillary reaction: constriction of the pupil in response to light that may be painful in inflammatory disorders of the eye.

older sister. She enjoyed travel and new experiences. Our children immediately took to her.

When I'd first met Birgitta, she told me she had had a fantasy that she was going to America. "And here I am!" she said, laughing.

A week after she moved in with us, the kitchen smelled of homemade bread, saffron cookies, and fresh-roasted coffee.

One day after we'd arrived in Florida, Birgitta, the children, and I were relaxing on the sand, very close to the water, just beyond the reach of the waves. The sand glimmered white with pink shadows. The ocean directly in front of us glittered. It was a spectacular Miami sunset: light peach and purple clouds crowned the red horizon, the sun itself a huge ball of flame.

"What a lovely sunset," I said.

"It's lovely," Birgitta said, "but I don't like watching a sunset . . . It still frightens me." An inward sadness clouded her blue eyes. "When I was growing up," she said, "a sunset could paralyze me with fear. I was afraid that the sun would disappear forever. I hated and feared the long months of darkness. . . ." She smoothed a lock of blond hair that had blown across her face and rushed on: "I had nightmares all the time," she said. "I had them even with my eyes open." She glanced at me and smiled. "I have retained some of those fears. . . ."

"By now you should regard the sun as a reliable friend," I said.

"But I don't." She shook her head. "I still can't take its reappearance for granted."

For a while we were silent. Then Birgitta went on: "When I was a child, I always woke up before dawn on Sol-Tag and stepped on the porch to see the sky lighten up. The porch was not sheltered. It was like an ice palace, open to the fury of the winds. I used to bundle up in all my woolens—sweaters, scarves, and mittens . . . It was cold—bone-chilling cold—and yet I did not mind it. Seeing the sun rise on an icy morning was simply beautiful, a white beauty covered with sheets of gold. The pines and all the evergreens shimmered with rainbows. I had to be there just to look and feel and know that the sun was back." Birgitta spoke with a rush of emotions. Her eyes, so very blue, were beaming with those memories. Many more words might have followed had she closed her eyes to relive those glorious moments.

In the ensuing silence I envisioned an image of my own. It was the day I left my parents' house to come to America. It was March 3, 1941, the day the German soldiers came into Sofia. For an instant I saw myself standing by a window in my mother's kitchen, gazing at the beautiful spring morning outside. As far as Vitosha Mountain in the distance, every detail of the landscape stood out, distinct against a blue sky. The ground was covered with half-thawed snow that glittered under the reflection of the sun. By the low stone wall that sheltered the early spring flowers from the mountain winds, there were clusters of radiant snowdrops. That year, the March sun was warmer than usual and had stirred the snowdrops and even awakened some jonquils from their winter sleep. It seemed safe for me to focus on the flowers during those heartbreaking moments.

Mother walked into the kitchen and put her arms around my shoulders. Hugging me tightly, she smiled at me gently. "Everything will be all right. The war can't last forever. Before you know it, we'll come to see you in America . . . America! Think of it!" (Poor Mother. She deceived herself that the war was coming to an end. She died before she could see America.) Mother's eyes were brimming with tears. It was hard for her to keep her fears from welling to the surface. Her voice took on a tone of indescribable sadness when she said, "My girl . . . my girl . . . your dreams began here, and now you'll start a new life, with new experiences and new dreams." With a sidelong glance at the flowers, she made an effort to smile. "The snowdrops are a bit early this year," she said. "They came early to please you. . . ."

When I was a child, Mother remembered, I was the one who always found the first snowdrops in the melting snow. Unable to suppress my excitement, I ran about the house crying, "Spring is here! Spring is here!" My happiness was focused on a certain consciousness of the rebirth of nature and the miracles of re-creation. I accepted those miracles with joy rather than reasoning. Those feelings have remained unchanged. . . . I remember those days as times of reverence for life that extended to my everyday experiences. The

>**22** **Florida**

spring flowers were symbols of hope and continuity, with no beginning and no end. They were like Mother's stories about her mother and her grandmother—one generation after another—and about life that flows and stretches from yesterday to tomorrow.

Thinking of these things, I glanced at Birgitta. For an instant I envisioned two small girls with eyes of identical blueness—one huddled in her warm woolens, smiling at the white of dawn, and the other searching for snowdrops in the melting snow. I recognized the likeness in Birgitta and me, however different our origins had been. The girl and I were both aware of nature in a deeper sense. We both had something of substance to fall back on.

Ingrid broke the long silence. "What are rainbows made of?" she asked Birgitta.

"Oh, rainbows? Rainbows are made of sunlight shot by water drops, I think. I'll make rainbows for you in the springtime."

"How will you do that?" Al asked, yawning.

"I'll show you when we water the garden with the hose." Then she looked at Ingrid. "If you're good, I'll let you jump over the rainbows. When I was your age," she said, "I believed that rainbows are made in fairyland and they foretold good things to come."

"Do you still believe that? Do you?" Ingrid asked.

"I suppose I do." Birgitta blushed when she answered.

"You love the sun," Ingrid said thoughtfully.

"Of course I love the sun. Who doesn't? The sun is our friend. It brings us health and happiness."

"My teacher told me that the Frost Giants don't like the sun!" Al interjected. "They are giants of darkness. They disguise themselves as wolves and run around the sky to catch the sun and swallow it."

"Tomorrow will be sunny," Ingrid chimed in. "I heard it on the radio."

"That's good; that's very good," Birgitta bubbled in her appealing Norwegian accent. "I'll be happy, and I won't be tired!"

"Why won't you be tired?" I asked, puzzled by her comment.

She shrugged. "I don't know. I am never depressed when the sun is shining, and I am never tired when I am happy."

"Do you get depressed because you miss the light? The warmth?"

"It's more than that," she answered. "Medical scientists in Norway are studying the effects of light on the human brain and how it affects human behavior. They are encouraged by statistics and by observations." She paused for a moment and then said, "When it is dark in Tromsö, our hearts are saddened. We all feel weary on those sunless days. It has always been like that. . . ."

"When you are sad, think of something happy to cheer you up," Al said.

"I do." Birgitta ruffled up his blond curly hair. "I think of a sunrise."

Martha, curled in a tight ball, had fallen asleep with her head on my lap. Al and Ingrid were yawning. I thought they looked exhausted and ready to go to bed, but I was wrong. The next moment they were tumbling in the sand and laughing. Martha stirred. Her eyes opened dreamily. She looked toward the ocean. Trembling slightly, she touched my hand to be sure she was awake. She sat up with an expression as if she could still see something that only she was able to imagine—something that had perhaps appeared in her dreams. Then she looked from face to face before reality was kindled in her eyes. She smiled when I put my arms around her, hugging her close. I bent and kissed her.

"It's time to go to bed," I called to the children.

Al's face became sullen. "I don't want to go to bed," he said.

"I'm not a bit sleepy," Ingrid said, yawning.

"I slept already," Martha said, rubbing her eyes.

"Look, look!" Ingrid cried, pointing to a flock of sea gulls circling low in the air. The gulls were glaring at us with shining round bead eyes, screeching and flapping their wings like children looking for attention.

"The sea gulls have come to play with us." Martha clapped her hands excitedly. She tried to imitate their screeching, and we all laughed when the gulls responded.

"No more stalling," I said in a voice stricter than necessary.

"Off to bed. I'll come to kiss you good-night as soon as you have your pajamas on."

Birgitta rose up. "Come now, children," she said. "I'll tell you a story after I tuck you in bed."

Ingrid's eyes brightened at the promise of a story. Birgitta picked up Martha in her arms, and Ingrid and Al tagged after her. I watched them walk over the gravel path lined with palm trees and gigantic red poinsettia bushes. Several times the children turned around and waved, and I waved back. I felt unusually tired; raising my arm seemed as difficult as lifting a bag of sand.

There was a cool breeze coming from the ocean. I decided to stay there for a few more moments to enjoy the peace and quiet after the children had gone.

In the short time that I had been there, the weather had changed drastically. A strong wind was blowing along the beach, and the ocean looked black under the shadow of the gathering clouds. Each time a wave swept over the beach, it appeared threatening. I was getting ready to leave when I saw a woman clad in a white dress walking on the beach. It was Gloria Swanson, the movie star. On our first day at the Flamingo Hotel, Ms. Swanson had walked over to us and introduced herself to the children and shook hands with them. She said she liked children. Ms. Swanson was a small, graceful woman, not notably beautiful but elegant and poised. She had short brown sassy hair with skin pulled tightly over her cheekbones and dusted with a delicate pink powder. I'd heard a woman at the swimming pool say that she was in her early sixties. She looked much younger. Only her eyes betrayed her true age. Unprotected by wrinkles, they were like deep pools of water in which an infinitude of memories were stored. One felt compelled to look into them.

As Ms. Swanson walked closer, she smiled and said, "Good evening."

I opened my mouth to respond, but no sound would come. I nodded, trying to make a civilized appearance. Ms. Swanson paused for a moment and asked, "Are you all right?" I nodded again and smiled to reassure her. She walked away.

I tried to clear my throat, but that was not the problem.

Then I remembered that once before my voice had disappeared like that in Holland, only to come back. Remembering this filled me with courage.

When I tried to get up, I could not move. My body felt lifeless. I was experiencing an exhaustion that defied description. It was a feeling for which I had no name. I didn't know what to do, and it was getting darker and darker. With a desperate effort, I crawled on my hands and knees before I could stand up. I was unsteady on my legs, and I swayed about until I reached the entrance of the hotel. I felt pathetically grateful to have achieved that. Before I went inside, I turned around for a moment to cast a glance at the ocean. The place where I had sat only minutes before was covered by water.

As I struggled to push open the heavy glass door, a cry escaped my throat. "Oh, Mother!" I uttered in desperation, aware that I was at least capable of speech. I could not believe what was happening to me. This illness was testing me in strange ways, I thought, and I didn't know what to do about it.

Sitting alone by the ocean that evening was an indescribable experience. I do remember, though, that in those moments of panic I somehow was aware that some inner strength would not allow me to succumb without a fight. In retrospect, I believe that this experience was the beginning of an awareness that I would manage to cope with this illness through self-discipline and personal effort.

The lobby of the hotel was crowded with men in tuxedos and women in long gowns adorned with precious stones and diamonds. The Flamingo Hotel was a lovely place. Its name was appropriate for close by there was a park with hundreds of pink flamingos strolling gracefully, like characters out of a fairy tale.

The manager of the hotel, a Mr. Jim Smith, also owned the Wentworth-by-the-Sea in Portsmouth, New Hampshire. Mr. Smith and his wife had a large following from New England and Canada, with some guests coming from as far as Scotland. Occasionally there were stars from Hollywood and titled persons from England among the guests.

As I made my way to the elevator, looking completely out of place in my damp, wrinkled sundress, I could barely keep my balance. Holding the door of the elevator, Michael, the bellboy, smiled at me. "You must hurry and change for the dinner dance. We are expecting Clark Gable." I managed a smile. Clark Gable was the last thing on my mind.

I entered my room utterly exhausted. I sat on the edge of the bed to catch my breath, then undressed and took a bath. I lay in the cool water, resting. The thought of trying to get out of the tub was fatiguing. As I lay in the water, a golden flood of moonlight streamed through the open window. I remember thinking, It's so dark by the ocean . . . so frightfully dark. . . . It was so extraordinary, as if it had never happened. I wondered what on the face of the earth could be wrong with me.

The next morning, I would have slept around the clock if it hadn't been for the children bouncing on my bed. They were all excited. Birgitta was taking them on a boat ride to see live crocodiles. It was after eleven.

"C'mon, Mommy, get up." Martha put her small arms around me. "Come with us," she pleaded.

"I feel tired," I said. "I feel dead tired."

"You are always tired," Ingrid said.

"How can you be tired when you are still in bed?" Al asked.

"I don't know why I'm tired," I snapped, "but I am."

"I'm tired after I play tennis," Ingrid said.

"That's a good feeling," I said, "but it's different when you wake up tired. It's morbid." The last words I mumbled to myself.

After the children left, I suddenly felt guilty for not going with them. Perhaps I shouldn't have told them how I felt. Perhaps I should have tried a little harder and gone with them. But how could I pretend that I was not tired or in pain or dizzy or uncomfortable when I was experiencing all those things and more? A sigh escaped me. I cannot keep up with anything anymore, I thought. I'm lucky if I can do work for an hour or so, and then I have to lie down. At times I feel so tired, as if my brain fogs over. This condition keeps me in constant thought and endless self-examination. How will this illness further disturb my life? I wondered. How will I handle new stresses? I wiped the sweat off my face. Poor Martha—she was afraid to go without me to see the crocodiles. Perhaps the other children had similar fears. They're still so small . . . I thought. They need a well mother. In the past months my symptoms had come and gone unpredictably. It was one horrible awakening after another. My husband and children had never accepted my illness, and I was aware of our shared tensions and all the sour moments we were experiencing. I worried about it a lot. Did the children blame me for problems over which I had no control? How did my husband feel? What did he think? Maybe he didn't think about it? How could he find time to think about anything? I felt a sudden irritation. He's all business. Such thoughts and questions were racing through my head and would torment me with the fantasy that it was I who had the power to set things right. I tried to put these thoughts aside. It seemed like a whole complicated set of feelings that were too overwhelming to analyze at the moment; but I was left with the nagging thought that perhaps there was something that I could do to resolve some of these creeping problems.

Strong sunlight was reflecting on the ocean and pouring through the wide-open balcony door. There were rainbows on the wall. I smiled. Perhaps things would change. Perhaps I was exaggerating. Perhaps my strength would come back and I'd forget all about it. I tried to stretch my legs. They were as stiff as logs.

I was brushing my teeth, looking with surprise at my pale face in the mirror. I was completely white. This was unusual, for Birgitta and the children were getting a tan and had that healthy glow that comes from being by the seaside. In the past, all I had needed was a glimmer of sun for my skin to darken. Now I had been in the sun for a week and nothing had happened. Why? I didn't know. It seemed so strange. I felt a sudden inexplicable suspicion of the sun, as if it had suddenly become my enemy. I was by no means certain that there was a connection, but doubt and worry merged into an aching anxiety. For an instant I tried to imagine what it would be like if I no longer could walk in the sunlight or work in the garden, play tennis, or do all the other things I had enjoyed doing with the children during sunny hours. Could the sun penetrate deeper than the skin and cause some internal problems? I wondered. At that point in medical history, the role of UV radiation was not entirely understood. It would take years before some knowledge would surface about how UV light could precipitate disease with or without skin changes.

More thoughts reverberated through my mind. I was struck by a disease that had no name and symptoms that were difficult to explain. And this dreadful fatigue and exhaustion! It invaded my being like cement.

I dried myself and put on a swimsuit. Despite my warning instincts about the sun, I wasn't ready to seek the shade and was determined to go to the solarium and test the sun. I rang for breakfast, then went onto the balcony and looked out. The ocean was blue. But the colors of the night before were still trapped in memory. The experience of the previous evening was still alive inside me, troublesome and gnawing.

I went back into the room. There was a knock on the door. I went over to it and opened it. It was the waiter with my breakfast. The fragrance of coffee filled the room. Lately, most smells were making me feel sick to my stomach. But I could still enjoy the smell of coffee. The telephone rang. It was my husband. "How are the children?" he asked. "And you?"

"We're all fine," I answered.

"I wish I were there," he said. "It's zero degrees in Boston. You must be all nice and brown," he added in a wistful tone.

"Birgitta and the children are, but I'm not."

"Why is that?"

"Heaven only knows!" I said. "Perhaps my body has changed."

"It better not," his voice teased. "You're not having a good time," he said. "Do you want to come home?"

"I don't know what I want anymore."

"What's wrong?" he asked.

"I don't know. I get tired . . . I get tired very easily. The sun tires me. It tires me even to talk. I don't feel like myself anymore." I spoke rapidly, my voice getting higher and higher with frustrations, not able to be reasonable over the telephone. "It's nothing that I can explain." There was a pause. "I'm not angry with you," I said. "I'm angry with my frustrations."

"Try to relax," my husband said calmly.

"How can I?" I snapped. "I feel like a battlefield ravaged by bullets. One day they attack my legs, the next my voice, my arms, or my entire body." (Those words, uttered in innocence, would remain central to the problems I would develop. The metaphor I used in a burst of emotions would gain realistic dimensions in the field of autoimmunity and immunology. Physicians would describe an illness such as mine as "a chronic civil war within the body."* They would describe the "bullets" that I spoke of metaphorically as antibodies that could attack a person's own body instead of foreign invaders such as bacteria or infections.)

After I put down the receiver, I slipped on a sundress over the bathing suit, took two aspirins with another cup of coffee, and left the room.

As soon as I got outside into the sun, the feeling cropped up again stronger than before. The sun! I must be careful of the sun! Why this subconscious warning of danger; I had no explanation. "Why should the sun hurt me?" I murmured to myself. I could not see any reason.

I walked slowly along the sunny path, the day warm and bright around me, the sea air exhilarating, and yet all this sickness and pain . . .

The large terrace that was called the solarium was shielded from observers, and women lay naked side by side for hours under the broiling sun, tanning themselves.

I didn't mind lying naked, surrounded by equally unclothed women. Since my childhood, I had gone with my mother to the mineral bath in Sofia. The bathhouse was an imposing structure of a Byzantine style, surrounded by beautiful gardens. It was adjacent to a picturesque mosque with a high minaret where the Imam chanted his prayers.

*Michael Crichton, M.D. 1966. *Five patients: The hospital explained* (New York: Alfred A. Knopf), p. 146.

I lay on the solarium floor next to a young woman by the name of Joan, who had long straw-colored hair and wore black sunglasses. Joan lay in the sun all day long and came to life only at night. Sometimes, she told me, she danced until dawn. I envied her for having enough energy to indulge in such activity. Lying next to Joan, whose body was the color of bronze, I looked even whiter than before.

I fell asleep in the solarium, unprotected under the blazing sun. When I awoke an hour later, I was bright red all over. I felt a little chill. The solarium attendant cautioned, "Be careful not to burn. The sun can murder you today."

Little did she know that in the future I would remember her words with fear and apprehension.

During that night I developed a 101 degree temperature and slept poorly. The following morning, my body was covered with a bright red rash, and my face had broken out in blue blotches. Toward evening, two angry red sores appeared on my forehead. Each one was half an inch in diameter, and they were sensitive to the touch. The waitress in the dining room commented that I had "sun poisoning"—a term I had never heard before, but by now I was willing to accept any diagnosis. After a few more days in Florida, I put Birgitta, Martha, and Ingrid on the train, and I took Al on the plane with me—a first flight for both of us.

One hour after we were in the air, I had to remove my shoes; my feet had swollen to a grotesque size. When Al remarked a couple of hours later that Boston, with all its lights, looked like a Christmas tree, I sighed with relief to be home.

5. Sunlight and the Lupus Patient

The Physician's Point of View

WHAT is the mystique of the sun and its healing powers? After all, heliotherapy has been used successfully for the treatment of tuberculosis, psoriasis, depression, neonatal jaundice, rickets, and jet lag. Many ancient cultures oriented their temples and their festive occasions toward the sun. The Sun God, in its many guises and variations, stood for justice. Kings were proclaimed the Son of the Sun. Modern priests (travel agents) praise the virtues of sunshine, invoke us to come, en masse, to southern temples (resort hotels), and promise a tanned, healthy body.

They conjure up images of warmth, fertile lands, green plants, colorful flowers, tranquil beaches, peace and quiet, rest, feeling content. How inviting! How tempting to think that a week, or more, of a vacation in the sun will dispel all troubles, all aches and pains. It seems that all our friends, neighbors, and relatives at one time or another have benefited from such a vacation.

How does the lupus patient respond to a physician's order to "stay out of the sun" in a sun-oriented culture? When no explanation follows, no exploration of the consequences of exposure, the patient is justifiably perplexed. Many ask: If I felt so good basking in the sun last summer, achieved a glorious tan, why am I no longer

able to do so? And many lupus patients often report *no* ill effects
from sunlight! But they all want and deserve an explanation. Let us
begin that explanation by examining the nature of light.

Light consists of the visible spectrum of the rainbow, the
invisible spectrum of infrared rays that provide warmth, and the
invisible UV spectrum. Light involves both hue and intensity. It can
be natural (the sun) or artificial (e.g., light bulbs). Sunlight consists
of 7 percent UV light, 52 percent visible light, and 41 percent infrared
light. UV light consists of three types: UV-C (200–290 nanometers),
which is used as a germicide and, although it has no discernible effect
on the skin, can damage the retina through prolonged exposure; UV-
B (290–320 nanometers), which causes sunburns, tans, aging skin,
and a lupus rash; and UV-A (320–400 nanometers), which causes an
immediate tan and occasionally a lupus rash. The major source of
UV-A and B is the sun; minor sources include sunlamps, some fluorescent lights, projector lamps, some old TV sets, TV studio lights,
some photocopying machines, and welder's arcs. (Computer terminals
rarely emit significant amounts of UV light.) The maximum amount
of UV light comes from the noonday sun, in midsummer, near the
equator, at high altitudes. While UV-B and C cannot penetrate glass,
some UV-A can do so. UV-B easily penetrates clouds and fog and
reflects off sand and snow, which accounts for sunburns acquired on
cloudy beaches and in cold, bright, snowy regions.

It is UV light that causes the problem of rashes for the lupus
patient. Some (or all) of the following mechanisms may be responsible
for the process: (1) UV light causes damage to the DNA and/or
proteins in the skin, the patient makes antibodies to these altered
molecules, and the antigen-antibody reaction attracts other humoral
factors (e.g., complement) and cells and causes a local inflammatory
reaction (a rash); (2) UV light causes significant alterations in cellular
membrane phospholipid metabolism that may affect inflammation; (3)
UV light causes an increase in production and release of cytokines,
including IL-1, which can cause fever, local inflammation, increased
antibody production, from cutaneous keratinocytes and Langerhans
cells; and (4) UV light stimulates the evolution of increased numbers
of suppressor T cells. The severity of cutaneous reaction will depend

on the intensity of the UV light source, how close one is to it, and the duration of exposure. Biopsies of lupus skin lesions demonstrate antibodies and complement and mononuclear cells. If the skin involvement is severe, it may cause a systemic reaction, including fever and arthritis, presumably through the formation of immune complexes in the skin, which then "escape" to settle in other parts of the body (namely, the kidney, joints, brain) and cause more inflammation.

How does one determine "photosensitivity" in view of the fact that approximately forty diseases are associated with photosensitivity? For the lupus patient it means the development of characteristic rashes. Only about one-third to one-half of lupus patients are photosensitive. Normal individuals vary as to their degree of photosensitivity. Type I persons always burn and develop little or no tan. They have very fair skin, red or blond hair, blue eyes, and freckles. They are usually of Celtic origin. Type II persons always burn, tan minimally, and have fair skin, blue or hazel eyes, red or blond hair, and freckles. Type III persons burn moderately, tan gradually, and have blond or brunet hair. Type IV persons burn minimally, tan easily, have dark eyes and hair, and are of Mediterranean, Oriental, or American Indian background. Type V persons rarely burn, tan profusely, and are usually brown skinned. Type VI persons never burn and have deeply pigmented skin and are of black origins. If you aren't sure of your type, use a sunscreen and spend a few minutes in the sun early in the morning or late in the afternoon. If no rash develops, gradually increase your exposure levels, but stop if you develop a rash. Always avoid sunbathing and the noonday sun (good advice for *everyone*!). The level of tolerance may increase or decrease without warning; therefore, prudence and care are necessary to protect against becoming symptomatic. Photosensitivity does not mean feeling ill while being in the sun, that is, feeling chilled, nauseated, and/or dizzy, for those symptoms usually represent typical photophobia and/or dehydration in hot weather.

How can the lupus patient who is proven photosensitive, acquire protection from UV light? Total avoidance is impractical. Common sense dictates that depending on the degree of photosensitivity, you should avoid the noonday sun, especially near highly reflective surfaces such as water, sand, and snow, and wear protective garments made of tightly woven fabric. Textured acrylic sheets over fluorescent lights (diffusers) will block out most UV light. Photosensitizing medications, drugs, substances (including phenothiazines, sulfonamides, tetracycline, and certain fungicides), whiteners, and fragrances should be avoided. While PABA esters are sun blockers for most individuals, they are photosensitizing for others. Sunscreens containing PABA, PABA esters, cinnamates, homo-methyl salicylates, and anthranilates will block UV-B. Benzophenones will block UV-A and B. Titanium dioxide and zinc oxide are total blockers. Sunscreens/blockers come in different grades (SPF = sun protection factor). The higher the number, the greater the degree of protection. They can be worn under makeup; titanium dioxide and zinc oxide come in different skin-colored tints. These agents should be used on areas exposed to UV light (i.e., face, neck, chest, arms, hands). Lip balms containing sunscreens will protect the lips. Sweat, water (pool, lake, ocean), and evaporation will decrease the products' effectiveness, and reapplications may be necessary. Sunscreens/blockers are best put on at least one hour prior to exposure. Some people are allergic to PABA, and it may be prudent, therefore, to test for allergy by applying some to a small test area of skin two or three days before general application to determine sensitivity. A rash would be considered an allergic reaction.

What is a typical lupus rash? It may be simply a blush or swelling or scaly red lesions over the bridge of the nose and cheeks (the butterfly rash) or elsewhere. It rarely itches. It usually disappears, but may recur, especially with UV light exposure. Continual recurrence may cause permanent scarring. Discoid lupus can cause ulcers, scabs, areas of increased or decreased pigmentation (vitiligo), and telangiectasia (small blood vessels that appear as red streaks on the skin, especially on the face, which represent scars and not inflammatory lesions).

My clinical experience has shown that lupus patients present additional skin manifestations: livedo reticularis: a spasmodic condition of very small blood vessels that shows up as a reticular red pattern on the skin, especially in cold weather; Raynaud's phenomenon: spasm of larger blood vessels that causes the fingers (and/or toes) to blanch, ache, and then either return to normal color or turn blue, dark, or red, becoming painful before returning to normal color—Raynaud's is aggravated by stress, smoking, and/or cold weather; ecchymoses (black-and-blue marks): bruises resulting from bumping into objects or occurring spontaneously—usually due to clotting problems; periungual erythema: redness about the base of the nails; purpura: little red dots usually either on the arms or legs due to either a low platelet count (and bleeding into the skin); hives and/or vasculitis (inflammation of blood vessels).

The cutaneous lesions mentioned above are noticeable and usually require a physician's examination to determine their cause. Mrs. Aladjem already had had a number of skin problems that suggested lupus. She even had a biopsy of a skin lesion at the elbow, which was nondiagnostic. Today there are specific tests to recognize lupus of the skin that were not then recognized.

How is a lupus rash treated? Education and prevention are probably the best medicines. It is the physician's responsibility to educate the patient regarding the importance of using sunscreens and the patient's responsibility to follow directions that can prevent lesions. But what if the lesions do develop? Most lesions respond to natural hydrocortisone or to more potent synthetic corticosteroid ointments (for dry skin) or creams (for oily skin). More stubborn lesions respond to antimalarial medication or injection of the skin lesions themselves. Prompt aggressive therapy will usually prevent scarring.

Light striking the retina initiates a chain of signals to the pineal gland and the hypothalamus. The series of signals controls our biologic clocks. Lack of light for appropriate periods of time can upset Circadian rhythms, resulting in endocrine imbalance. Lack of UV light exposure or vitamin D intake will lead to rickets. Psychological implications of light deprivation include melancholia, depression, SAD (seasonal affective disorder), an increased sense of stress, and at the extreme, suicide. SAD, which manifests itself during autumn through spring and is characterized by depression and weight gain, often responds to treatment with full-spectrum artificial light (e.g., glow light). Emotional and physical adjustment to light deprivation is probably the most difficult battle a lupus patient must face in our sun-worshiping culture.

People dealing with any chronic illness are prone to the fatigue caused by stress and depression. I want to emphasize that the lupus patient need not (indeed *should* not) become housebound out of fear of a flare-up. Rather, I encourage active participation in everyday living, both in the workplace and socially. The workplace of a lupus patient should be well lighted, provide a pleasant environment, and contribute to a sense of productivity and well-being. Frequent mini-vacations (a long weekend away, a day trip) can be beneficial—in the shade. Swimming can be just as pleasurable in an indoor pool. Strolls in a shaded garden in the early morning or evening can be soothing. I encourage my patients to apply sunscreens automatically prior to exposure and to exercise caution and good judgment regarding anticipated exposure. The current literature reminds us that tanning is unhealthy for *anyone* and can lead to premature aging, leathery skin, and cancer. Above all, I encourage optimism in my patients. I help them focus on their achievements rather than on their inabilities. And although I urge their families to support all efforts at "normal" living, I stress that understanding and compassion during a flare-up is a vital part of treatment. No one likes to feel ill.

Mrs. Aladjem was wise enough to pack up her bags and head home. Enough of Florida! The sun was clearly becoming her enemy.

6. Fatigue
The Physician's Point of View

FATIGUE—everyone complains of fatigue. Frankly, I used to get "tired" hearing of the subject. But over the years, as I've learned to listen to my own body signals as well as to patients' symptoms, a "fatigue pattern" began to evolve. There are times when we have lots of energy and other times when we have none, can't move, can't lift a finger, much less the rest of our body. What is the cause and what are the implications regarding treatment? What is normal versus abnormal fatigue?

To define abnormality, one must define normality. All of us have good and bad days. To me a simple definition of abnormality is when the number of bad days exceed the number of good ones—or put simply, when there are more bad days than there used to be. Why the shift from energy and enthusiasm to fatigue and listlessness? It could represent an increased work load (job, children, school, house, marriage), lack of sleep, depression, unhealthful habits (smoking, alcohol, fad diets, sedentary living, drug abuse), internal conflicts, (e.g., inaccurate perception of one's role at work and/or at home), deconditioning (the medical term for being out of shape), "tired blood," chronic mononucleosis, use of certain medications (including pred-

37

nisone), any inflammatory disease (including lupus), many systemic infections, and other factors.

A skilled physician will try to determine the cause of the symptom of fatigue and not summarily dismiss the patient either with an aspirin and/or Valium in hand (although these medications do have their place) or with a hasty referral to a psychiatrist (although a course of psychotherapy may be indicated). Each of these remedies may be appropriate for a particular patient. One needs to ascertain whether an organic disease and/or a functional disorder are the primary cause(s) of the fatigue. In SLE, fatigue due to inflammation often responds to treatment with NSAID (see Introduction, p. xxx) or corticosteroids.

Holly Atkinson, in her book *Women and Fatigue* and in other publications, provides many helpful hints on how to avoid fatigue. How to decrease a work load? Learn to say no. Perhaps an assertiveness workshop would help define where you feel manipulated or "put upon." Get family members and friends to help you just as you helped them in the past. Stop being a perfectionist. (Who cares, besides you, whether your house is spotless and every meal superb?) Exercise! Increase your heart rate by 50 percent three times per week. Routine household chores do not qualify. Work up a sweat by swimming, jogging, bicycling, aerobics, vigorous walking, whichever one you like to do! You'll sleep better and feel better about yourself. Curb unhealthful habits such as smoking, drinking alcohol, taking drugs (not medications), and fad diets. Carve out time to pamper yourself each day. Read, write a long-overdue letter, lunch with a friend, soak in a tub. Get in touch with your energy levels. You'll accomplish more on days when you have a high energy level. Get in touch with your feelings. Anger, dissatisfaction, resentment, and inner conflicts dissipate energy. Seek the cause(s) of these feelings, resolve them (perhaps with the aid of a professional), and get on with your life. Sigmund Freud talked of the twin pillars of life: love and work. He stressed that it was vital for one's emotional and physical well-being to blend (not just balance) the two. If they are in conflict, stress results, and the body will be drained of energy trying to cope with that stress.

To return to Mrs. Aladjem and her exhaustion—she was on an extensive trip through Holland and was caring for her husband

and children (one of whom became ill), enough to make anyone tired! But Mrs. Aladjem had done all that before without abnormal fatigue. Some significant changes had developed on this trip. What did headaches, the lost voice, the fevers, the red nose, all indicate?

Trained as a scientist, I instinctively search for the molecules that cause a disease and use proper medications to effect a cure, but I'm also concerned with how someone reacts to the symptoms of a disease. As a physician, I know that the synthesis of both the measurable molecules as well as the "gut" feelings need tender caring to make a person feel well again. How would any of us respond to symptoms of fever, headache, exhaustion, rashes, etc? We wish they would vanish and wonder what we can do to accomplish that. Take two aspirins and call the doctor in the morning? Rest and hope the symptoms will disappear? Fortunately, many illnesses do dissipate no matter what we do or do not do, and we never know (or very much care) what caused them. The conditions that do not simply disappear create anxiety, stress, internal conflicts, and exhaustion and prompt us to either consult a physician or cause us to spiral downward into inaction.

7. Return from Florida
The Patient's Story

THE moment I stepped off the plane at Logan Airport, a cold, icy wind enveloped me in a new blanket of pain. My head whirled, and my stiff joints grew stiffer. With Al tugging at my skirt, I struggled to reach the terminal. My husband exclaimed with alarm at the eruptions on my face. "I couldn't tolerate the sun," I said, trying not to further alarm him.

"That's strange." He observed my face more closely. "All your life you've loved the sun so much." When we got home, he urged me to call Dr. Fried at once.

First thing in the morning, I went to see our physician. He, too, was troubled by my worsened condition. My swollen legs and ankles seemed to puzzle him more than the eruptions on my face. Dr. Fried prescribed acetazolamide.* The drug reduced the swelling but did not eliminate it completely. The headache, nausea, and dizziness persisted; I felt almost as sick as I had on the boat coming back from Europe. When Dr. Fried suggested that we increase the

*Acetazolamide: a sulfonamide diuretic (causes increased urine formation or excretion). Trade name: Diamox.

dose of acetazolamide, I felt reluctant to follow his advice. I told him I had a weird feeling that drugs were worsening my affliction.

In the days that followed, my dizziness got worse, and I developed an impossible itch all over my body. The itch was driving me out of my mind. My two little girls were taking turns in scratching my back.

Next, an angry rash appeared on my arms. Dr. Fried decided to send me to a skin specialist in Boston. The Boston doctor prescribed a powder and a thick paste to be applied daily to the rash. After each application, the eruptions worsened. The UV light that he used on it increased the rash, the itch, and the pain throughout my body. I sounded like a madwoman when I tried to explain to Dr. Fried that whatever I was taking by mouth or applying to my skin was killing me.

Dr. Fried and I discussed the matter further. He declared that, once and for all, we had to determine the exact nature of my problem. "You have so many complaints suggestive of rheumatoid arthritis, I think it's time you saw a specialist." He recommended Dr. Zenith of Massachusetts General Hospital in Boston. "I'll make the arrangements right now." He picked up the telephone and made the appointment for four o'clock that same afternoon.

I parked the car in front of Dr. Zenith's office on Commonwealth Avenue. The temperature hovered around zero. My limbs ached in the worst way imaginable—my knees wobbled. Wondering if I could make it to the front door, I rested against the outside wall of the building. I managed the front door. Then I had to face the elevator. Opening that door was impossible—I had no strangth left to lift my arm. Totally frustrated, I fought to hold back tears, when a man appeared and rescued me and we rode up together.

Dr. Zenith, a slender man in his mid-forties, noticed my weakened state immediately and rushed to offer me a seat. He said that I shouldn't be out on such a cold day. I admitted that I couldn't struggle against the assault of the weather. On cold days like this I felt like a car with a frozen motor. "But even when it is warm, I don't feel any different," I said.

"I can understand that," he offered in a sympathetic tone.

After he completed the patient-history phase of the interview, Dr. Zenith asked me to lie down on a wooden table with a comfortable two-inch mattress and began the physical examination. He spent over half an hour examining my muscles and swollen joints and checking my reflexes. My reflexes were satisfactory, my lungs were clear, and the liver and spleen appeared to be of normal size. When I was seated again in front of his desk, he casually inquired if I had any problems other than my physical ones. I must have looked rather surprised, for he hastened to ask, "Are you depressed?"

"By the disease, you mean?"

"Well, what we usually mean by 'problem' is"—he hesitated—"do you get along with your husband?"

I shrugged slightly, failing to see the connection.

"Do you have any money problems?" he persisted.

"Money problems?"

"Can you pay your bills?" He observed me for a moment, then dropped the subject.

When my examination was over, Dr. Zenith suggested that I take two aspirins* every three hours. "It's important to take them regularly," he advised. "Take the aspirins with a glass of milk," he added, and promised that the salicylate would alleviate my pains. After two days of taking sixteen aspirin tablets per day, my stomach turned sour. The milk, instead of helping, gave me cramps and diarrhea.

At my next visit, Dr. Zenith made a tentative diagnosis of rheumatoid arthritis. He said that my sedimentation rate was elevated, which suggested possible inflammation in my system. I also had a rather low white blood count, and there was no albumin† in my urine.

He handed me a slip of paper. "Here are some of your appointments I have arranged. The results of these studies should

---

*Aspirin: in 1763, it was discovered that an extract of the willow bark was effective in relieving the pains of rheumatism. Willow extract owes its therapeutic efficacy to a substance that is called salicylic acid—from the Latin name for willow, *salix*. A chemically modified form, acetylsalicylic acid, is marketed under the name of aspirin. For reasons still unknown, aspirin proves helpful for relieving pain.

†Albumin: "white protein"; an important protein of human blood serum that may be found in the urine in diseases of the kidney.

help us make a more definite diagnosis. Your first appointment is tomorrow at Massachusetts General Hospital in the Arthritic Therapeutic Department," he said, and stressed that the hydrotherapy there was superb. The application of water, such as whirlpool baths, and the exercise should help. He remembered to ask me how I had managed with the aspirins. I told him that the aspirins made me sick and so did the milk.

"The milk, too?" He seemed surprised. "Milk intolerance is uncommon in this country." He shrugged and suggested that I try Gelusil tablets instead of the milk. "It's an antacid control," he explained.

I asked him what the elevated sedimentation rate meant. Dr. Fried had mentioned that, too.

"An elevated sedimentation rate is usually associated with inflammation or some underlying complication or infection," he said. "But, in your case, I don't anticipate anything serious. Your hematocrit, hemoglobin, serology, and all your other blood values so far are normal." Dr. Fried had reported that my myasthenia gravis* test, thyroid tests,† and chest X rays were also normal.

In the car I looked at the slip of paper Dr. Zenith had given me in his office. I read:

> Wednesday + Friday—Mrs. J., Physical Therapy
> Hematology routine‡ LE?

The letters "LE" did not stand out on the slip of paper. In fact, they appeared quite innocent. But through the ensuing years, they were to lose their innocence.

---

*Myasthenia gravis: a disease in which nerve impulses are not properly transmitted to the muscle cells. As a result, muscles all over the body become weak.

†Thyroid tests: basal metabolism, radioactive iodine uptake—tests to determine whether the thyroid gland is over- or underactive.

‡Hematology routine: routine tests to count the cells of the blood. The LE cell is a white cell that has eaten the nucleus of another white cell; the latter appears as a blue-staining spot inside the first cell.

8. The Need for Consultation
The Physician's Point of View

HOW nice it is to come home. We feel secure seeing, feeling, and smelling all the familiar surroundings. We settle into our comfortable routines. The problems of the trip are put behind us, remain but an unpleasant memory, and are often best forgotten. Better to focus on the future, on happy children in school, happy family times. How easily that dream is spoiled by physical problems. How hard it is to begin a pleasant day when one is affected by inflammation of the joints (arthritis) or of the periarticular tissues (the tissues around joints). How hard it is to get out of bed on a cold morning when we feel so comfortable under nice warm quilts. Why face the cold air and floor? Why face all those chores you have to do when staying in bed is so much easier?

Illness can have a devastating effect on a sleeping/waking routine. When sleep is interrupted by pain or by nightmares (reflections of inner conflicts), we truly have not had a night's rest. A tired person has trouble facing a day of chores. Illness forces us to face our inability to continue as we were. Mrs. Aladjem is experiencing that frustration. She tries a few standard remedies for her aches and pains: aspirin, hot tea, a hot bath. They help only temporarily, and then the symptoms recur. She turns to a friend for help.

To whom do we frequently turn when we don't feel well? A good friend, a close relative, a loving spouse, a friendly neighbor, a sympathetic physician, media advertisements, the *Merck Manual*, and foundations. All offer advice. But who is giving the right advice for a particular person at a particular time in the course of his or her disease? For just as often as the advice from several sources may be similar, it may be conflicting. Most people try a variety of "home remedies" before calling a physician, which is probably reasonable behavior under most circumstances.

Mrs. Aladjem took the middle road. She turned to a friendly neighbor who was also a physician! He did what many physicians do when in doubt about a diagnosis: He admitted the patient into the hospital for diagnostic tests. (This was at a time that physicians now refer to as "the good old days," when patient care was primary and cost containment not yet an issue.) Now, however, under new guidelines for diagnostic related groups and related federal guidelines, physicians can no longer admit a patient for a diagnostic workup. Although convenient for patient and physician, the federal government tells us it is too expensive. Patients must now schedule repeated office visits as well as outpatient laboratory and X-ray appointments. It often seems as if hospitals and federal regulations have become silent partners in depriving patients of optimal care.

How does a physician diagnose lupus? It may be helpful at this point to review the early symptoms of SLE. Lupus may present itself in various ways. The onset is usually undramatic, gradual, with vague feelings of disease until some specific symptoms of lupus develop. However, it should be noted that early symptoms of lupus mirror symptoms of any acute or chronic illness and may simply disappear. These early symptoms include:

- Fever
- Fatigue
- Loss of appetite
- Weight loss
- Aches and pains
- Swollen glands

- Nausea and vomiting
- Headaches
- Depression
- Easy bruising
- Hair loss
- Edema/swelling

What a physician suspecting lupus is looking for are more specific signs, something measurable, observable, rather than just described. These specific signs include:

A rash over the cheeks and bridge of the nose
Discoid lupus lesions
Rashes after exposure to the sun or ultraviolet light
Ulcers (not chancre sores or blisters) inside the mouth
Arthritis—i.e., specifically, swollen, painful, inflamed joints
Pleurisy—confirmed by auscultation and/or X ray
Seizures
Psychosis
Anemia
Raynaud's phenomenon
Bald spots
Hives

How frustrating it must be to have some of these symptoms only some of the time (typically not when you're in the doctor's office!), and not know what causes them, rendering them untreatable. What can a patient who suspects early lupus do to help the doctor make a diagnosis? Keep accurate at-home records that track the symptoms (including photographs of a typical "flare"). Seek a physician who listens and believes. Physicians often consider themselves primarily scientists. They want and need to be objective, to diagnose correctly and treat appropriately. They need to be able to see, feel, hear, and measure something that can be defined as abnormal. It is often hard to take a history and determine what is real, what is imagined, what is normal, what is abnormal, for if the imagined is all too real to the patient, *that*, then, is the patient's reality and must be dealt with accordingly. Good listening is so important, as is watching a patient relate a story, for words, facial expressions, and mannerisms tell us how a patient feels about the symptoms. It is important for a physician to believe the symptoms if only because the patient believes in them. The art of medicine is blending the signs and symptoms, heart and mind, together not only to determine the correct diagnosis and specific treatment but also to help the patient (and family) deal with a potentially altered life-style. Kind words, sincerity, and a clear, comprehensible explanation of what is physically occurring in the body will allay fantasies and fears. Occasionally, circumstances may indicate ancillary treatment such as psychotherapy and/or anti-depressants.

9. Massachusetts General Hospital

The Patient's Story

MASSACHUSETTS General Hospital is located in downtown Boston near the Charles Street Jail and the West End Bridge. Approaching the bridge from the Cambridge side, I tried to remember if it was the one referred to by some Bostonians as the Longfellow Bridge after the lovely poem "The Bridge." As I drove across the Charles River, I dredged up the lines "I stood on the bridge at midnight, / As the clock was striking the hour . . .," and promptly missed my left turn at the busy rotary.

Inching my way with the traffic, I landed not at the hospital but in Scollay Square, right in the heart of Haymarket. Never had Boston seemed so colorful to me, so Bulgarian. I found a strong likeness to market day in Sofia, on Fridays, when the farmers brought their produce for sale. Here, too, the sidewalks were lined with old-fashioned grocery stores, and the cars could hardly move between the pushcarts heaped with fruits and vegetables. The market men made lots of noise in broken English. When I stuck my head out the car window, I detected at least three foreign accents—Greek, Armenian, and Italian. The air smelled of trotters marinated in bay leaves and vinegar and of stale blood from the butchers' shops. The smells nauseated me.

A feeling of disgust swept over me as a man pulled a large carcass half wrapped in brown paper out of the rear of his truck. The sight brought to mind how, as a growing girl, I had hated to go with Mother to the market, for that always included stopping at the butchers'. It made me sick to look at the butcher's white apron splattered with blood and at more blood dripping from his meat counter into a chipped enamel bucket on the floor.

Only last week Dr. Fried had asked me if I ate a balanced diet. I did now, but for years in Bulgaria I had refused to eat meat. It was a fad, Mother said, and Father teased me that I was doing it to show my support for Mahatma Gandhi, my hero. But now that I look back on it, I was more inclined to blame Abe Rott, the butcher, and the glazed eyes of the lambs that stared at me from every corner of his shop.

Another episode came to mind. When I was seven or eight years old, I liked to play in a neighbor's garden. The place belonged to a widow with gray hair and piercing black eyes, and she was bursting with energy. The neighbor's name was Mrs. Peneva. Mrs. Peneva tended to her garden from early morning until the sun went down. When she finished her chores, she sat on a low wooden stool, sipping Turkish coffee from a small gold-rimmed cup. Mrs. Peneva was very proud of this cup. It was a gift from Queen Joanna of Bulgaria in recognition of Mrs. Peneva's Red Cross work. Mrs. Peneva taught me how to water some of her flowers with a watering can that was just right for my size. On occasion she would let me feed the chickens in the back of her house. The squawking of the chickens as they followed me around filled me with excitement. At such moments, a smile flickered on Mrs. Peneva's lips. She would say that I was making more noise than the chickens, and she looked as happy as I was. One day I was sitting in the tall grass, munching sunflower seeds, when I saw Mrs. Peneva trying to catch a chicken, holding a long shining knife in her hand. What was she going to do with that knife? I was too scared to imagine. Then Mrs. Peneva caught a frightened, flapping chicken and cut its head off. After that, I kept well away from Mrs. Peneva's garden.

Lately I had been remembering childhood scenes. They drew

me out and in some ways helped me to face the new challenges with a little more understanding.

I reached the parking lot of the hospital by 9:20 A.M., ten minutes before my appointment. The walk to the main entrance was endless, and the distance from there to the Arthritis Department ridiculous. Even a healthy person would collapse. In the waiting room a ten-year-old boy watched me with curious black eyes from his wheelchair. His father, a sturdy-looking man dressed in Esso coveralls, offered me a piece of gum after he had given one to the boy and put two in his own mouth. I took it.

The black woman sitting on my right appeared well until I saw her fingers curled like eagles' claws. I imagined they were twisted by pain, mercilessly. The thought made my flesh creep. The black man beside her glared into space with heavy red eyes, as though he were attending a funeral. In the few minutes I sat there, I began to feel like one of them already. I was getting depressed. When a redheaded nurse came to the door and called my name in an Irish brogue, I was ready to flee from the place in horror. I followed her hesitantly through a ward swarming with cheerless arthritic patients. As I walked along behind the nurse, breathing in the patients' pain and helplessness, I felt defeated.

"Suppose I become a cripple, too? Suppose my fingers curl in like the black woman's? Suppose, suppose . . . What's the use, forget it," I snapped at myself. Behind another door the exercising gym was crowded with more crippled and dejected people—a nightmare. Dante must have had a similar sight in mind when he described his walk through the lower realms of the next world, I thought. How else could he have imagined such misshapen bodies, such tormented expressions, such eyes so full of doom?

"You look as if you expect to see the d-i-v-i-l," the nurse said as we entered a room divided into cubicles by curtains.

"You mean Lucifer?" I mumbled, trying to keep up with her fast pace. She pointed to a bed table where I was to lie down. Shortly after I stretched out on the uncomfortable table, a tall, heavyset intern came to question me about my symptoms. While he spoke to me, he checked my reflexes. After a few minutes, he moved on to the next cubicle, where a black man was groaning. The nurse took over. She showed me for half an hour how to exercise every muscle and joint in my body while lying flat on my back. On my way home, I felt more depressed than ever.

During one of my visits to the hematology laboratory, I overheard two technicians talking. They were unaware of my presence in the next room.

"Golly, I feel sorry for that woman with the foreign accent—the one we did the LE prep on," one said. "It was positive."

"Positive?" the other asked in a strange way. Then I heard her again: "I don't know what an LE cell is."

The first answered, "It stands for lupus erythematosus. The doctor said it's a horrible disease—it's incurable."

"I've never heard of it."

"You're not the only one. The doctor said he'd seen only a few cases in the past few years, and they were all in the terminal stages."

Although the voices remained implanted in my mind, I did not then associate myself with the "woman with the foreign accent." At my next appointment in his office, Dr. Zenith received me in a friendly way, but I felt a slight uneasiness in his voice when he began to tell me about the results of my blood tests.

"Something in your blood is puzzling us," he said. "We found a few cells which are suggestive of SLE. The test raises some questions of systemic involvement."

"SLE?" I repeated the letters, not hearing the rest of Dr. Zenith's words.

"That's short for systemic lupus erythematosus," he said, then looked at me for a moment. "The cells we found are only suggestive, not diagnostic, of lupus. We shall repeat the test."

I was stunned. The conversation I had overheard at Massachusetts General flashed through my mind. "What does lupus erythematosus mean?" I asked, feeling as if I had started to die already.

Dr. Zenith spread his palms. "Frankly, we don't know much about the disease—not yet, anyhow. We think it has a tendency to alter blood vessels and connective tissue; it could affect the kidneys . . ." He shrugged a little. "I wish I could be more specific. For the moment, the affliction is not recognized with much accuracy. I guess with lupus the first diagnostic act is to suspect the disease."

"Is there any treatment for the disease?" I asked.

"Not really," he said. "If the condition becomes acute, we manage to control it with cortisone."*

"So, it's incurable," I mumbled to myself. I didn't know what cortisone was, but I asked him if I could be given this medication.

"No, no, not at the moment," he hastened to answer. "Truly, we spent hours the other day examining your blood again, but we couldn't find another abnormal cell."

He had an ascetic, angular face with clear, penetrating eyes. It was hard not to believe him. He reminded me to continue with the aspirins, do the exercises they taught me at Massachusetts General, keep to a no-salt-added diet, and try to rest as much as possible. Later he helped me get on the elevator. Before he closed the door, he said, "Sometimes all of a sudden the patient begins to feel better for no special reason at all. I've seen it happen with other patients."

On my return home, I sensed some excitement. "Mommy is home . . . Mommy is home!" Martha was running from one room to another, and I could hear Ingrid and Al shushing her. Before I took my coat and boots off, all three children were coming down the wide stairs dressed in party clothes. Each was holding a gift wrapped in colorful paper and tied with big bows. As if on cue, they started singing "Happy birthday, Mommy," with bright, glowing faces.

I had forgotten it was my birthday, and I stood there holding back my tears.

Birgitta poked her head through the kitchen door and wiped her hands on her white kitchen apron. "Happy birthday," she said with a broad smile. "You're a special person to be born on this day."

"How's that?" I looked at her curiously.

---

*Cortisone: a potent hormone of the adrenal glands; the pure compound was first discovered in adrenal secretion by Dr. Edward C. Kendall of the Mayo Clinic and by Dr. Tadeus Reichstein of Basel, Switzerland, simultaneously in 1936. It is now synthesized as a pure chemical.

"It's Sol-Tag, the day the sun comes back to Tromsø. We all celebrate your birthday back home. Even the children don't go to school on this day." She smiled at the children. "Instead, they stay home and eat cookies and drink hot chocolate. While you open your presents and see who sent you all these beautiful flowers," she rushed on, "I'll bring in some hot chocolate and cookies. . . . The children and I have baked them."

Surrounded by the children, with their glowing faces and their warm arms around me, I could feel new life pouring through my veins. In those few moments all I wanted was to stay alive, not only for my sake but also for the sake of my children. I wanted to get well more than ever before.

Shortly, Birgitta reappeared carrying a tray of hot, steaming chocolate and yellow saffron cookies in the shape of stars, sprinkled with sugar. "You are fortunate to be born on this day!" Birgitta looked at me with an earnest, thoughtful scrutiny and continued in a calm, matter-of-fact voice, her blue eyes studying me attentively. "You see," she continued, "my grandmother, Hella, has a favorite fairy tale which has been passed on word by word in our family for generations. The story is about a good-natured fairy with golden hair and a face that gleams like the sun. Her name is Destiny. The fairy lives down over hills and dales and through fjords, on a tiny island probably toward the northernmost point of the sea.* The trees on that island are thousands of years old, with twisted branches entangled by the strong Arctic winds. When Destiny walks through those woods at night, the golden glow on her face lights up the farthest corners of the island."

From time to time, Birgitta glanced at the children, whose eyes were wide open with wonderment, and said, "The birds on this island sing all night long, and the forest animals smile in their dreams." Birgitta spoke slowly, her voice low and convincing; it held the excitement of a person who is certain that her story holds some magic to affect the children's imagination. Then she glanced at me with a

*From an itinerary of Walter Heller, September 13, 1986.

pointed emphasis. "On Sol Tag, Destiny, who looks so much like the sun, gives out the gift of healing among the infants born on this day. This gift will help you take care of yourself."

Amused, I smiled at Birgitta. "It's a marvelous story," I said, "but I'm quite sure that Destiny forgot to give me the gift."

Birgitta looked hurt. "Destiny never makes such mistakes. Hella would be very angry with you for daring to doubt Destiny's diligence on this very special day."

"I don't want to anger Hella," I said, "but if I had such a gift, I would have been well by now, don't you think?"

Birgitta glanced at me and said bluntly, "You have the power of your gift, and you must use it."

I shook my head dubiously. "I hope you're right, Birgitta."

"You're a strong person." She beamed encouragement. "Such strength doesn't go away! It always returns in time of need. You see," Birgitta said, "in the multitude of newborn infants there are usually some who are stronger than the others." She laughed now good-naturedly. "These are the ones who are born with strong genes!"

It was my turn to laugh. "Perhaps you're right," I said. "I was the strongest of the pack. I weighed twelve pounds at birth and came in a sack. According to my grandmother Mays, this in itself was a good omen."

Birgitta's wisdom and confidence surprised me. I had to admit to myself that her words had an effect on me. One has to believe in something, I thought. Destiny . . . hope . . . even magic . . . anything to help one live from one day to another.

My eyes were closing with fatigue. The visit at Massachusetts General Hospital had drained me of all energy. Birgitta said gently, "You'll feel better soon . . . you'll see." She suggested I lie down on the sofa in the study and rest before dinner. I did just that. Shortly, I drifted into sleep. I saw Destiny in my dream. She appeared faceless, golden. She followed me around, reflecting my own image. Like in a twilight, the images were vague, but not so vague that I did not remember that in the dream Destiny became me and a sense of hope and security was born of this metamorphosis.

When I woke up, I kept my eyes closed for a long time. I

thought of Birgitta's story, and I thought of the dream. Everyone has something that helps them from birth to death. But one needs wisdom for a deeper understanding of one's self. New hope rose inside me. I reflected some more. This illness was not only assaulting my body; it was also striking at my self-image. It was a challenge. Physical and mental discipline was necessary to meet this challenge. It needed lots of effort, but what was life without effort?

After dinner that day, Birgitta brought to the table a large, fluffy cake that she and the children had decorated with a bright yellow sun. When we lit the candles in the darkened dining room, the cake glowed. The inscription on the cake read, "In Search of the Sun." I asked Birgitta what was the meaning of those words.

She said, "When one searches for the brightness of the sun, there is hope for joy and for happiness."

"In search of the sun," I repeated to myself. Does hope promote wellness? Theologians speak of hope—but what do physicians know about hope? Do they understand the effects of stress on the human body? The effects of resignation? Of hopelessness? Of apathy and despair? The questions seemed to come from some great hollow in me, as if my subconscious had suddenly erupted.

While we were eating the cake, Birgitta looked at Al and said, "Your teachers will probably tell you about the three spirits of Destiny that live in Norway. They are named Urd, Verande, and Sculd. Those spirits decide the fate of every human being. They know what was, what had been, and what was to be. To every newborn infant they will grant a life of luck or a life of misery; a short life or a long life. Those spirits spin a thread of life for every human being."

"What kind of thread?" Al asked.

"The thread is mostly gray and coarse. But sometimes they spin threads of some brighter colors. And if you're a prince, they spin a thread of bright gold."

"I wish I was a prince," Martha chimed.

"You're silly," Ingrid said. "You can never be a prince."

"Why not?" Martha asked.

"Because! Because you're a girl."

I thanked Birgitta for the cake and told her that it was not often that one received a gift so wonderful that it also carried a promise for a brighter future. "I shall always remember this birthday," I said, "and I shall think of you with affection."

Several months went by. My sickness seemed to go on forever. Pessimism was not part of my makeup, but as matters grew worse, I began to lose hope and started to feel insecure. How does one keep from despairing? I kept asking myself. Was I ready to accept defeat? Was I going to give in to melancholy?

Dr. Fried came periodically to our house to give me the vitamin B_{12} injections. I suspected that the good man did so to keep up my morale and prevent me from succumbing to apathy. Everyone in the family grew fond of him, and he returned our feelings. The children anticipated his visits as much as I did. He used to bring them a few sugar candies in small envelopes, pretending to be their doctor. And my husband's face always brightened after he returned from walking Dr. Fried to his home next door. He, too, needed some moral support.

During this time, my system began to retain fluids, and I felt very dizzy. The radiators in our house were the old-fashioned kind —painted a bright silver—and if I looked at them for a long time, their shape appeared distorted. The same would occur with the geometric design of silver and gold in the wallpaper. The bizarre floating sensation and difficulty in focusing seemed like a hallucination. I could not bring myself to mention the radiators or wallpaper to anyone. In a voice filled with anguish, I told my husband about another maddening experience.

"I know that I'm not crazy," I said emphatically, "but you may wonder after I tell you. If I reach for a book or a plate, I sometimes feel that they move farther away and I'm not sure that I can make the contact. I know that I'm not crazy," I repeated, "but I feel like I'm going out of my mind."

"Stop saying that you're not crazy." My husband assumed a joking tone. "That's what crazy people do. They're usually the last ones to admit it." Then he became serious. "There must be a reason for your peculiar symptoms. Explain all this to Dr. Fried. But," he teased some more, "don't insist that you're not crazy."

I burst into tears. "I don't want to see a doctor again. They don't seem to know what's wrong with me. Every time I'm given a medication, I feel worse instead of better. Anyway, what do I have to lose?" Just as my husband was about to speak, I rushed on, "And furthermore, with all the odd symptoms I'm experiencing, I don't want to discuss my illness with anyone. Whenever you or I try to explain what's ailing me, we become so involved and so foolish sounding—it makes me feel uncomfortable. More than that, it makes me feel crazy." The last words came out as a screech.

"We won't talk about your sickness anymore if that bothers you." My husband took my hand. "But please stop worrying about it," he remonstrated. "You don't owe an explanation to anybody. So there." He looked as distraught as I was.

When, however, after a few more days of misery, my husband became increasingly worried and insisted I see a blood specialist, I reconsidered my decision.

10. Fear of Disease
The Physician's Point of View

NOTHING is as inevitable (and traumatic!) as birth, death, and paying taxes. Surely one can add illness to the above, with its accompanying trips to the doctor. As far back as childhood, few of us have pleasant memories of visits to physicians. Examinations, prodding, poking, pulling—and the shots that weren't supposed to hurt! We begin our medical memories with negative associations of disease and physicians. We have trouble differentiating between the illness (a negative concept) and the physician (whom we should regard with a positive attitude). Was a lollipop at the end of the visit enough to counteract the bad impression? Probably not!

Why do we conceive of disease as bad? Semantically, the word itself suggests negative connotations, that is dis-ease. Why do we not regard dis-ease as merely a troublesome episode in an otherwise fulfilling life? While this may be true for some, many consider disease a personal punishment for a wrongdoing and/or overindulgence. Others regard disease as merely "bad luck" or a germ caught from someone else. In any case, disease is considered diminishing. In a larger sense, disease can create a sociological and economic drain on society. A sensitive physician recognizes these residual associations of disease/doctor and helps to dispel the myth of the relationship by stressing his role as a healer and guide to long-lasting health.

Mrs. Aladjem's visit to a physician at the Massachusetts General Hospital is a chronicle of the many fears that patients face. Even now a visit to a hospital evokes fears of death and dying. Only two hundred years ago a hospital was considered a place where one went to die. Regrettably, despite innovative lifesaving technological and scientific advances, this concept lingers. Ideally, a hospital and a doctor's office should represent havens of hope and alleviation of suffering. But to most of us, a hospital or a doctor's office still symbolizes the dreaded examination, the poking, prodding, pulling. You bare your body and soul to the physician. Nothing remains private; nothing is deemed sacred. Physicians' questions seem irrelevant at best, too personal at times. One hundred years ago physicians examined patients but conducted no tests. Some now do tests to the exclusion of a thorough physical exam. Fortunately, most physicians still do both. Tests allow a physician to better understand what is going on inside the body in places and ways that cannot be reached. Tests assess the structure and function of all the organs in a way that no history or physical examination can hope to accomplish. But who likes to have blood drawn, to put on a johnny, half covering a naked body, and stand in front of an X-ray machine in a cold room, hearing and sensing the penetrating rays? Unless the patient has confidence in the physician and maintains a positive attitude, examinations can truly be an ordeal. When examinations end, new fears arise: Why do they take so long? When will I hear the results? What will the results mean? If the results are inconclusive, will I need more tests?

What does disease mean to people? To one it may mean the discomfort of a "common" cold—a runny nose, headache, and sore throat. But the knowledge that it will only last a few days makes it bearable. A short-term illness is relatively easier to endure because of its limited duration. A chronic illness, however, is a heavy cross to bear, for such a diagnosis implies that this problem may never become just an unpleasant memory. It may mean a physical deformity, a gnarled hand, a limping walk, a curved spine, a cutaneous scar—

deformities that one cannot (easily) hide. Anxiety often compounds the fear that a deformity may cause embarrassment to the family, neighbors, and employers. Some deformities make it more difficult to keep house, make meals, go shopping, dress oneself, have children, enjoy sex, keep a job. Some disabilities may not be physically visible but may affect some vital organ. For example, if the kidneys, heart, and blood are not functioning normally, one may appear healthy but feel ill. Some disabilities may be psychological. In this age of stress and tension, fears and phobias abound. Millions of people, adults and children alike, suffer from crippling anxiety attacks that prevent them from leading "normal" lives. Who would not term this syndrome a dis-ease? Caring, continued, candid discussions between patient and physician can help allay many of these fears. Physicians must learn to listen "beyond the words," sense what the patient is feeling, and assess when short-term therapy or joining a support group is indicated as an adjunct to medical treatment. Admittedly, patients have the more difficult task of shedding the old image of physician as an aloof god and developing a willingness to share embarrassing concerns and anxieties. Often, the mere(?) unburdening brings relief and reassurance, as the physician clarifies the cause(s) of the symptoms and together they develop possible solutions.

A justified concern of many patients is medication. The media, reflecting current medical theory, encourages modifying our diet and/or life-style, to be illness-free. Failing that, chained to a disease with no known cause or cure, the lupus patient reluctantly becomes dependent on medication, with its possible side effects. Rashes, diarrhea, nausea, and drowsiness are common side effects of many medications. But the risk/benefit ratio for most medications is very high. Therefore, when I prescribe a particular medication for a patient, it is because I've deduced from my readings and from my clinical experience that the expected benefit will exceed the potential risk. I make a point of explaining what benefit I expect from the medication and what the possible side effects may be (carefully trying to avoid a self-fulfilling prophecy).

Granted, no one likes to take medication for a long time, much less forever. Each pill is a reminder of an unwanted illness, a dependency, a potential flare-up. This scenario can be psychologically crippling. Again, maintaining a positive attitude, focusing on what the medications enable you to do and not what the disease is preventing you from doing, will help.

There is another subtle fear that a patient often has to face, as did Mrs. Aladjem, that is, the fear that a diagnosis cannot easily be made, the symptoms not explained, or a specific treatment recommended. A corollary fear, just as frightening, is that an incorrect diagnosis is made and inappropriate medication, whose side effects are worse than the original disease, is prescribed! Coping successfully with these fears requires a joint effort by patient and physician. Patients should select a physician who is respected in the medical community as having documented expertise in the particular specialty required. Physicians should prescribe conservatively, monitoring for side effects both physical and psychological, and maintain an open dialogue with the patient.

Fear can be a very disabling syndrome. To her enormous credit, Mrs. Aladjem maintained a positive attitude and sought the advice of a specialist at another hospital in hope, not fear, that her symptoms would be explained, clarified, and specifically treated.

11. Children's Hospital Medical Center

The Patient's Story

OUR pediatrician was a renowned blood specialist and a professor of pediatrics at Harvard Medical School. Through the years, we had built a steady friendship, and I valued his judgment. After much deliberation, I phoned Dr. Louis K. Diamond. I asked him if he would consider doing some blood testing on me to determine whether I had LE. I told him the results of my blood test. Between suitable pauses, he asked me a few questions to give himself time to reflect, then said yes, he would see me the following morning.

Dr. Diamond was also the associate physician in chief of the Children's Hospital Medical Center in Boston, and his office was located on the fourth floor of the main building of the hospital. At ten o'clock the next morning Dr. Diamond welcomed me, eager to hear more about my condition. His face reflected a sad gentleness that I assumed he had acquired through his many years of working with suffering children. With his courteous manner and impeccable dress, he gave the impression of an old-fashioned European gentleman.

"I'm glad you called me," he said, holding a chair for me. "You look well," he added amiably. "I see no lupus."

"I'm afraid I've panicked," I murmured.

He looked down at my face and smiled. "I never would have suspected you of panic."

"It's an impossible situation," I said. "I'm getting tired of seeing so many doctors. Besides Dr. Fried, I have seen a skin specialist, an eye specialist, a thyroid specialist, a myasthenia gravis specialist, and a rheumatoid arthritis specialist—I am reaching the point where I don't want to see another doctor."

He didn't reply to that but went behind his desk and sat down. He pulled out a pad of paper from his desk and for a moment remained quiet, as if wondering how to begin. His office overlooked a terrace filled with pigeons. Two well-fed birds came close to the window and stared at Dr. Diamond in an expectant way.

Dr. Diamond jotted something down and then opened his diagnostic questioning by asking how I felt.

"I feel tired, dreadfully tired. At times I can barely lift my arms."

He nodded with a sympathetic look. "I'll be more than happy to do a complete blood analysis on you. But I must warn you that since you are a grown woman, I can conduct only a limited examination. Anyhow, we'll talk about this later," he said, and then asked, "Besides being tired, do you have any other symptoms?"

"God, yes. I feel dizzy most of the time." Dr. Diamond wrote this down. Suddenly I was anxious to tell him everything that was wrong with me. When he looked up again, I said, "In the past year I have been more susceptible to infections than I can ever remember."

"What do you mean by 'infections'?"

"I have a constant sore throat—a very peculiar one. It hurts and it doesn't! It's hard to describe."

Dr. Diamond looked up from his notebook.

"And I have recurring bouts of nausea. This plagues me more than anything else. I can't stand it!"

"Any skin problems?" He focused his eyes on my face.

I described the redness that had appeared on the exposed parts of my body.

"The V around my neck in particular has turned an angry

red, suggesting sunburn." I showed him the redness, which seemed to puzzle him.

Then Dr. Diamond asked, "Did you have proper nourishment as a child?"

"What do you mean?"

"Did you have enough to eat?"

"Yes, as far as I can remember, I was a well-fed child. Bulgaria used to be famous for growing fine fruit and vegetables," I added, a little puzzled by his question.

He looked up briefly from his pad of paper, then turned to a fresh page and looked at it as if he were reading something important. "All right," he said, "tell me something about the health of your family."

"My grandmother on my father's side died of asthma at sixty-eight." While he was writing this down, I said, "I loved that grandmother dearly. I was only ten at the time of her death, but I can still recall my distress. Mother used to say that I took after Maia spiritually and physically. Maybe I also inherited some of her allergies, although I have never had asthma."

Dr. Diamond smiled discreetly, then bent down to write as I continued.

"On my mother's side, my grandfather died of a heart attack, and my grandmother lived to be very old—she had her last baby at the age of forty-nine." Dr. Diamond chuckled and asked if I were conscious of any special diseases among other members of my family. All I could remember was that my mother and father had each lost two brothers with TB. "Mother always overprotected us as children against colds for fear that we might catch the disease. My only brother is fine. My mother has mild diabetes; my father has atherosclerosis."

"You must be getting tired," Dr. Diamond said. He put his pen down on his desk and asked if I would like a glass of tomato juice before we continued. I nodded, and he went out and brought back two large glasses of cold tomato juice. "Just a few more minutes of questioning," Dr. Diamond said when he put his glass down. He wanted me to recall some of my childhood diseases.

I remembered mumps and chicken pox and, when I was

eight, double pneumonia and hepatitis, which kept me from school for half a year. I told him I used to have bronchitis and a chronic runny nose that I was constantly reminded to wipe. I also remembered that at age nineteen I had a deep abscess under my right arm that had to be opened under general anesthesia, and I told him of the skiing accident after which I had developed erysipelas. "I felt dizzy all the time," I said, and stressed once more the miracle drugs I was treated with. "The ankle has bothered me ever since." I paused for breath. "Several weeks after the skiing episode, a sore the size of a quarter appeared on the right calf of my other leg. That oozed pus for months and months. I still have the mark."

"That's interesting." Dr. Diamond became more animated. "Do you have any idea what those miracle drugs were?"

I didn't. In Bulgaria, doctors did not discuss such matters with their patients. I mentioned the erysipelas I'd had in Holland at the onset of my present disease and the sulfonamide the Dutch doctor had given me. "Somehow every time I am given these drugs, instead of feeling better, it seems to me I feel worse." I listened to myself repeat the same words that I had spoken when Dr. Fried had administered the acetazolamide.

Dr. Diamond did not interrupt me at all. Only when I finished, he said, "Tell me more about the sore on your leg."

"A question of TB of the bone was raised," I recalled, "but meanwhile, the sore healed, and nothing further was done about it."

"I'll look at your scar later when I examine you." Dr. Diamond leaned back in his chair. "Then what happened?"

"I came to this country and was married, and it seems like I have been seeing doctors continuously ever since. I am beginning to feel uncomfortable talking endlessly about myself. It must sound to you like a dull autobiography."

"With an uncommon condition like yours, the doctor assumes the role of a detective, and any detail, however trivial or remote, may hold the key to the solution of the mystery. Let me tell you, before we come up with a correct diagnosis, you'll probably have to repeat your story more than once." He meant every word—as I found out countless times later.

"You arrived in this country, you were married," he read aloud from his notes. "Did you have normal deliveries with your children?"

"More or less. I was married five years before Al was born. I needed a small operation to conceive." I paused to remember what followed immediately after. "After the delivery, a kidney infection developed."

"Did that clear up right away?" Dr. Diamond asked.

"I had a fever for a while, then I was given—" I suddenly stopped.

Dr. Diamond looked up from his pad of paper.

"I was given something to combat the infection, and I developed a horrid-looking rash. I had lumps all over my scalp."

Dr. Diamond wrote with hurried strokes, then said, "Go on."

"A year and a half later, Ingrid came along. This time the bleeding continued for some months, so I had to return to the hospital for a D and C."* I heaved a long sigh and went on talking in a monotone. "Two years later, I had a miscarriage. But in four months I was pregnant again with my last child. This pregnancy began with bleeding, which eventually stopped. The delivery was extremely difficult. Labor had to be induced, and I was given several blood transfusions. Martha turned out to be a healthy eight-pound girl with a wonderful disposition."

"I know," he said, grinning. "She's a charmer. But how did you feel when you returned home from the hospital?"

I told him how I couldn't walk for months after I returned from the hospital with Martha. I developed phlebitis† in both legs. The skin became ulcerated, and a year later, the veins had to be stripped. I cringed at the memory. "The incisions did not heal properly, and staphylococcal infection set in and lasted for over six months. The exhaustion during the pregnancy, during the delivery, and after I took the baby home is very hard to describe," I said. "There are no words to describe it—no words to describe such fatigue. But I

*D and C: abbreviation for dilation of the cervix and curettage of the uterus.
†Phlebitis: inflammation of a vein.

was fortunate," I said after a breath. "I had a skilled obstetrician who was also a very kindhearted man. It helps at such times to have a doctor who is also your friend."

Dr. Diamond smiled comprehendingly. "Would you go through the experience again?" he asked with a testing look in his eyes.

"The answer is yes—if I could still have the same good medical care and if I could get rid of this fatigue and exhaustion."

"You have a nice family already," he said. "You must concentrate on that."

"I know," I said. "When I look at my children, all being healthy and well, I count my blessings. That brings me just about to the beginning of my present difficulty," I said, then reluctantly repeated to him the current symptoms that I already had gone over with Dr. Fried and Dr. Zenith.

A petite nurse walked in with a tray filled with tiny tubes. She drew an ounce or so of blood from my arm and pricked my finger for some smears. As she did so, Dr. Diamond phoned Dr. Zenith's office and asked if he could see the positive LE prep I had mentioned. Dr. Diamond could not hide his annoyance when he was told that one of the technicians at Massachusetts General Hospital had lost the preparation. A few minutes later, a trim, vivacious young woman entered and introduced herself.

"I'm Dr. Heally, Dr. Diamond's assistant." She extended me a friendly hand. "I'm here to help with your examination."

Dr. Diamond indicated that Dr. Heally would take over. I followed her to a small room next door. She helped me undress, then pointed to an examining table and told me to lie flat on my back. She moved a chair close to the table and started the customary tedious examination. I had to answer more questions as she went over every inch of my body. When she finished, she covered me with a crisp white sheet so that I could be seen only from the chin up and called in Dr. Diamond.

He came into the room and felt the lymph nodes on my neck, then lowered the sheet just enough to put his hand first under one arm, then under the other, to check for more nodules. It took some skill to manipulate the sheet so that my spleen, liver, and abdomen could be felt without exposing an unnecessary inch of flesh. At the end of the examination, he confessed that he hadn't examined a grown woman since his medical-school days, which made Dr. Heally laugh and me turn crimson.

Dr. Heally reported to Dr. Diamond that I appeared to be in good shape. Except for a bunion on my left foot and the redness of the V of my neck, she hadn't come across anything impressive. We made my next appointment for Saturday morning, two days later, when Dr. Heally was to measure the sugar level in my blood. Dr. Diamond said by then all my other blood values should be back. I left his office with a glimmer of hope.

On Saturday, Dr. Heally was already waiting for me in Dr. Diamond's examination room. She greeted me with a friendly smile. "How do you feel?"

"Tired, just plain tired."

She confessed that she, too, was worn out, having studied all night for her medical board exams. "There are literally thousands of facts to remember! It's murder!" she exclaimed. I agreed that some exams were sadistic in nature and should be modernized, along with other things in the educational system.

"God should hear you in a hurry, before I collapse from the tension."

Dr. Diamond peeked in and asked how his grown-up patient was, then hurried off before I had a chance to answer. An hour later I was in his office once again. This time we sat down to talk at the other end of his large room. He informed me right away that my blood picture was good. "I did all the tests myself," he said, "and everything looks fine." He sounded genuinely pleased. "The cell we found is not the typical LE cell; there is a slight morphological dissimilarity. We come across such cells more frequently than the true LE cell." I could feel my breathing quicken. "In my opinion, you don't have systemic lupus," he said, and nodded to confirm his words. "You might have a related condition to lupus, but even that will have to be determined by more specific tests."

"Dr. Diamond," I suddenly asked, "what does an LE cell look like?"

He asked me to move closer to the round coffee table and drew a small circle on the cover of an old *Life* magazine. He carefully filled in some shadows inside the circle. "That's roughly how an LE cell looks under the microscope," he said. "Some of the white cells have large, abnormal bluish lumps inside them. We call these cells LE cells."

"You're a fine teacher," I remarked.

"I like teaching," he replied, "and I like to explain to my patients all I can." He adjusted his glasses with extra care and said, "Recently we've found positive LE cells in patients who are hypersensitive* to penicillin, tetracycline,† and the anticonvulsants.‡ In some instances, penicillin can produce lesions of polyarteritis nodosa,§ a disease resembling lupus," he explained. "And at Robert Breck Brigham Hospital, over twenty percent of the rheumatoid arthritis patients have LE cells. They were admitted as arthritic cases but probably have something that is at least related to lupus."

This was the first time that I had heard of Robert Breck Brigham Hospital. It is the arthritic hospital in Roxbury—not to be confused with Peter Bent Brigham, which was next door to Children's Hospital Medical Center. "The presence of an occasional LE cell is not reliable evidence of SLE," Dr. Diamond continued. "In a few diseases that overlap with lupus, we can now find LE cells. Several other conditions can mimic systemic lupus, and some criteria are merely suggestive of the disease and should not be applied dogmatically." I was absorbing every word.

"I find it difficult to cope with my illness," I blurted out. "My friends and family see me well one moment and in distress the next. They must be questioning my sanity." I paused. "I need understanding of what's going on," I said. "It's frustrating . . . I wonder how this is affecting my family."

"Do they resent your being ill?" Dr. Diamond asked.

---

*Hypersensitivity: a form of allergy generally mediated by antibodies, a special group of blood proteins.

†Penicillin and tetracycline: antibiotics.

‡Anticonvulsants: drugs used to reduce frequency of convulsions.

§Polyarteritis nodosa: inflammation of the large arteries.

"I don't know if that is the proper word," I said, "but the children mind when I can't drive them from one place to another. My husband, too, is missing my vigor and my desire to do the things I used to enjoy—we used to enjoy. What makes it so difficult is that I look so healthy. I feel tired of having to explain all the time. . . ."

"You do look a picture of health," Dr. Diamond said with a smile.

"I don't want to be sick," I said in a low voice. "I want to be well. I'm willing to fight, but . . ."

"But what?" Dr. Diamond asked.

"But I must know what I'm fighting. My symptoms of pain, dizziness, and fatigue are not specific," I said. "I can't show anything to the doctors except my swollen fingers and rings that are getting tighter and tighter."

"The fact that you cannot show any signs of disease does not mean that you are not suffering," Dr. Diamond said. "What is important to me at this moment is how you feel. When you tell me that you're dizzy and tired and in pain, my job is to find out why you feel the way you do and try to help you. Let's hope that things will improve rather soon." His words had an encouraging sound to them.

"I must find a name for this illness of mine," I said.

"If you must," Dr. Diamond said, "we could call it a cousin of lupus." His voice became firmer when he added, "However, your condition is not something that you can manage by yourself. That would be foolish!" He sounded for a moment as if he were talking to a child. "You need a skillful physician who will become interested in your case and be willing to spend lots of time on it." He observed me for a moment, waiting for my reaction, then went on. "I have a doctor in mind, but for the next year he is engaged in special research in Puerto Rico. But we cannot wait a year. For now we should get in touch with Dr. George W. Thorn at Peter Bent Brigham Hospital. I hope that he will consider taking your case." When I didn't openly react, he continued. "Dr. Thorn doesn't see many patients; he, too, is engaged in research. His field is endocrinology."*

*Endocrinology: the study of the glands of internal secretion.

I had no idea what endocrinology was, but I agreed to see Dr. Thorn because of my implicit trust in Dr. Diamond's judgment.

Pleased, Dr. Diamond wrote down the names of some vitamin pills for me to take: folic acid, B_6, ascorbic acid, and a few others, all to be taken in large doses for a few weeks. I was to continue to see Dr. Fried and get the vitamin B_{12} injections. Since I had complained about taking aspirins, he told me to try Bufferin for my aches. "If that doesn't work, Alka-Seltzer might," he said with a chuckle. "Both are actually aspirin buffered with excess sodium bicarbonate."

As I left the Children's Hospital Medical Center, I walked a little straighter. The fright that had hounded me since I had overheard the two technicians at Massachusetts General lessened. The solid enemy of lupus became fragmented in my mind into several diseases of various strengths. Today each one of them was worth fighting. It seemed easier to think that I could overcome a condition related to lupus than the disease itself.

Dr. Diamond's promise of eventual recovery stimulated a feeling of expectancy. I was beginning to feel hope—hope that generated some new energy in my system.

12. Taking a Medical History
The Physician's Point of View

HOW do you feel when symptoms persist, week after week, waxing and waning, but never really disappear? What do you do after seeing physicians, specialists, and "authorities," none of whom offers a definitive diagnosis, much less shares his mystification with you! I repeat: A good physician is one who is available, communicates well with and offers hope to a patient, acknowledges the limit of his own knowledge and expertise, and, when puzzled, seeks consultation with another physician. The perceptive patient will recognize and respect these attributes in a physician rather than consider them inadequacies. Conversely, dissatisfaction with one's physician usually results in "shopping around." The issue of consumerism, so currently popular, is no less relevant to personal medical care than to household products. We are each responsible for obtaining what we consider best for our own bodies. So often I hear of an individual who "physician hopped" until one doctor finally made the "correct" diagnosis, that is, told the patient what she or he wanted to hear. However, was the diagnosis medically sound, was it only what the patient wanted to hear, or was it simply (?) that the disease evolved to the point that it could be recognized—by anyone? These are difficult questions to answer. In the final analysis, trust is the essential factor that cements the patient/doctor relationship in the treatment of chronic illness.

How does a physician determine what is ailing an individual? How does he decipher the code, the signals that a patient gives in an oral history, prior to a physical examination? My medical students are encouraged to read Agatha Christie as a good example of learning to look, listen, and search for clues. Accurate diagnosis is similar to solving a mystery. Taking a history from a patient is a combination of listening (sensitively and perceptively) and asking pertinent questions, many of which may appear irrelevant to the patient. Explaining the process of differential diagnosis often eliminates resistance to prolonged questioning. A history begins with a description of the symptoms that resulted in seeking help. Each sentence may evoke a question from a physician. A dialogue begins, a routine that is familiar to many of us. The hypochondriac, presenting pages and pages of medical history, may try the patience of the physician who is looking for objective rather than subjective information. A delicate balance of evaluation is often difficult to maintain.

On a first visit, I usually discuss the health of the patient's parents and other family members and whether any of them have had lupus or a related disease. I explain that there is an increased frequency of lupus and related diseases among relatives of lupus patients. Predictably, a concern shared by many young lupus patients is pregnancy and the hereditary risk of a child developing lupus. The actual risk is about 5 percent; that is, about one in twenty children born to a lupus parent will develop lupus. The risk is low, but sadly, not zero. Understandably, genetic "facts" create fear, tension, and anxiety in the young lupus patient.

Regarding pregnancy: If the risk of having a child with lupus is small, what are the risks associated with the pregnancy itself? Many of us have ambivalent feelings about pregnancy. While we would like to regard pregnancy as a joyous occasion, the culmination of the sharing that a couple can achieve, we cannot forget the typical accompaniments—morning (noon and night, for some) sickness, weight gain, low back pain, fatigue, and swelling of extremities. How does

a lupus patient react to these tugs and pulls on her emotions—
wanting a baby but dreading the pregnancy? Lupus patients who are
considering pregnancy are advised that while 10–15 percent of *all*
pregnancies end in miscarriage, the percentage rises to about 30
percent in lupus patients. Exacerbation of the disease may also occur
during and/or shortly after delivery. The pregnant lupus patient,
therefore, has good reason to be fearful and needs a compassionate
physician-obstetrician team for medical and emotional support
throughout the entire nine months. Frequent appointments, phone
calls, hospitalizations (if needed), and lab tests are but some of the
willing sacrifices lupus patients make. The "dynamic duo," that is,
the physician and obstetrician, while playing supportive roles, do not
necessarily enjoy the same positions vis à vis the patient. The physician
monitoring the lupus may still be (subconsciously) negatively associated with the disease. The obstetrician, however, is associated with
a joyful experience and outcome—a healthy baby! Is it all worth it?
Seeing the smiles on the faces of the parents and involved physicians
after the delivery of a healthy baby answers the question!

Mrs. Aladjem had many of the complications of pregnancy
seen in lupus patients. She was given good medical care, but complications arose. Dr. Diamond deduced that Mrs. Aladjem's fevers
and severe infections after her pregnancies were more frequent and
severe than normal. They reflected either a local problem (e.g., recurrent sinusitis due to a blocked duct) or a systemic defect in the
immune system due to a deficiency of immunoglobulins, complement,
white blood cells, or other factors. Here at last was the clue he
needed! Patients with lupus usually have more infections than do
healthy individuals, as a combination of these defects. Lupus patients
are also caught in a further dilemma. The infection, whether bacterial
or viral, may cause a lupus relapse. Sulfonamides and penicillin, normally used to treat the infection, may also cause a relapse. Furthermore, the corticosteroids used to treat many lupus patients may make
them more susceptible to infections. Therefore, a history of recurrent
bacterial infections is objectively significant. I explain all these potential
problems to lupus patients and insist that they contact me when they
develop symptoms of an infection so that I can (1) determine whether

it is indeed an infection or a relapse of lupus, (2) determine the cause and type of infection, and (3) treat the infection quickly so as to prevent a relapse. I observe the patient carefully for signs of a relapse, ready to react aggressively and quickly.

Fever (temperature over 100 degrees) is another symptom of concern to physicians and patients. I insist that patients call me when a fever is above 100 degrees, and together we try and determine its cause. Did it develop suddenly? Was it associated with a chill? This combination usually suggests an infection. If it developed gradually over a few weeks, it suggests a relapse. A sore throat, runny nose, and headache suggest a common virus. A cough that produces yellow sputum suggests a bacterial bronchitis or pneumonia. A burning sensation on urination suggests a urinary tract infection. Acute diarrhea usually represents either food poisoning or an infection—chronic diarrhea is more likely due to lupus. Gradually increasing headaches with fever and inability to flex one's neck suggests meningitis. Taking a careful history is important. Listening is critical. Depending on the presumed cause of the fever, I may wait and watch, prescribe aspirin, antibiotics, or corticosteroids, depending on the circumstances. The message for the patient with a fever? Contact your physician. The message for the physician? Listen carefully, and take action, if necessary.

When Dr. Diamond questioned Mrs. Aladjem about her past history, he also asked about her diet. Why is a physician concerned with what a patient eats? Some diseases are caused by a deficiency of certain nutrients: iron deficiency anemia, pellagra, and rickets are but a few such diseases. Dr. Diamond was particularly interested in the possibility of pellagra, whose photosensitive rash may resemble that of a lupus rash. However, a normal intake of grains, cereals, and/ or meat all containing vitamin B_3 (niacin) will prevent pellagra. Taking a dietary history may also reveal unhealthful eating habits: too many calories, too much fat, not enough calcium, too much, or too little protein. Although these factors may have little direct relevance to lupus, a thorough physician is concerned with the overall good health of the patient and will endeavor to take a dietary history and recommend changes if necessary. Patients naturally rebel against what they imagine will be bland, tasteless food and not enough of it! Explanations of the benefits of low sodium, reduced calories, increased calcium, etc., often require repetition. It is difficult to alter ingrained familial eating patterns and dietary habits. Physicians must continue to advise, convince, and cajole, often for years, before a dietary change can be considered permanent.

At the close of Mrs. Aladjem's detailed history-taking session, Dr. Diamond is considering a diagnosis of lupus. He recommends a thorough physical examination, followed by specific laboratory tests. We leave them not yet defining her disease but closer to doing so and determined to search further. The investigation continues. So does Mrs. Aladjem's spirit of determination.

13. The House on Prince Street
The Patient's Story

Patients' participation based on sound medical information can be of much help to the doctor.
—Dr. George W. Thorn

A bed, a patient, a doctor, a nurse, and a cook do not
constitute what the French call a Hôtel Dieu in the way
that Mark Hopkins, the student, and a bench might
conceivably constitute a college.
—David McCord,
The Fabrick of Man

DRIVING back to Newton from Dr. Diamond's office, I crawled
along at 30 mph, still dwelling on what I'd been told. Dr. Diamond
had given me new hope, but I still had to find a way to arrange my
life in such a way that I could spare all my strength for the family.
Instinct told me that I'd have to change my way of life, perhaps even
sell the big house we were living in. Even with Birgitta's help, the
demands of the house overwhelmed me. My increasing weakness
seemed to make the simple walk from one enormous room to the
next almost impossible. What a dreadful thought—to have to sell
our home! The idea horrified me. My husband would be most unhappy.
To him the place had become a symbol, the planting of his roots in
America, an anchor for his family. Besides, what Bulgarian ever thought
of selling his property? A house stayed in the family for generations,
complete with mothers-in-law, grandparents, and ancestral ghosts.

As I drove, I thought of how our house must have looked
seventy-five years ago when it was built by a prominent Boston
Brahmin family with taste and money to lavish on details; it must
have been charming then. But when we bought the old English Tudor,
it was worn and badly needed repair. We enlarged and brightened
the kitchen by knocking out a wall and adding a window. Two of

the three bathrooms needed new tubs and showers. The ceilings on both floors were sagging in places and ready to cave in. The furnace had to be replaced, as did every shingle on the roof.

To carpet, curtain, and furnish our house to look American, yet instill a European air, took time and imagination. We started by choosing Kirman rugs like those back home and hung a few paintings done by friends. We mounted the blue-and-white tiles that I had brought from Holland around the dining-room fireplace. For the mantelpiece, I chose the two large old jugs from my Delftware with silver mounts, gifts of Mr. Van de Vettering, one of the directors of my husband's company. I added a claret bottle and two old sack jugs. Blue plates with patterns of pastoral scenes graced the dining-room walls.

In every room, on almost every shelf and table, the Delft blue was on display. Every form of Delft was represented: candy dishes, fruit bowls, vases, candlesticks, and all sorts of figurines.

Initially I bought everything and anything in Delft blue, including imitations. But gradually I became more selective. I started collecting pieces that were signed and numbered and painted by hand. Most of the pieces I had dug out of shops in small old Dutch towns. On one occasion I bought two exquisite music boxes from an old Dutch couple. They play old-fashioned waltzes and Dutch children's songs.

Every detail of the Delft blue pieces, however simple and straightforward they may look to the casual observer, conveys a peaceful charm. As symbols of human necessities, such as candlesticks, pepper mills, and flower containers, they are like a visible story about family life, with its feelings of caring written right into them. The delicate shades of blue and simple lines and shapes add charm no matter where I place them. I have a deep sense of appreciation for each piece that we own. The shades of blue evoke curiosity about the human spirit and its creativity. Somehow it makes it easier to look upon another hour with some serenity.

After having lived for ten years in urban Cambridge on busy Massachusetts Avenue, I now appreciated the trees, the shrubs, and the large piece of sky I had rediscovered. From my new kitchen window above the stove I could see the south wall of the garage covered by climbing flesh-colored roses, each flower the size of a peach. Beyond, at the edge of the lawn, the wooden fence was covered by a mantle of scarlet rosebuds. The heavy garlands of tiny beauties hung loosely to the ground. The rhododendron bushes by the front walk were huge. From the living room, the blossoms appeared like clouds of pinks and mauves and deep purples.

The house that had been at first too formal, too somber, too large, and too dilapidated suddenly became too beautiful for words, but it was still too big and taxed my strength. A horn blared, and I jumped in my seat.

"Watch your driving, dummy!" a woman shouted from a car. She angrily waved a white-gloved hand at me and shrieked, "Who the hell gave you a license?" The gray sedan flew by me. I realized I was driving at a snail's pace, wobbling in the middle of the road.

A week after I saw Dr. Diamond, Dr. Thorn's secretary called me to arrange for an appointment. His office was at Peter Bent Brigham Hospital in Boston, a relatively small but very important hospital connected with Harvard Medical School.

Three days later, on a Friday, I went to see Dr. Thorn. I had reached Peter Bent Brigham twenty minutes before my appointment with plenty of time to park, or so it had seemed. I circled around the hospital for more than ten minutes but couldn't find a space. Suddenly I noticed a vacant spot in front of the Harvard Medical Library with a large sign that read "No Parking at Any Time."

The bear is afraid, but I'm not, I thought, remembering an old Bulgarian saying, and started to park. Halfway in, I heard somebody growl loudly, "Hey, lady, can't you read?" An old and very annoyed policeman came to my car window. "Hey," he said again, "What do you think you're doin'?"

Despite his loud voice, the man looked more like Santa Claus than a ferocious guardian of the law. "I'm not hiding anything," I said. "I'm parking."

"What do you mean you're parkin'?" His voice rose another octave. "Are you out of your mind?"

I told him that I had no choice. I had an appointment with

Dr. Thorn in exactly five minutes, and I intended to keep it even if I had to break the law. "Anyway"—I gave him a smile—"I have never broken the law before in all the sixteen years I've been driving."

"Oh, yes, you have," he fumed. "It's just that no one ever caught you. You can't leave the car here. We'll tow it away."

"But I will," I insisted. Choking with rage, he threatened to summon me to court for not only deliberately breaking the law but also flaunting the fact. Something about the policeman's expression made me tease him. I don't know where my strength came from to be funny that day. Casually, I remarked that he could take me to court but that would not concern me; it would be strictly an issue between him and the Dutch government. "What do you mean?" He looked astonished.

Keeping a straight face, I said, "My husband works for a Dutch concern, and I'm driving the company car." But then I quickly apologized for teasing him and asked him if he would please help me find a place to park.

I shall never forget the way he glared at me. He looked as if he were facing a demon, and I heard him mutter under his breath, "When I left Ireland thirty-five years ago, me ol' mother warned me—'Jack,' she blasted, 'if you go o'er the oceans an' leave me, Jasus, somebody you'll see the live Divil in person!' This is the day, lady. By gorry, I feel sure of it!" he said. But just the same, he helped me park the car across the way. He also had to help me climb the few back steps of the hospital. I was in more pain than ever—my whole skeleton was in agony.

Dr. Thorn, a man in his early fifties with bright red hair and a freckled face, looked more like a young intern than a world-renowned Harvard professor and the physician in chief of a famous hospital. When I entered his office, I couldn't walk unattended. He helped me to a chair and told me that Dr. Diamond had written him a long letter about my affliction. "We'll see what we can do to help you," he said, settling behind his large desk. As he proceeded with the usual medical questions, his face radiated unusual intelligence. His mind was quick, with a flair for sharp insights, and he had an infinite passion for detail.

In less than an hour, Dr. Thorn managed to make me feel as if I were an associate working with him rather than the object of his investigation. He demanded all my cooperation to facilitate his task. His eyes twinkled as he promised in return to explain to me all the tests that would be taken. "That's the only way you'll become a member of the team," he said. "Patient participation based on sound medical information can be of much help to the doctor." His magnetic personality and confident air made me think of him as a man who would stand up against the pitiless strength of nature and fight back.

Dr. Thorn had written down all the information he needed; he became quiet, as if he had run out of words. Then, in a slightly changed tone, he said, "Can you enter the hospital sometime early next week? Today is already Friday," he quickly reminded me. He studied my face as if to reassure himself that I understood the importance of his request. When I was slow to answer, he stressed that it was vital for him to determine the functions of my kidneys. "Have you ever had a bone-marrow test?" he asked. I shook my head. He said not to worry about it; it would be no more unpleasant than drawing blood from a deep vein.

I agreed to enter the hospital but said I preferred to return home each night to be with my children. I felt it was important to maintain a normal home atmosphere for the family—they shouldn't have to worry about my being ill.

Dr. Thorn hesitated briefly. "This is not the hospital's policy, but perhaps we'll let you go home once or twice. But let's see."

I accepted his tentative promise, admiring his skillful parrying of my question.

Satisfied, he wrote something in his notebook, then looked up again. "Let me warn you about Peter Bent Brigham. It's a research and teaching hospital. Besides the regular doctors, you'll have to cope with flocks of inquisitive young medical students and interns—that's how these young doctors learn."

This marked the beginning of a long association lasting over fifteen years with Peter Bent Brigham Hospital.

Just as Dr. Thorn predicted, my stay at the hospital was a unique experience. Parades of doctors, nurses, dietitians, and medical students flocked through my room from early morning until late at night. There was constant activity. I had nothing private left about me. My life history was recorded repeatedly. Blood was drawn until no more veins could be raised. Bone marrow was taken from my hip as well as from my chest. An elimination diet was instituted to determine any possible food allergies. The search for clues continued. Every morning, Dr. Thorn and his assistants stopped in to see me. I listened carefully to their brief discussions, which took place by the foot of my bed.

On one of these visits, a young doctor from Utah did all the talking. His expression was unusually keen. In a soft but confident voice, he said that in his opinion the sulfonamides could precipitate systemic lupus in cases previously diagnosed as discoid lupus, a condition that affects only the skin. He added that there was some evidence to implicate sulfonamides in triggering other diseases that could be called cousins of lupus. The reference to "cousins" recalled Dr. Diamond's words, which was reassuring to me.

When most of my tests were back, Dr. Thorn related the results to the group by my bedside. "All the tests seem fine," he said in a light tone, "but the patient continues to feel miserable." He glanced briefly in my direction. "That's not very helpful, Mrs. A., is it?" Then, almost immediately, he turned to his young assistants. "The patient has not had any fever. She has no skin lesions, no renal involvement; the urinalysis came back this morning perfectly normal, too." He cleared his throat and continued. "The EKG,* chest film, GI series,† and IVP‡ were all normal." Gazing out the window, he continued his soliloquy. "Blood pressure—one forty-five over eighty; no anemia. The LE cell preparation has been negative three times, and the leukopenia§ persists. The bone-marrow biopsy gave no further clue to the nature of the white-cell problem." He glanced at his notes once more. "The white count is three thousand, with a normal

---

*EKG: electrocardiogram.

†GI series: gastrointestinal series; an X-ray examination of the esophagus, stomach, and small intestine.

‡IVP: intravenous pyelogram, an X-ray examination of the kidneys.

§Leukopenia: low white-cell count.

differential, and the sedimentation rate is still slightly elevated." He shook his head a little and said, somewhat unconvincingly, "Despite all the fuss about the white cells, our findings are not impressive— nothing to get excited about." Then he instinctively shifted gears as if to avoid my dwelling on the obvious white-cell trouble and stated with an air of finality, "I am really pleased to find her kidneys functioning so well."

A young intern with sleepy eyes and curly black hair commented that suspicion for lupus should be attached to any female who had sunburn, like the one I had had in Florida, that failed to clear in the usual time. Another intern, who spoke with a strong southern accent, couldn't see how anyone could ever pin down SLE in a case such as mine in which the LE prep had been negative, then positive, not following any pattern. Furthermore, to him the disease was even more mysterious, for he had never seen a case. Dr. Thorn admitted that it was a rare condition but pointed out that among rheumatoid arthritis cases there was a significant percentage of hidden lupus. These words also brought to mind what Dr. Diamond had told me.

The next day, Dr. Thorn called in an infectious-disease specialist for consultation. His Harvard accent was so pronounced that I mistook him for an Englishman. He also spoke fluent French. He seemed fascinated with philology and infectious diseases. He explained that at one time or another infections had been implicated as a cause for lupus, erythema nodosum,* and other mysterious afflictions. "Even though this view is no longer considered tenable," he said, "we have recently treated several patients with autogenous vaccines† with favorable results." He applied several patch tests on both of my arms and, before he left, assured me in French that all would end well. Twenty-four hours later the TB skin test was positive, as was the one covered by the streptococcus patch. The latter became very sensitive and angry looking. The possibility of hypersensitivity to

*Erythema nodosum: painful red bumps on the skin. A skin manifestation of several diseases, including lupus.

†Autogenous vaccines: vaccines made from the patient's own bacteria, as opposed to vaccines made from standard bacterial cultures.

streptococci,* while suggestive, had not been proved. Although I remained puzzled by these results, my hope increased.

The infectious-disease specialist prepared a vaccine that he planned to give twice a week indefinitely. Dr. Thorn prescribed small daily doses of penicillin to be taken alone with 5 mg of prednisone.† When he discharged me from the hospital, we agreed that I should see him once a week until my condition cleared up. Hopefully, that would be soon.

Throughout the year in which I was seeing Dr. Thorn and getting the strep vaccine, the disease seemed relatively quiet. Yet the throat irritation still bothered me occasionally. I accepted the burden of a mild chronic affliction, something Dr. Fried had stressed at the onset of my disease, and I stopped worrying about the prognosis.

After Dr. Thorn had given me the autogenous vaccine for six months, I was gradually weaned away from it and all other medications except for the vitamins. At least for the time being, there seemed to be no cause for concern.

---

*Streptococcus: the round organism (coccus), a very dangerous bacterium that may cause sore throats and skin infections, as well as other infections such as nephritis, inflammation of the kidneys, rheumatic fever, and inflammation of the heart and joints.
†Prednisone: the chemical name for a steroid hormone.

14. The Months Went By
The Patient's Story

AT the end of the year, Dr. Frank H. Gardner, the hematologist*
whom Dr. Diamond originally recommended, returned from Puerto
Rico. He accepted my case. Thenceforth, I was to see him once every
month. A tall, pleasant-looking man, Dr. Gardner possessed the same
interest in detail as Dr. Thorn, and like Sir William Osler, he valued
the importance of getting to know his patient well so he could better
help him.

Dr. Gardner had a way of drawing me out; he gave just
enough of himself to create a warm two-way relationship.

The hematology lab at Peter Bent Brigham was at the rear
of the hospital. From the front entrance I used to pass through a
labyrinth of stuffy corridors with innumerable heavy doors that I was
too weak to open. One day I counted seven such doors as I walked
closely behind a heavyset nurse to whom I was grateful for patiently
holding each door.

When I went the back way, I could count on Jack, the
policeman, to find me a parking space and help me with the heavy
door to the freight elevator.

*Hematologist: a specialist in the study of blood.

The hematology lab consisted of several small and dingy rooms where people constantly bumped into one another. The long, narrow corridor, with two wooden benches where I had to wait, was always hot and stuffy. At times, especially in summer, the place smelled of urine and other unidentified but equally unpleasant odors that emanated from the labs.

Tubes, funnels, scales, measuring cups, pots, and the like cluttered the labs where Dr. Gardner drew blood from my arm. The room looked more like an old-fashioned Bulgarian kitchen. The centrifuge in a corner of the room reminded me of a washing machine. In that crowded but friendly atmosphere, Dr. Gardner did his research while training many young hematologists.

His office, across the hall, was sparsely furnished, with a large desk, a leather chair with a high back to support his large frame, another chair for the patient, and an old-fashioned brown wooden examining table. The window behind the desk faced a sooty wall covered with faded ivy leaves. The depressing view was more than offset by the warmth and excitement of the Gardner group, all of whom helped me in one way or another to bear my ordeal. Sipping an occasional cup of coffee with Dr. Mitsu Laforet, the only woman doctor on the research team, had the effect of psychotherapy on my emotional stress. Her friendliness instilled confidence in my faltering spirit. She and I have remained friends. Good friends.

Dr. Gardner stubbornly searched for the LE cell and watched for changes in my blood. At the time, my white count fluctuated between 2,500 and 4,000. The sedimentation rate stayed about the same, mildly elevated. Dr. Gardner reported periodically to Dr. Thorn and Dr. Diamond about my progress. The diagnosis, for my ears, was leukopenia.*

Each day I felt better, though I was still too weak to enjoy physical activities the way I had before I became ill. I learned how to budget my strength, and my hope of getting well grew all the time. Reading and writing provided a continuing intellectual interest, as did music. My love for these pursuits had originated in my early

---

*Leukopenia: reduction in the number of leukocytes in the blood, the count being 5,000 or less.

teens. Exploring symphonies and old church music kept me in a hypnotic trance then and still does. Occasionally I delight in searching for the vibrations that stimulate the muses. Whenever I get in such a mood, I remember Mother telling me that anyone who doesn't write poetry at eighteen must be a fool and anyone who does after thirty is a still bigger one.

The wool business did well. My husband imported wool from Australia, New Zealand, South Africa, and South America and sold it all over the world. His business interests expanded to keep pace with the medical and household expenses, and his attitude of "things will be better by tomorrow" sustained my optimism. After a while, I found myself wondering if any other kind of life existed.

Since Birgitta had returned to Norway to become a bride, we had a new household helper from Ireland. I was convinced that keeping a girl in the house was vital not only for my own good but also for the good of the entire family. The help preserved the image of a smoothly running household—meals on time, clean laundry, and a tidy home. I could save what little strength I had to do things with the children. My family never saw me as the cripple I was at the time.

Mary, our new housekeeper, added a little extra to the spirit of our home. She had astigmatism in both eyes, large flat feet, and must have weighed close to two hundred pounds. Her heart proved to be equal to her size. I always remember her seated at the big oval kitchen table, feasting with a crowd of never fewer than five children, with several contented animals lying near her feet. The week Mary came to us, we had adopted Mev, a handsome six-month-old golden retriever. We already had Wuzzy, a ferocious orange cat, two huge white rabbits with pink eyes, and two parakeets that never made a sound. Mary's feet were never too tired to attend to the needs of a child or to dance an Irish jig with Ingrid and Martha. While her dancing was less than ethereal, she glowed with enthusiasm and moved with the precision of a clock. The house shook to its foundation. Miraculously, none of my Dutch plates fell off the wall, though at times they threatened to do so.

Having animals in the house pleased the children no end.

The only creature showing signs of strain that year was Mev. An American dog by birth and early training, it took him some time to realize that by adoption into our family he was expected to behave like a Bulgarian dog. In Bulgaria, dogs were outdoor adventurers. They had to earn their keep by guarding their master's house or tending the sheep. But Mev couldn't care less what dogs did in Bulgaria. He resented being restricted to the kitchen and struggled for equal rights in the house. The children sympathized with him, and eventually the "beast" became the ruler of our household for the next fourten years—*Vox populi, vox Dei!*

15. Canada

The Patient's Story

> It is termed lupus [wolf], for that it is, say some, of a ravenous Nature, and like that fierce Creature, not satisfy'd but with Flesh.
>
> —D. A. Turner

NOVEMBER found my husband in Holland on business. Before he left, we had agreed to go skiing in Canada for a week during Christmas vacation. The children shared our enthusiasm for the sport. School closed, my husband returned, we packed; then children, Christmas presents, and all boarded the Friday midnight train for Quebec. The next noon, we left the train under low, pale-gray skies and in freezing air. The family accused me of having exaggerated my description of the delights of Quebec.

Perhaps I had let myself be carried away by memories of a springtime visit when I entered Quebec via a St. Lawrence River steamer, I admitted. Martha was heartbroken. Her older brother and sister had told her that Canada was on the way to the North Pole where Santa had his toy workshop. The child expected to have at least a glimpse of Prancer or Dancer, if not of Santa. Instead, the streets of the old town seemed desolate. Martha's blue eyes peered through the car window at gaudy Christmas decorations and Santa Clauses selling gasoline. The taxi driver's radio was tuned to a soft melody. Ingrid, who was then the poet in the family, starting reciting, "'Twas the night before Christmas, and all through the house, not a creature was stirring, not even a mouse."

Our lodge proved to be twenty miles out of Quebec City. The tedious ride over country roads packed with ice and snow took at least an hour—it grew colder and colder. As we drove through the mountains, icy winds seeped through the cracks of the ramshackle taxi. I felt chilled to the bones. Some extra woolens next to my skin would have been a godsend. When we reached the lodge, the Laurentian Mountains were spread wide open only a few hundred feet away. The vista was breathtaking, and so was the cold air. We rushed into the lodge to a pleasant surprise. Two friendly crackling fires greeted us in both our rooms. The air smelled of birch and mountain evergreens. I stretched out on the bed, with all the children bouncing around me, and fell asleep until suppertime.

By the next day, to everyone's delight, the sun came out of hiding and shone for the rest of the week. On the ski slopes the wealth of snow surpassed all our expectations. For a change, the masses of sugarlike powder were not a mere nuisance to be shoveled away.

While the family skiied, I roamed through the nearby hills, admiring the huge pine trees. Their lush green colors contrasted sharply with the whiteness of the snow and the powder-blue sky. The pine needles, loaded with crystals of ice, shimmered in the sun's rays—millions of iridescent rainbows. I thought of Birgitta and her pine trees in Norway. I shall always remember the girl; she was such a wonderful person.

The day before our vacation ended, I took a long walk downhill toward Quebec. As I walked amid the winter beauty, I felt very much alive. With every step I took, I felt a shiver of delight through my body, and I praised nature's magnificence and those glorious moments. I walked for a long time, as though I had forgotten I would have to return. It was a lovely day. As much as possible, I tried to avoid direct sunlight by walking hunched over under the heavy branches. When the sun went down, the temperature dropped below zero. The return trek seemed endless. My ears and nose were stinging, and my feet felt like sticks of ice. I could hardly lift them —only the fear of being frozen kept me moving. I reached the lodge totally exhausted.

"Mommy looks blue," Ingrid cried out.

"She's purple," Martha chimed in.

Rubbing my frozen ears, I told them that as I was coming up the hill, the wind had turned into a dragon with fiery claws that bit into my cheeks and chased me all the way back.

Martha put her warm little hand to my cheek. "The nasty creature burned your skin like fire."

"She's teasing," Ingrid said. "There are no such things as dragons."

"Who saw a dragon?" Al barged in, waving a Ping-Pong paddle.

"Mommy did!" Martha's tears glittered in her eyes.

"You're silly!" Al scoffed, and told us to hurry to the dining room before it closed. The next morning, I awoke before daylight with a splitting headache and a raging fever. My shoulders, neck, arms—every inch of me—ached. Later, when my husband brought me a cup of steaming coffee, my hands shivered so badly I couldn't even grasp the cup. Thinking that I had a severe cold, we remained at the lodge two extra days. After that, I felt well enough to start homeward.

When I returned home, I was at a loss to explain some of my symptoms. The lymph nodes had become enlarged on both sides of my neck, and I succumbed to nausea once more. I also developed a rash on my face that covered my nose and both cheeks in an oddly shaped pattern. My palms and fingertips were speckled with dark blue spots. The nail folds were fiery red, as if hemorrhaging.

The moment I entered Dr. Gardner's private office at the front of the hospital, his eyes focused immediately on my face. I sensed his bewilderment. "What in heaven have you done to yourself? You have a rash on your face—a red butterfly."*

I tried to smile. "A red butterfly? Why the poetic name for the nasty rash?"

"We call it that because it occurs symmetrically on the cheeks

*Butterfly rash: a form of double-wing-shaped skin rash around the nose and cheeks indicative of lupus.

and extends over the bridge of the nose. It does look like a butterfly! Have you been in the sun again?" He kept his eyes on my face.

"No!"

"There is a tendency for lupus to get worse after one has been exposed to sunlight or even artificial ultraviolet rays. You should shield your face and body from ultraviolet light." The word lupus took on a special meaning. I recalled reading that the disease had been named lupus because the ulcerations on the skin resembled wolf bites—a common occurrence in olden times. I reached for my pocketbook mirror to see if my rash resembled such bites but did not take it out. Yet I knew that I could not avoid all mirrors. I thought of the rearview mirror in the car that I so often used to look at myself as well as the cars in back of me.

"Tell me what happened," Dr. Gardner asked, recognizing my anguish.

I described our trip to the Laurentians. "The sun was strong on the ski slopes," I said, "but I made an effort not to expose myself. I walked in the shade."

"You got the reflection of the sun off the snow," he said. "Such rays increase the degree of the skin's exposure. At high altitudes, the penetration of sunlight is more intense than it appears. People with blue eyes and light skin like yours should not fool with the sun, lupus or no lupus. . . ." He advised me that even on an overcast day I should always wear protective creams or a hat.

"What now?" I asked mechanically.

"We must be realistic." He shrugged a little. "Things will get worse before they get better." As he drew the usual sample of blood from my arm, he said, "Don't look in the mirror for a while."

"You must have read my mind," I murmured.

He told me that he had faith in my ability to keep up my morale. I hoped he was right, for at times I felt sure that my well of spiritual resources was running dry. Before I left, he scribbled two prescriptions: one for prednisone— a 5 mg tablet every six hours— and another for .5 percent hydrocortisone ointment—10 mg in a tube. I was to rub the hydrocortisone vigorously into my skin to make it more effective. With that instruction, I left his office.

"Things will get worse before they get better." I kept hearing his words as I emerged through the old-fashioned doors and the stately portico of Peter Bent Brigham. At the end of the front walk, a distance of no more than a couple of hundred feet, I felt drained of all energy. Sweat broke out on my face, and I was overcome with dizziness. I had to sit on the curb before I could hail a taxi. A short distance away a group of children were arguing in shrieking voices. Looking at them, I wondered fearfully, if worse comes to worst, what will happen to my own children?

When I entered Dr. Gardner's office a week later, he said, "You have a moon face. Your cheeks are swollen from the prednisone."

"A sun face would have been more appropriate with the butterfly rash," I said, and sat down on the chair in front of his desk.

"But are you feeling better?" he asked, observing my face. The red spots were still there, and so were the blue blotches on my palms. The glands on my neck were as swollen as ever. The one on the right stuck out like a cherry. Dr. Gardner pulled out my file from the cabinet next to his desk and wrote down his observations.

"I'm pleased with your tests." He raised his head briefly, then thumbed through some lab slips and read the tabulations aloud. "Your hematocrit is forty-three; hemoglobin, thirteen point four; white count, four three four oh; polys,* twenty-nine; lymphs,† twenty-one; BUN,‡ eleven; uric acid, four point eight; sedimentation rate, twenty-two." He closed the folder with meticulous care and said, "You still haven't told me—how do you feel?"

"I feel fine." I paused. "No, as a matter of fact, I feel terrible." My lips trembled as I told him that I dreaded making an appointment for fear that I wouldn't be able to keep it. "My symptoms change from hour to hour," I said. "No matter how well I feel in the morning, I'm liable to collapse in the afternoon. But worst of all, I have a morbid feeling that I'll never regain my confidence . . . I'm thinking

---

*Polys (polymorphonuclear leukocytes): White blood cells.
†Lymphs (lymphocytes): white blood cells.
‡BUN: blood urea nitrogen. When the kidneys fail, the BUN rises, as does the level of uric acid.

seriously of selling our house, Dr. Gardner, and moving into a smaller place."

"What does your husband think about that?" His eyes never left my face.

"We haven't discussed it yet," I said. "He'll need time to get used to the idea."

"I wouldn't be in a great hurry," Dr. Gardner warned. "Sometimes a patient with symptoms like yours suddenly feels better for unexplained reasons." His tone of voice sounded the same as that of Dr. Zenith's at the beginning of my illness.

But the thought of selling the house had taken root in my mind. In the next few months, as my illness grew progressively worse, I decided that I could not go on living without contingency planning. Even if my health improved, maintaining our large house would mean constant dependence on outside help. In truth, my chief concern centered on my family and my desire that if my condition eventually were to take me away from them, they would be able to manage by themselves. But these thoughts I kept to myself.

I was crying when I finally confessed one day to my husband that the hardships of a large house had become impossible. Try as I would, I had to admit that my ebbing strength no longer proved equal to the demands.

We deliberated back and forth for several months. Finally, my husband agreed that perhaps it would be better to sell the house. After a brief search, in the fall of 1957, we bought a smaller house in Wellesley, Massachusetts. Our new home was located high up on a hill, surrounded by aged shady trees, lots of lady slippers, squirrels, and singing birds. I envisioned how the place would look when I could dig with my own hands and plant in the soil. Here I could have a garden of my own that I could start from scratch. What fun! In my new house I knew that I could handle all my ups and downs a little more easily; here, I thought one could never be lonely with floor-to-ceiling windows overlooking the woods and the open sky. In my new bedroom I could lie in bed and watch the moonlight creep across my garden.

Our new home was within walking distance of Tenacre Country Day School, where two of our children were second-year pupils. "No more daily driving back and forth to school for me!" I cheered when Ingrid and Martha left in the morning to walk to school, with Mev trailing after them. In the long run, my instincts for self-preservation proved right—every measure that eliminated fatigue and stress provided extra ammunition for my battle ahead.

We were scarcely settled in Wellesley when I had to reenter Peter Bent Brigham Hospital for a reevaluation of my condition. The rash on my face that had originated in Canada faded with time but did not disappear as Dr. Gardner had expected. My neck glands remained stubbornly swollen. The day I entered the hospital, I had a mild fever and the ever-present nausea, which made me miserable.

When Dr. Thorn heard I was in the hospital, he came to my room. He regretted the turn of events. He reflected that he had thought all my problems were solved, or nearly so. Dr. Diamond came every day; Dr. Fried, every third or fourth day. Dr. Gardner called in several other doctors for consultation. During this stay more medical students than before walked in to see me. Each one was curious to glimpse my butterfly rash; lupus was still such a clinical rarity. These inquisitive young men tried to palpate my spleen, liver, and kidneys with vigorous strength, as if the secret of my affliction could be found buried in the folds of my flesh. One young charmer, built like a football player, appeared hesitantly at my door. He watched me from the corner of his eye, as if not sure that he were in the right place. In a high-pitched voice he inquired if I were the patient he was looking for. I asked if he were expecting to find a living cadaver.

"Gosh," said the young man as he advanced close to my bed, "how would I know? You are my first lupus patient." He admitted that he was surprised to find me looking the picture of health.

His mentioning lupus brought a lump to my throat. The doctors had managed to make the disease sound nebulous enough to dull its sharp edges, but I still shuddered whenever I heard it called by name.

The intern settled himself in a narrow wooden chair and jotted down name, age, race, sex, orientation, cooperativeness. He flashed a disarming smile in my direction and asked if I would help him write a paper on my case.

My gaze moved from his gray narrow eyes, which appeared ready to dissect me, to his big, powerful hands. "I'll oblige and tell you all you want to know," I agreed, "if you will promise not to touch me. I ache all over, and I've been feeling cold all day long. The slightest change in temperature makes me shiver."

"My grandmother is like that, too," he said with another grin. "She has arthritis and can predict the changes in the weather by the twinges in her little toe."

He consented not to examine me, and we talked for nearly three hours.

The young lupus enthusiast came back two more times. I even translated two articles on leukopenia from Russian for him while I was in the hospital. Months later, Dr. Gardner, who was teaching fourth-year medicine at Harvard, commented on the student's excellent paper.

On the evening before my discharge from the hospital, I heard Dr. Gardner's voice down the hall. He was talking with one of Brigham's doctors, who repeated several times, "Your patient is really quite sick. Her kidneys are severely damaged. With that degree of damage, she doesn't have much of a chance."

It was obvious that they were talking about me, but for some reason, they had not muted their voices. After the first moment of shock, I was glad I had a chance to react to their grim words alone instead of playacting in their presence. I did not have to pretend that I was brave. I asked myself what to do. What was there to do? What would keep me going? I still had the doctors on my side; they were going to help me all they could. I still had the children to take care of. Every day I survived helped them grow a little more. "I must find the strength to carry on," I whispered to myself. I had to. I had no other choice.

Dr. Gardner walked in and informed me that the latest tests showed some kidney damage. "The ability of the kidneys to clear certain substances from your blood is impaired," he said. "We will have to repeat the tests, of course."

His dwelling on the word "kidneys," despite the fact that it was not news to me, still had a frightful effect. I became light-headed. The room spun around, and my mouth became terribly dry. I asked him what were my chances?

"The prognosis is not hopeless—not hopeless at all. The kidney damage may reverse itself. Sometimes it happens. There is hope." The last words he pronounced in an almost cheerful tone that doctors so often adopt, knowing well that something is terribly wrong with the patient.

I tried to fasten to his last words, but I had read very thoroughly the book called *Lupus Erythematosus*, edited by Dr. E. L. Dubois, a professor of medicine at the University of Southern California. The book claimed that it was hardly possible to survive with lupus once it got to the kidneys.

Dr. Gardner drew blood from my arm and slipped a rubber band around the test tubes, then dropped them into his pocket. He pulled up a chair and sat down like a friend. "Stop worrying," he said. "I believe that cortisone will take care of the problem."

"Cortisone is not curative," I said.

"It's not curative," he agreed, "but the hormone* can change some of the effects of the disease before irreversible damage occurs."

I assumed from his words, that the hormones could prolong life and asked him how long a patient with lupus could live on cortisone.

"In all honesty, I can't answer your question," he said. He explained that doctors seldom followed a lupus patient from the onset of the disease through to the terminal stages. The cases that came to medical attention were usually the grave terminal ones; their life span varied from five to ten years. "Patients with lupus seldom stay for very long with the same doctor, which makes it difficult to follow the disease," he said. "People feel discouraged when the doctor is

---

*Hormone: from the Greek "to excite"; hormones are chemical messengers that excite a response in other tissue.

unable to provide a prompt cure, and the doctor gets discouraged, too, when he cannot establish a quick diagnosis and effect a cure." He stressed that until recently mild lupus cases were rarely diagnosed, much less followed intensively.

When I asked him what was the major threat to life in lupus, he answered, "The kidney involvement could be a continuing threat to life."

The room was hot. By now Dr. Gardner's crimson face matched the flamboyant red vest that he frequently sported under his otherwise conservative tweed jacket. He rose from his chair and told me that my blood samples would be packed in dry ice and flown to the Rockefeller Institute of Medical Research in New York City. "They have developed a more sensitive way of checking the serum protein," he said. "Let's wait until we hear from them." I could never lose my sense of the miraculous. His not being quite sure of a diagnosis injected a new hope. I held on to that hope like a child.

Somehow I relaxed for a moment. I even managed to tell him a Bulgarian joke about a village priest who had to send a specimen to Sofia via his pretty maid. On the way, the girl slipped and broke the bottle. Frightened, she filled a new bottle. The returned diagnosis was "Pregnant."

Dr. Gardner sent samples of my blood many more times to New York City, Los Angeles, and "down east" to Waterville, Maine. Dr. Gardner never missed an opportunity to listen to another opinion from an authoritative colleague, and he told me that whenever he attended a medical meeting, he carried my medical case history in his briefcase. He was always ready to discuss my plight with whoever showed an active interest in lupus.

Listening to Dr. Gardner's footsteps fade down the hall, I felt grateful for his interest. He and the other doctors at Peter Bent Brigham Hospital seemed to combine knowledge with warmth and informality. I was privileged indeed to have such a share of their care and attention.

On my third day in the hospital, an old symptom recurred. The subcutaneous nodules under the extensor surface (outer side) of my elbow reappeared. They felt tender. Also, smaller, harder nodules showed clearly on my fingers. Now a doctor would surely see them before they vanished!

Several doctors examined the nodules. Their divided opinions echoed the confusion of my disease. One doctor thought that they were the same as those found in patients with rheumatoid arthritis; another agreed with him but thought that in rheumatoid arthritis the nodules usually did not regress, as mine did, without medication. A third declared that in his opinion these nodules definitely were a sign of systemic lupus, for in rheumatoid arthritis the nodules did not regress at all, medicine or no medicine!

An hour later, a staff surgeon came in and sat at the edge of my bed. He carefully examined my elbows and fingers and detected some soft-tissue swelling in my joints.

Half an hour later, a nurse wheeled me into the operating room, and the same surgeon removed a tiny lump from the lower inner side of my left index finger. All I felt was the prick of the Novocaine needle.

The next morning, the surgeon stopped by my door and reported that the pathologist had found a mild inflammatory reaction but nothing more specific. "The biopsy was not interpreted as giving evidence of SLE," he said. "If I were in your shoes, by now I would pack up and leave the place before they thought of other tests to do."

I told him that the thought had occurred to me more than once.

A couple of days later, Dr. Gardner told me that he had asked a lupus specialist from California, whom I shall call Dr. Koenig, to come see me. "He'll be in sometime this afternoon. We'll see what he has to say." Dr. Gardner, who always liked to explain things, added, "Dr. Koenig seems to think that patients with SLE can be helped by regular fresh white-blood-cell injections."

"What do you mean by regular?" I asked.

"Twice a week—indefinitely—who knows?" he answered with a quizzical expression. "The rationale of the white-blood-cell injections has not been proved conclusively."

"Do you have any idea how these injections work?"

"Not really. Dr. Koenig is basing his theory on the premise

that some enzyme causes damage to the DNA* and that normal white cells supply a missing factor that inhibit the damage."

"DNA!" I was frequently amused by Dr. Gardner's assumptions that I understood medical terminology as well as all the members of his staff.

"DNA is a vital constituent of every cell. It is the genetic substance, the identity of the cell," he explained.

Dr. Koenig arrived that same afternoon. He walked into my room with quick strides. Following him were Dr. Thorn, Dr. Diamond, Dr. Gardner, and a large group of interns and medical students. Dr. Koenig, a medium-sized man with a very serious expression, examined me with quick, nimble fingers. I observed his every motion, wondering if he was aware that I was still a breathing woman under the hospital covers.

"How do you feel?" he asked with a friendly look.

"Okay," I nodded.

"How is your appetite?"

"The cortisone makes me feel hungry all the time."

He turned to Dr. Diamond, who was standing closest to him. "Your patient looks well."

"But she doesn't feel too well." Dr. Diamond, always attentive, gave me a reassuring look. He turned to Dr. Koenig. "Don't let her deceive you. She has pride."

One young student winked at me. I smiled back at him. From the conversation at my bedside I learned that the Los Angeles County Hospital, an institution with 3,500 beds, had a lupus research laboratory. Several thousand LE cell preparations had been performed there on many individuals in the past several years. Dr. Koenig also mentioned that in several other hospitals in the country LE cell tests were randomly performed on all patients in whom SLE or other rheumatoid diseases were suspected. At one point, Dr. Gardner interjected that since he had started handling my case, he was tempted to perform the test on all women who presented diagnostic problems.

Dr. Koenig suggested a regimen of increased doses of cor-

*DNA: deoxyribonucleic acid, a large complex molecule composed of chemicals called sugars and nucleic acids.

tisone plus 5 cc injections of fresh white blood cells twice a week. The latter treatment was very new and had not yet been used in Boston. The next day, Dr. Gardner prepared a fresh white-cell concentrate in his laboratory and gave me the first of a long series of painful injections that were bearable only because I hoped for their success. A week later, I went home with no fever but feeling sicker than ever.

16. Hospitalization and Tests
The Physician's Point of View

I REMEMBER the first time I was a patient in a hospital. I was admitted to have all my wisdom teeth removed. I felt that I was on an impersonal assembly line, and days later, after being pressed, prodded, banged, and molded, I was dismissed. Hospital life has its own rules, patterns, culture, to which physicians, nurses, etc., have spent years adjusting. A patient is expected to adjust to that environment instantaneously upon admission, disregarding the impersonal stares of admissions financial officers, X-ray technicians, phlebotomists, etc. Often these jobs are boring, routine, and repetitious, and they account for lackluster facial expressions that we, in our anxiety, misinterpret as disinterest. Nurses fare better in the PR department. Trained to make you comfortable even while stripping you of your clothes, helping you into johnnies, assessing your vital functions, and dispensing medication, they are usually all smiles. Sharing your fears and anxieties regarding being in the hospital will usually elicit extra TLC from a nurse—back rubs, extra pillows, frequent inquiries into how you're feeling. What, then, is the physician's role? From the patient's point of view, a physician is one who appears for only a few minutes each day. Patients wonder about their physician's whereabouts: Is he in the building or off on a trip, golfing, vacationing? Is he thinking of me? Of some other patient? When you are in the hospital, you expect your physician to come by each day. If such a visit does not occur, you are entitled to an explanation. Physicians usually evaluate each inpatient daily, often frequently, depending on the severity of the illness and its acute nature. Chronic problems, varying little from day to day, do not require as much medical attention as psychological support. A daily visit is often the focus of the day for the patient and provides that psychological uplift.

From the physician's point of view, he must act as primary coordinator of the many people and processes involved either directly or indirectly in the evaluation and care of the patient. Interacting with the physician are nurses, interns, residents, consultants, specialists, phlebotomists, X-ray technicians, physiotherapists, dietitians, social workers, medical students, and laboratory technicians. Some of these people you will see frequently; many you will not. Many patients want to interact only with their "private" doctor and want nothing to do with interns, residents, and medical students. In a complex illness like lupus, having many professionals involved is a bonus to the patient in shared "brain power." When physicians make rounds with interns, residents, and medical students, the questioning and examining can become rather stressful to the patient. From the patient's viewpoint, this sharing of information and opinion is not always handled sensitively or thoughtfully. Fear sets in when a word or two is overheard. What are they saying? Is it good or bad? Will there be more tests? More injections? Am I getting better or not? Am I going to die? Do I have cancer? When can I go home? These are the thoughts that race through a patient's mind. Although making rounds is medically practical and educationally sound, and discussing each patient ideally improves his or her care, it is vital to do that talking out of sight and earshot of the patient. I have found that returning after rounds, explaining the consensus, and encouraging questions allay many patients' fears. Medical students can be a particular boon to a patient. Young, eager to learn, and friendly, they will often spend time with you and serve as your advocate with the rest of the medical team. Although not yet as knowledgeable about your illness as the intern, resident, or private physician, the medical student's role is a vital one in easing the patient's fears and keeping lines of communication open.

Signs and symptoms, no matter how eloquently described, are insufficient to pinpoint the diagnosis. We must therefore resort to and rely on modern technology and laboratory tests to acquire objective measurements that indicate what is occurring in the body. Testing, always testing. You see a lupus doctor and all it seems they do is test. Some lupus doctors only test the patient and do not even take a history, listen to the patient, or even examine them. Why all this rage for testing? Because immunologic tests have been made so sensitive that the blood tests often show abnormalities even before a patient develops symptoms. The blood tests often aid in distinguishing symptoms that may represent a lupus flare from those of some other disease (e.g., a fever). However, the sensitivity and specificity of these tests do not excuse physicians from meeting their responsibility of dealing with the patient. How do patients respond to testing? They do not particularly care for the needle stick, the endless vials of blood tubes, having to urinate into a tiny bottle. These are the physical discomforts. The psychological ones tend to be worse. Fearing that the tests will reveal bad news—especially when you are feeling better and thought you had just gotten over a relapse—can be very stressful. The frequent testing is a reminder of the chronic nature of the disease. Basically, the patient only hears snitches of what the doctor says— and it boils down to either good or bad news. Good tests bring a sigh of relief, until the anticipation develops for the next round of tests, days, weeks, or months away. Bad test results mean more tests, and particularly more medication—with its potential for side effects and its constant reminder of the problem.

While blood tests are easily tolerated, being repeatedly jabbed with a needle and having tubes of blood taken day after day are debilitating. As a physician, aware that the body manufactures new red blood cells each day, I can reassure my patients that anemia is unlikely to develop. Although X rays are less painful than blood tests, concern about radiation increases anxiety in patients. Fortunately, the newer machines tend to emit less radiation. When preliminary tests do not yield as much information as a physician requires to reach a diagnosis, a biopsy is often recommended. Procedure and risk/benefit of a biopsy are issues that should be discussed in detail and at length by patient and physician. Organ tissue, when examined microscopically, will often reveal the characteristic tissue and cellular morphology diagnostic of a specific disease. Some biopsies are relatively painless (e.g., punch biopsies of the skin, bone marrow, and pleura). Other biopsies can be somewhat hazardous (e.g., liver, kidney) and are therefore usually only recommended when information anticipated from the biopsy far outweighs the risk of the procedure. Biopsies of other organs (e.g., brain, heart) are done less frequently because of the potential hazard to the patient. Other tests performed to assess various organ functions include blood counts (bone marrow), urinalysis (kidney), blood tests (many organs), EKG (heart), X ray (many organs), EEG (brain), etc.

Mrs. Aladjem's test results indicated an elevated erythrocyte sedimentation rate (ESR). What does that mean? Perhaps nothing, but it may suggest an inflammation somewhere in the body. Mrs. Aladjem also had a low white-blood-cell count (leukopenia), which is often associated with viral diseases, overwhelming infection, enlarged spleen, use of certain medications, and lupus. Mrs. Aladjem's physician made two recommendations: vitamin B_{12} injections and a consultation with an arthritis specialist. The vitamin B_{12} injection probably did little good because vitamin B_{12} is only useful for vitamin B_{12} deficiency—pernicious anemia. However, vitamin B_{12} has an acknowledged placebo effect for the following reasons: It must be given as an injection, which is psychologically more powerful than simply prescribing a pill. It has a lovely deep cobalt-blue color and colored medication impresses.

Diagnosing lupus is less difficult than it was thirty years ago, when many physicians were only vaguely aware of the disease. The diagnosis was usually only considered when someone appeared with an obvious butterfly rash or florid systemic symptoms. The only laboratory test for the diagnosis of lupus, the LE cell test, had only recently been described. It was tedious to perform; a physician or technologist had to sit at a microscope and study each slide for an hour, and there was disagreement on the best way to prepare the slides. Some experts felt that one could not make a definitive diagnosis of SLE unless the test was positive. Yet there were lupuslike symptoms in individuals whose tests were negative, or weakly positive and then negative. Furthermore, some patients with rheumatoid arthritis, Sjögren's syndrome, liver diseases, and related syndromes also occasionally had a positive LE cell test. Did these individuals also have lupus? Many experts thought so at the time. We now recognize that the test was misnamed. It is not specific for lupus; in fact, many patients with lupus never even have a positive test! For these reasons we no longer do LE cell tests to determine lupus. However, back in 1956 it was often difficult to diagnose lupus, especially since the patient often appears in good health.

Lupus nephritis is a primary concern to a physician treating a lupus patient, for as recently as thirty years ago, kidney involvement was the most common cause of death in lupus patients, perhaps because renal disease usually presents little, if any, symptoms until there has been considerable damage to the kidney. Lupus nephritis is basically an inflammation of the kidney due to lupus. There are a number of different types of lupus nephritis: mesangial, focal proliferative, diffuse proliferative, membranous, and membranoproliferative. These different types generally cause few symptoms and little distress. However, if the nephritis becomes severe, it may cause symptoms associated with hypertension (e.g., headaches); loss of large amounts of protein in the urine, causing weight gain and edema (a watery swelling) of the feet and ankles (the nephrotic syndrome); and/or nausea when the kidneys are functioning at less than 15 percent of normal capacity. If most nephritis is not severe or symptomatic, how do we recognize it? We perform tests that measure kidney function, that is, urine tests, blood tests, and combinations thereof. Immunologic tests of complement, immune complexes, and anti-DNA antibodies are also often useful to monitor the patient at risk for renal disease. Kidney biopsies determine what type of renal involvement exists, its extent, and how active (inflammatory) it is, and we are thereby able to recommend specific therapies. Lupus nephritis is generally treated with corticosteroids, usually prednisone. If excessive side effects result, or there is an inadequate clinical response, immunosuppressives may be used.

One of the most difficult aspects of lupus for the patient is enduring the tedium of endless tests, anticipating a diagnosis that will explain nagging symptoms that have persisted for weeks, months, perhaps years. How do people in an age of anxiety and instant gratification cope with the necessity for patience? Some go from doctor to doctor, becoming depressed and/or anxious, even taking to bed; others read up on their possible illnesses in medical textbooks or talk to friends, family, a clergyman, or physician while maintaining outside nonmedical interests. Feeling "down," a natural result of illness, is expected. Health-care specialists all know that nondepressed individuals handle disease better than depressed patients do and encourage activities that lift the spirit, divert the anxiety, and lessen the depression.

The patience required by a person awaiting a diagnosis cannot approximate the patience demanded of a researcher. I have been engaged in lupus research for twenty years, seeking clues and answers, trying to piece the puzzle together. I have not yet achieved that goal but keep searching, finding satisfaction in the knowledge that what I and others have learned has benefited the treatment, survival, and happiness of many lupus patients and their families.

Now that you have settled into the hospital and tests have been completed, you await your doctor's visit and the information that will confirm your diagnosis. When the doctor appears serious, troubled, and perplexed, you spiral downward with anxiety, fear, and depression and steel yourself for bad news. However, in Mrs. Aladjem's case, Dr. Thorn's expression was one of confusion, for he continued to feel frustrated in his attempts to reach a definitive diagnosis. At this point in a patient's experience, the physician can be reassuring by listing all the diseases that are clearly eliminated and encouraging continued exploration, stressing that it is often impossible to diagnose a disease definitively in its early stages. Is there harm to more waiting? Usually not in lupus—assuming that the various tests indicate no organ damage. Furthermore, those vague symptoms often simply disappear, and one never knows what caused them! Somtimes, even though I do not know what is wrong, I will suggest a therapeutic trial, choosing a regime that I hope will help and that I know has little chance of doing any harm. This is just what Dr. Thorn and the infectious-disease expert recommended for Mrs. Aladjem—a trial of low-dosage prednisone, vitamins, and a streptococcal vaccine. Today we might still try the prednisone, but vitamins and the vaccine have not been proved effective treatment in lupus.

What can we learn from Mrs. Aladjem's stay in the hospital? She had a candid, concerned, compassionate physician who strived to uncover the cause of her illness while trying to keep her as comfortable as possible. He even permitted her to go home evenings (when tests were not being performed) to be with her family! She began a therapeutic trial, continued to be observed, and still awaited a specific diagnosis.

17. Nicotinamide

The Patient's Story

> The search for drugs was in the past a purely empirical
> venture. And, despite lofty attempts at a rational ap-
> proach to this problem, its greatest achievements are still
> the result of chance or at best of trial and error.
> —René Dubos,
> *Mirage of Health*

THE fresh white blood cells and cortisone did not produce the
hoped-for effect in me. The clinical picture remained unchanged.
After a few weeks of the increased dose of cortisone, I retained over
ten pounds of fluid, a common side effect. Dr. Gardner prescribed
acetazolamide (Diamox) as a diuretic. In about a week I developed a
sore on my right arm—identical, it seemed to me, to the one I had
developed on my leg in Sofia during my bout with erysipelas. I recalled
again the miracle drug I had been given in Sofia and mentioned it to
Dr. Gardner.

Without a word, he made a quarter turn in his chair, pulled
a thick volume from the shelf on the left, and opened it on his desk.
I detected a trace of excitement on his face as he finished reading.
"I thought so!" he exclaimed. "The Diamox I gave you is chemically
related to sulfonamide and probably is capable of causing the same
side effects. We'll have to change the drug. You must be terribly
allergic to sulfonamides. Very few people would have reacted to such
a minimal dose. From now on, we must be absolutely sure of everything you take. A drug sensitivity like yours will get us into trouble
wherever we turn."

Was it possible that the sulfonamides did not just worsen

my condition but had actually given me the disease? What a frightening
thought! I looked up at Dr. Gardner and asked him if the sulfonamides
had been available in the late thirties.

"Yes, they were," he said.

"I wonder . . ."

"You could be quite right." He guessed my thoughts. "The
'miracle drug' you took in Bulgaria could very well have been a
sulfonamide."

"What makes one person allergic to one drug and not another?"

"What makes one person susceptible to an infection and
another immune?"* he echoed. "We know so little. We often learn
by our mistakes." After some moments, he added, "Allergic people
like you seem to do better on no drugs at all. Too often we over-
medicate people for minor complaints. We should be more careful."

Haunting questions came to my mind. Had the "miracle
drugs" in Bulgaria started my trouble? Had the sulfonamides given
in Holland unmasked my condition for the second time? Were the
doctors in Boston, however well-intentioned, giving me the wrong
drugs to relieve my symptoms? Did the powder I applied to my rash
and the medicated cream I applied to my sores contain sulfonamide?
Were there other hidden routes by which sulfonamide could enter
my body that even the doctors were not aware of?†

"God, there must be thousands of people all over the world
who react as I do. Or am I just one of the few unlucky ones who
cannot take a very useful medicine?"

Dr. Diamond had told me that penicillin and several other
commonly used drugs could produce LE cells with similar systemic
manifestations like mine.

"Dr. Gardner," I said, "suppose the sulfonamides are at the
root of my problem and what I have now is a type of lupus caused

*Immunity: the power to resist infection or invasion of bacteria.

†In February 1972, an article in a Boston newspaper reported that over one
hundred billion meat animals and poultry had been routinely fed sulfonamide, penicillin, tetracycline, and other antibiotics during the past two decades.

by sulfonamides—would that change the prognosis? Would I stand a better chance to get well?"

"It is reasonable to hope that everything would clear up if we remove the source of the trouble. It would be interesting," he said, "to see how many other patients have the same problem. It could shed light on the nature of lupus itself."

When I got up to leave, he asked, "By the way, how is your weight?"

"I'm retaining lots of fluids, but I also must be gaining real weight. My appetite is uncontrollable. All of my clothes are too tight. This only adds to my depression."

"Cortisone does that," he said, getting up himself.

"Does what? Retains fluids or accentuates my problems?"

"It can do both."

"So, now I can expect to lose my mind, too." I half smiled.

On my way out, Dr. Gardner said he was sorry he couldn't offer me anything for the moment to alleviate my problems—he could only sympathize with me. However, he assured me that once we withdrew the cortisone, my weight would return to normal and my outlook would improve.

Returning home that afternoon, I found Dr. and Mrs. Floyd Black waiting for me in my living room. For the second time in my life, these dear people would prove to be my saviors. I had known them since my youth in Bulgaria. Dr. Black had been the president of the American College in Sofia when I left home for the United States. He had helped me obtain my American visa and was personally responsible for my being in this country. When he retired in 1955, he and his wife came to live in Arlington, Massachusetts.

Mrs. Black's keen eyes sensed my low spirits. "Poor girl," she said in her motherly voice. "You don't feel too well?"

"No, I don't," I admitted, on the verge of tears.

"I know that you don't like to talk about it, but what do you call this illness of yours?"

Dr. Black gave me a long look, then removed his heavy-rimmed glasses to wipe them. For the first time in all these years I saw his eyes. They were a special blue, the color of water that had absorbed the sky.

"I feel like a hypochondriac whenever I talk about it," I mumbled.

"Poor girl," Mrs. Black repeated.

"The doctors believe that I have systemic lupus erythematosus. But they don't know much about the disease. They think it is incurable," I said, and started to cry.

"That's strange." Mrs. Black's voice quivered with feeling. "My nephew had systemic lupus erythematosus in Bulgaria more than thirty years ago."

I wiped my eyes and looked at her in surprise. She was the first person outside the medical profession whom I had heard pronounce correctly and without hesitation the words "lupus erythematosus." This was the first time that I'd heard of someone who had actually had lupus.

Dr. Black confirmed her statement. He said that Jordan, their nephew, had been working for the American College in Sofia when he was stricken with lupus. Today he was still healthy and sound. "He lives practically next door to you, right here in Wellesley," Dr. Black said with an encouraging smile.

"You should call Jordan up this very evening," Mrs. Black urged excitedly. "His sister, who is a doctor in Sofia, treated his lupus with some simple medication, and he got well!"

"At least well enough not to have mentioned lupus for more than thirty years." Dr. Black glanced at me with one of his mischievous expressions.

I wanted so much to believe that they were not in error. My doctors in Boston had no records of any lupus patient who had survived for such a long period of time. Still, I had to explore every possible clue. Immediately after supper, I telephoned Jordan. The Blacks had already alerted him, and he volunteered to come to our house for a cup of coffee.

That evening, when Jordan, sturdy and well, walked into our living room, I tried to hide my excitement. His dark complexion and heavy accent marked him as a true Bulgarian. Martha was somewhat disappointed that the nephew was so old. He was at least fifty. To her, someone's nephew had to be closer to her own age.

Jordan was reluctant to speak of his illness. Only after he understood my predicament did he open up. We began to compare notes. Most of the symptoms I mentioned, he had also experienced; only in his opinion, his ordeal had been worse than mine. During that evening, Jordan confessed that at one point his suffering had reached such a degree that he believed death to be his only salvation. I knew then that his case must have been graver than mine.

Jordan said that in 1937 he had gone to Geneva, where the doctors diagnosed lupus from a biopsy* from his cheek. He pointed to a faint scar under his left eye. His sister, who had been working at the same hospital, had cared for him. Once the doctors had established the diagnosis, she began to treat him on the advice of her colleagues in Sofia with a simple medication that brought about a remission. Whenever he anticipated a slight relapse, he fell back on the same medication, and all went well again.

I listened to Jordan with a strange feeling of suspense. I mentioned that I had understood from the Blacks that he had had the disease during the German occupation of Bulgaria in 1941.

"Yes, I had it then," Jordan said, and explained that living conditions were trying during those times and may have had something to do with causing the relapse of many diseases, lupus included. His relapse had lasted for many months, but despite some ups and downs, he had been well ever since. I was eager to hear the name of this remarkable medication. At that point, I was willing to accept witchcraft if witchcraft would help me.

"What's the name of the medication?" my husband asked seconds before I did.

"Nicotinamide," Jordan said. "It's a vitamin referred to as niacin; it's one of the B complex. It's more commonly known as a preventive medication for pellagra.† That's what saved my life!"

"Can one take niacin pills?" I asked, tempted already to rush

*Biopsy: a sample of tissue for microscopic study.

†Pellagra: a deficiency of niacin, one of the B vitamins, that causes diarrhea, dermatitis, and dementia.

to the drugstore and buy the magic vitamin as soon as Jordan left the house.

"It's possible," Jordan said, "but one gets better results if it is taken intravenously. You can take it also by injection into the muscle."

He suggested that I write to his sister, a physician in Bulgaria, to find out more details of his medical history. He thought that Dr. Gardner might find it of value to know if his condition were clinically similar to mine. "If Bulgaria were free," he said, "I'd advise you to go to Sofia to see Professor Liuben Popoff. He is a well-known dermatologist. The doctors might know of him at Peter Bent Brigham," Jordan speculated. "Professor Popoff is among the first to have used the antimalarial drugs successfully in rheumatoid arthritis and lupus." Half kiddingly, while bidding us good-night, he suggested once more that perhaps I should take the trip to Bulgaria.

"Go to Bulgaria?" my husband said after Jordan was gone. "How can one go to Bulgaria? The State Department won't grant protection to any U.S. citizen who wants to go there. Even if the new Bulgarian government would let someone in, there would be no guarantee they'd let him out again."

I lay down on the couch and closed my eyes. The nicotinamide grew in my mind as a symbol of new life. A trip to Bulgaria! All my emotions churned. Homesickness and sadness merged into pain. Nostalgic echoes from the past came back to mind. Surrendering completely, I fell to dreaming. As a growing girl, I had often seen myself traveling and exploring the world with curiosity. I was now in America, thousands of miles from home, and I suddenly longed to be back.

I thought of the mountains near Sofia and the pine woods where I used to spend every free minute of my life. I could almost hear the gushing springs breaking through the ice with thundering noises that echoed through the valley. Coming down the slopes on skis, chased by the spring winds, felt like flying into space. At night the stars hung low, almost within reach. I was tempted to pluck them for sheer pleasure but never had. I'd always left them there for the next time.

I could see Mother reading by the window in her low, cushioned chair. I had always suspected that besides the light, she'd chosen the window because of its closeness to the street. There the outside world began—the people walking, the children playing. To mother, the world was an extension of her home.

I was cold, but I closed my eyes a little tighter, afraid that I would break the spell. I could see the train pulling out of the Sofia railroad station. That evening, Mother's eyes had looked like emeralds, only greener. They shone like stars bathed in tears. As I watched her, I knew I would never again see eyes so wise, so human, and so tender. In them I clearly saw her soul and all her love for me.

German soldiers, their uniforms ornate with gleaming brass, packed the station, which was darker and more desolate than usual. The rhythmic clicking of the soldiers' spurs and the piercing whistle of the steam engine still reverberate in my mind. The air that night was heavily charged with fear and anticipation of impending disaster. The Germans had been in the country for only a few hours. I could not adjust to seeing so many young men carrying guns and pistols, objects reflecting hatred and savagery. The cold, icy expressions on their soldier faces, drained of humor and passion, even of cruelty, made them seem like phantoms walking in the semidarkness. The only civilians on the platform were Mother and Father and a few friends and relatives who had come to see me off. In a way, we looked like phantoms, too.

Father rushed to get me on the train. He walked with me from one compartment to another, looking for a seat. I was the only girl on that train; the other passengers were German soldiers. Eventually, Father found a place next to an open window, embraced me, and rushed out.

When Mother saw me, her voice trembled like a leaf. "Don't be—" The whistle's piercing sound muffled the rest of her words. The train gave a jolt, another whistle, and we were moving. Father found the strength to joke in those difficult moments, hoping to bring a smile to my face. "Don't forget," he called out loudly, trying to keep up with the train that gathered speed. "Act like a Boy Scout; forget that you're just a girl."

What a fantastic trip that turned out to be. To get to America from Bulgaria, I had to travel over the Black Sea to Russia, across the whole of Siberia to the Yellow Sea, to Japan, and over the Pacific to San Francisco.

In the past few days a letter had arrived from my brother. He reminded me that we had inherited our parents' good health. "Mother handed us her stamina, discipline, and perseverance, and Father his imagination. . . ." He was confident that I would make it.

My thoughts were derailed as my husband threw a blanket over me. "You seem to be shivering." He looked at me with a strange glance.

"I'm always cold," I whispered, trying to conceal my tears.

In bed, after he put the lights out, he said, "Perhaps you should go to Geneva and see some of Jordan's Swiss doctors. They might have a different approach to your problems. Often the methods of treating disease differ from place to place and the details are not known everywhere at the same time. The change might do you some good."

Long after he fell asleep, I lay there thinking. I could not risk going to Bulgaria in my condition. What if they kept me there? I tossed restlessly, unable to fall asleep. Go to Geneva?

During my next appointment with Dr. Gardner, I related Jordan's story of the nicotinamide. I asked him if he would mind writing to Jordan's sister. He said that he didn't mind writing but was skeptical of the vitamin. He knew that the vitamin was useful in the treatment of pellagra but not whether it might have any effect on lupus. After some reflection, Dr. Gardner said, "I'll give you the nicotinamide injections if you want me to." I could follow his thoughts: A placebo* has proved helpful in other diseases, so why not try a placebo in this one?

"I want to have the injections," I said.

"All right," he said, "but to treat you with nicotinamide would be the same as closing my eyes and, from a shelfful of harmless

---

*Placebo: an inactive substance given to patient either for its pleasing effect or as a control in experiments with an active drug.

potions, taking out just anything and giving it to you." Drawing a memo pad from the right top pocket of his white coat, he wrote down "nicotinamide," saying that this wouldn't be the first time he had made a fool of himself by experimenting. He put the pad back into his lab-coat pocket, which seemed to contain everything: pencils, pens, slide rule. On occasion I had seen there tubes filled with blood, and once he had managed to squeeze in a small plastic bag of plasma.*
"I'll do some inquiring about the nicotinic acid," he said, "but I'll only buy the idea when I have some clinical proof." He handed me a prescription for hydroxychloroquine, saying that some patients with lupus had responded favorably to it. He wanted to give it a try.

The hydroxychloroquine was supposed to reduce the light sensitivity of the skin. Its ability to do this, as is common with many other medical discoveries, had been found by accident. The drug is one of a group of malaria-control medicines that were first used on a large scale by the U.S. Armed Forces in the Pacific theater during World War II. Some very alert physicians noticed that discoid lupus cases seemed to benefit from the malaria prophylaxis. It was then reasoned that if discoid LE could be helped, perhaps LE would also be benefited by the same family of drugs. Dr. Gardner felt that hydroxychloroquine produced the fewest side effects of the entire group.

"What kind of side effects?" I asked.

He said that changes in vision had been reported in patients on prolonged chloroquine therapy. This meant that I had to be checked periodically by an eye specialist while on the medication. "It would be wise," he cautioned, "to take the medicine intermittently. Let's say, take it for four months, then rest for a few. You should take it during the summer months, when the sun is at its strongest." I asked if the eye examination would provide absolute assurance of safety.

He said no, but indicated that I should not worry because the dose I was about to take was probably not large enough to pose any problems. But one could never be sure. All sorts of problems, minor and major, had been reported with this drug. Every drug has

---

*Plasma: the fluid portion of the blood in which the blood cells are floating.

the ability to hurt someone. "But don't worry. Don't think about it; otherwise, you and I will be paralyzed and won't be able to do anything."

During that discussion about hydroxychloroquine, I had made up my mind. I told Dr. Gardner that I had just decided to take a trip to Geneva.

"I follow your thinking," Dr. Gardner said. "You want to see for yourself. Actually, I myself am rather curious about the nicotinamide. My only concern is over the possibility of your getting fatigued by the journey. But on the other hand, the change might do you some good."

Traveling had always satisfied a need for adventure in me, and I was glad the feeling had not diminished with my illness. Besides, I had to find out all I could about the nicotinamide. I seized upon the drug as a thread of hope.

Dr. Gardner gave me a white-cell injection that made a tetanus shot seem like a tea party. First came the burning, then a predictable soreness and swelling the size of a lemon that lasted until it was time for the next injection the following week. With the injection completed, he seemed to notice my pained reaction to it, and trying to cheer me up, he said he would try the nicotinamide as soon as I returned from Geneva.

Before I changed my mind about taking the trip, I asked him to give me the smallpox vaccination required by immigration law. Then I remembered Dr. Koenig's visit. I had gained the impression that something drastic might occur if I stopped taking the white-cell injections. When I expressed my worries to Dr. Gardner, he said that he had been planning to talk to Dr. Koenig about the possibility of stopping the shots. I had already had over one hundred such injections, and he didn't think they were helping much. And besides, he was concerned that I might get hepatitis. He explained that the type of hepatitis that concerned him was a disease transmitted by human blood products. If even one drop of plasma from a hepatitis carrier entered the bloodstream, the recipient could contract the disease. "The chance of getting hepatitis from one hundred blood donors sounds like Russian roulette, doesn't it?" Then he gave me the smallpox inoculations.

Two days after I had the smallpox inoculation, a terrific reaction set in. My arm swelled up. An angry sore erupted, raging like a volcano full of pus. My temperature rose to 101 degrees. For a few days it appeared as if I might have to cancel my trip. Dr. Gardner wondered whether the immunization had stirred up a new allergy. Other types of inoculations had been known to cause problems with lupus. Fortunately, the sore improved after a week, and I was able to go ahead with my plans.

Not sure that I could withstand the flight, I took a night plane with sleeping accommodations to London. From there, I flew to Geneva, where I was met by Madeleine and Noel Landru, close friends of ours who live in Voiron, France, forty miles from the border. They had reserved a room for me at a hotel in the center of town and suggested that I stay there for a day or so until I entered the hospital. I told them I would keep the room through my stay in Geneva. We made plans to drive out together to Chamonix in southeastern France for a ten-day holiday after my release from the hospital.

18. Therapy
The Physician's Point of View

TREATING a disease can be very simple or very complex. For a disease of known cause with an accepted specific therapy (e.g., a streptococcal pharyngitis treated with penicillin), a diagnosis is made in a relatively straightforward manner, medication is prescribed, and a patient usually responds. Complications are uncommon, and the patient fully expects to recover. The treatment of a chronic illness of unknown cause presents a far greater challenge to both patient and physician. While researchers continue to search for the cause and the cure, one must still deal with the potential ravages of the illness. Happily, much has been learned regarding the way cells and tissues are injured in patients with lupus, and rational therapeutic regimes have been developed to suppress inflammation, prevent organ damage and disability, and relieve pain. Therapy must be given in the context of emotional support, a topic alluded to in many chapters of this book.

How does lupus cause inflammation and tissue injury? Patients with lupus manufacture an excess of ANAs, that is, antibodies to substances within the nuclei of cells. Some patients also make antibodies to cells (viz., red blood cells, platelets, white blood cells) and antibodies to cytoplasmic organelles and proteins. Lupus patients appear to be genetically programmed to make an excess amount of these antibodies; various stimuli may trigger this process, including infections, surgery, UV light, and possibly stress. Excessive amounts of antibodies are made because the cells (called "suppressor T cells") that normally keep this process in check are not functioning adequately. The antibodies by themselves can cause problems when they attack and kill cells. For instance, antibodies to red blood cells attach to the cells, damage them, and cause splenic clearance at an accelerated rate. Anemia is the result of the body's inability to manufacture enough new red blood cells to replace the lost ones. A similar mechanism is involved when antibodies attack platelets. The consequence of a low platelet count can be bleeding into the skin (red dots called purpura, or bruises) or into other organs. Since the culprit in both cases is the antibodies, the goal of therapy is to reduce the amount of these antibodies in the blood. This may be accomplished with the administration of moderate to high doses of corticosteroids.

Cells in the body are always normally breaking down, dying, and being replaced by new cells. If the cell breakdown products, such as nuclei, meet ANAs in the bloodstream, they form an aggregate called an immune complex. This immune complex is normally cleared by red blood cells, which bring them to the spleen, where they are cleared from the bloodstream. Both clearance mechanisms appear to be defective in patients with lupus; thus, immune complexes may deposit in innocent bystander organs such as the skin, joints, kidney, lungs, brain, and other organs where their deposit results in inflammation. The immune complexes by themselves will cause inflammation only when they interact with other serum proteins called complement. Activation of the complement system causes the release of small proteins (called peptides), which attract more white blood cells to the site of the immune-complex deposit. The white blood cells then try and eat (phagocytose) the immune complexes and in the process release enzymes that can cause tissue injury. Ultimately the immune complexes are eaten up, and the cells promote healing. However, a scar may form, and the organ may not function quite normally again. Repeated attacks of inflammation, healing, and scarring can result in more severe organ impairment.

Therapy is aimed at intervening at multiple sites of this cycle: prevention of excessive antibody production, removal of antibodies, removal of immune complexes, prevention of complement binding or activation, prevention of white-blood-cell enzyme release, blocking of enzyme action, prevention of scar formation, etc. If no one medication is currently able to accomplish all these tasks, how do we determine the appropriate course of action?

Medications, natural or synthetic, are recommended when a physician feels that their potential benefit is greater than their potential risk. To minimize the risk and maximize the potential benefit, the physician must:

1. Consider what other medications are being taken and whether they will interact with new medications.
2. Determine a history of related allergy or intolerance. (One rarely develops a tolerance to medications unless one is using narcotics or barbiturates or one has a new disease or problem.)
3. Encourage the patient to take the medications as prescribed, not altering the dosage unless indicated.
4. Determine which medications can be taken prior to, together with, or after meals, at bedtime, or at intervals of several hours.
5. Encourage the patient to drink a lot of water (and little, if any, alcohol).
6. Consider how the medications may affect a life-style.
7. Consider the cost of the medication.

Before discussing the use of specific medications, it is important to consider a number of general principles regarding any medication. The physician must first consider the risk-to-benefit ratio. Each medication has a potential benefit, that is, it may make the patient feel better by alleviating, eliminating, or curing the disease. Unfortunately, no drug or medication is entirely free of risk, that is, side effects or allergic reactions. If one read the list of possible side effects in a package insert or in the official tome, the *Physician's Desk Reference (PDR)*, one would hesitate to take any drug. If all or even most patients experienced harmful side effects, we would discontinue the use of those medications. What the package insert usually fails to list is the frequency of side effects. If, in over 1 percent of patients, significant side effects occur, the drug may not be released. Some drugs that have caused significant side effects in even less than 1 percent of patients have been entirely withdrawn from the market, leaving in the lurch 99 percent of a population that could have potentially benefited from the drug. The FDA, in this overprotective, highly litigious, low-risk society, is trying to endorse only "safe drugs." Safe drugs do not exist. Even placebos have been mistakingly perceived by patients to cause side effects, such as headaches, fever, diarrhea, constipation, aches and pains, dizzy spells, and rashes in 15–30 percent of people taking them.

Now might be a good time to discuss the issue of placebos. All physicians agree that optimal care involves taking as much time as necessary and utilizing the resources needed to arrive at a diagnosis and suitable course of therapy. Although both patient and physican hope that whatever the patient has will go away on its own, physicians often feel pressured into action by an insistent patient. The resultant act is often prescribing a placebo. Are placebos a copout? In a way. But let's not discount their psychological effects. It's hard to imagine that a big, brightly colored pill or capsule doesn't possess healing qualities! However, some physicians who find themselves overscheduled use placebos to "buy time" as they seek a balance in time and effort spent on diagnosis, prescribing, and follow-up. When any one (or combination) of those three steps poses a problem for the patient or physician, each party should feel free to suggest a specialist. Searching for answers and seeking knowledge constitute good medical care and in the long run will benefit the patient more than a placebo, which may or may not harm. Open, trusting dialogue between patient and physician can only aid the continuing search for an explanation of the patient's symptoms and signs.

The current interest and fascination with vitamins as cure-alls must be addressed. Do we need vitamins? Definitely! Can one become vitamin deficient? Surely! Generally eating three reasonably balanced meals per day can prevent vitamin deficiency. Many products now available on supermarket shelves have added vitamins and other nutrients. Will taking extra vitamins help? Help what? Afford extra

energy? Relieve fatigue? They will not. Cure depression? Prevent colds?
Control lupus? No. Taken in excessive amounts, vitamins can be
extremely harmful, not to mention expensive! However, specific medical conditions call for vitamin therapy. Malabsorption syndrome,
osteoporosis, iron-deficiency anemia, and stringent dieting call for
extra vitamins and/or nutrients. Always tell your physician what vitamins you are taking and let him or her determine if they are
indicated. Perhaps they will have a placebo effect, if not a physiological one.

Many people seek natural products on the assumption that
a natural product will be safer and more effective than a laboratory-
manufactured synthetic. Thus Rousseauian ideal is usually wishful
thinking and may explain why this year's natural food cure is next
year's failure. I cringe every time I enter a health-food store and see
the rows of "natural products" of undocumented benefit.

Mrs. Aladjem drank herbal teas. Basically nonmedicinal, they
are aromatic, pleasant tasting, contain a mild stimulant, and made
her feel good. Placebos do have value.

19. Medications

The Physician's Point of View

MRS. Aladjem's treatment was comprised of the following: herbal teas, vitamins, aspirin, chloroquine, prednisone, potassium, Serpasil, atropine, and white-blood-cell injections.

Aspirin has been used as an anti-inflammatory and analgesic (painkiller) for nearly a hundred years. It is but one form of salicylates that act by inhibiting prostaglandin synthesis. The prostaglandins are small lipid molecules from phagocytic and other cells and are involved in varying aspects of inflammation, including dilating blood vessels, causing phagocytic cells to travel to a site of infection, trauma, or inflammation, etc. Prostaglandins also promote healing, as of a stomach ulcer, and are involved in uterine contractions. By suppressing inflammation and relieving pain, salicylates are particularly effective for arthritic and musculoskeletal manifestations of lupus. The dosage must be frequent, as the drug is rapidly metabolized. Since many salicylate preparations cause stomach irritation, many patients and physicians prefer other forms of anti-inflammatory and analgesic preparations. New NSAIDs such as ibuprofen, naproxen, diflunisal, indomethacin, sulindac, piroxicam, and others, similar to salicylates, irritate the stomach less and have a longer period of action per pill. *Note: Individuals allergic to aspirin (but not necessarily to other forms of salicylates) are also often allergic to the NSAID, despite the fact that they are promoted as nonsalicylates.* Allergy is a specific phenomenon manifested as a rash, sneezing, runny nose and/or eyes, wheezing, and, in particular, nasal polyps in respect to aspirin. Although NSAIDs have been tested on hundreds of people as equally effective, one can never predict which one will work best for a particular patient. A physician will usually try three of them for two weeks *each* to see which one helps an individual patient. NSAIDs also have the benefit of alleviating menstrual cramps for most women, an attribute not shared by salicylates. Other analgesics, with weak, if any, anti-inflammatory properties, include acetaminophen (Tylenol) and propoxyphene (Darvon).

For thousands of years, particular plants were known to possess qualities that alleviated symptoms of disease. Today many large pharmaceutical firms continue to screen thousands of plants worldwide for new drugs that may cure a specific disease. The yield may be about 1 in 10,000 plants tested—not a promising venture. One specific plant and its history is very relevant to lupus. The bark of the cinchona plant was recognized by natives of South America to alleviate the fever of malaria. After considerable international intrigue and subterfuge, cinchona bark was brought to Europe, and the active ingredient, quinine, was extracted. It not only alleviated the fever of malaria but also often effected a total cure. Physicians then applied its usage to other febrile and nonfebrile maladies. Predictably, the results were negative, and quinine fell into disfavor except as a remedy for malaria. When during the 1920s and 1930s it became apparent that some cases of malaria were unresponsive to quinine, chemists synthesized variants of the quinine molecule in an attempt to find more effective compounds. These were developed just prior to World War II and helped in large part to control malaria in the war zones. These drugs include quinacrine (Atabrine), chloroquine (Aralen), and later, hydroxychloroquine (Plaquenil).

Why were these quinine derivatives (now referred to as antimalarials) first used to treat lupus? Quinine was first used in 1894 for lupus, which was then considered a circulatory problem. By 1934, quinine was used successfully for the treatment of lesions, and by 1940, Atabrine yielded more favorable results. Widespread use of antimalarials only followed after medical journal articles in the 1950s appeared noting their efficacy in treating the lupus syndrome. How do the antimalarials work? They appear to stabilize the membranes of cells that phagocytose immune complexes so that fewer enzymes are released; they block the effects of UV light on the skin; and they may affect T-helper suppressor cells.

Antimalarials are now prescribed for the cutaneous and arthritic symptoms of lupus but do not appear beneficial in other manifestations of the disease. Most physicians prescribe hydroxychloroquine because it appears to have fewer side effects than the other antimalarials and is equally effective in most patients. When it fails to achieve the desired result, the dosage may be increased or experimentally combined, or other antimalarials may be substituted.

Mrs. Aladjem received prednisone, a form of corticosteroid. (I will subsequently refer to prednisone rather than corticosteroid, as it is the most commonly prescribed corticosteroid.) Corticosteroids are produced by the adrenal gland in response to signals from the pituitary gland, which in turn responds to various signals, including light, stress, and blood levels of corticosteroids. The adrenal gland normally makes cortisone (which mainly affects salt and water metabolism) and hydrocortisone (which affects mainly sugar metabolism and is an anti-inflammatory). The adrenal gland normally secretes about 25–50 mg of hydrocortisone per day; more when the body is stressed (e.g., as a result of infection, trauma, surgery, emotional problems, etc.). Chemists have modified hydrocortisone to develop preparations that can be administered intramuscularly, intravenously, topically, and especially orally, and maintain their efficacy for prolonged periods of time. The prototype drug is prednisone. It acts as a general anti-inflammatory drug by killing many of the mononuclear cells that either make antibodies or promote their formation. It also wipes out phagocytic cells and may act on the complement system, promote the clearance of immune complexes, and inhibit the action of enzymes released from cells. The greater the dose, the greater the effect, both beneficial and deleterious. As noted above, not all side effects develop in each person who takes prednisone, but the higher the dosage, the greater the likelihood. Prednisone is generally prescribed for significant organ involvement (such as of the kidney, lungs, brain, blood). The side effects may include increased appetite (and resultant weight gain), salt and water retention (and resultant weight gain), and as a result, the face may become round, and stretch marks may develop on the abdomen, arms, and legs. As a result of salt and water retention, blood pressure may increase (hypertension). Prednisone affects sugar metabolism and, in one who is genetically prone to develop it, may unmask diabetes. Prednisone increases acid and enzyme production in the stomach (causing dyspepsia and occasionally a stomach [peptic] ulcer); affects calcium and bone metabolism causing bones to become thinner (osteoporosis) and less structurally sound, making them prone to break or collapse; causes avascular necrosis (loss of blood supply to bones such as the hip, resulting in their collapse); and increases susceptibility to infections. Taking prednisone causes the adrenal gland to cease production until the dosage is decreased to a level less than the gland would normally produce (equivalent to about 5–10 mg/day of prednisone). In most individuals, as the prednisone dosage is decreased further, the adrenal gland will slowly begin functioning again. This may take weeks or months, or may never happen, relegating the patient to permanent prednisone treatment—not for the treatment of the lupus but to replace what a nonfunctioning adrenal gland would normally manufacture.

Prednisone can be given on a once-a-day basis or a number of times during the day. This decision and the dosage are based on the extent and severity of the lupus and the degree to which it has responded to a lower dosage or other medications.

Corticosteroids can also be given topically (i.e., applied to the skin) as an ointment (for dry skin) or cream (for oily skin) or as a gel. Topical steroids come in different strengths from hydrocortisone (to which most lupus skin lesions respond) to the fluorine-substituted steroids that are used for resistant lesions. The major side effect of topical steroids come from the fluorinated variants, which can cause skin atrophy and thinning if used for a protracted period. Therefore, it is recommended that they not be used on the face, or if absolutely necessary, only for short times.

Very large doses of prednisone are sometimes given in a very short period of time (pulse steroids). The rationale is to wipe out all of the ANAs quickly without risking side effects accompanying prolonged usage. Pulse steroids are usually only given for patients with moderate to severe renal disease that is unresponsive to more conventional therapy.

Potassium is a natural substance sometimes given to patients receiving corticosteroids, which can cause excessive potassium loss (a rare occurrence). Patients taking diuretics may also require potassium, since diuretics also cause an excessive amount of potassium loss. Blood tests are indicators of potassium levels and needs. Blood levels need to be monitored for overdose, a condition deleterious to normal heart function.

Immunosuppressives (azathioprin, cyclophosphamide, chlorambucil, methotrexate), another modern method of treatment, are a group of drugs initially developed for the treatment of various malignancies but used for the treatment of lupus for the last twenty years. They act primarily on the cells that make antibodies or influence their production. Treatment, therefore, results in lower levels of antibodies, at the expense of the white blood cells that defend us against infection, etc. It is not surprising, then, that their use increases one's risk to develop infections. As these medications suppress bone marrow, they may cause anemia. The dosage must be very carefully regulated to maximize benefit and minimize risk. The immunosuppressive cyclophosphamide may cause cystitis, hair loss, sterility, and malignancy, and methotrexate may cause liver problems. These agents are generally only employed when the patient has had an inadequate response to or unacceptable side effects from prednisone.

Techniques for "blood cleansing" go back to the middle ages, the days of blood letting and leeching. Thankfully, modern technology has updated treatment of blood-related disorders. Plasmaphoresis is a process by which a unit of blood (500 ml = 1 pint) is removed and the cells separated from the fluid plasma by centrifugation. The red cells are reinfused into the patient, while the plasma (containing the antibodies and immune complexes) is discarded. The rationale for reinfusing the cells is that they are basically healthy and the body would need days or even weeks to replenish them. Reinfusion is essentially a body's time/labor-saving device. The technique is well established, as painless as the prick of a needle, and complications are rare. Salt water usually replaces the volume of lost plasma to maintain intravascular volume. Predictably, removing the antibodies acts as a stimulus to more antibody production, which must be prevented by treatment with prednisone and immunosuppressives (see above). While plasmaphoresis was touted a number of years ago, recent careful studies (see below) have failed to demonstrate efficacy in controlled studies in either mild to moderate lupus, or in lupus nephritis. It should therefore still be considered an experimental technique best reserved for acute and/or very severe lupus characterized by high blood levels of immune complexes.

Many other medications may be prescribed for lupus, including antibodies (avoiding sulfonamides), sleeping medications, tranquilizers, and antiseizure medication. The latter affects prednisone metabolism, creating the necessity for doubling the prednisone dosage.

Of particular concern to me has been the treatment of lupus-related hypertension. It is essential to control the blood pressure of a patient with renal disease to maintain maximal renal function. Various medications, including diuretics, beta blockers, calcium channel blockers, and enzyme inhibitors may be necessary with different modes of action, either by themselves or in well-tested combinations. I encourage patients to have their blood pressures taken regularly at home and to keep an accurate record. Control of blood pressure will improve renal function and tends to prevent heart attacks and strokes.

Mrs. Aladjem also used Serpasil (reserpine), one of the first medications developed to control mild hypertension (rarely prescribed now, it has been replaced by more efficacious and safer medications) and atropine, a medication that was then prescribed to counter the potential stomach-irritating effects of Serpasil and adrenocorticosteroids. Mrs. Aladjem also received white-blood-cell injections, a form of treatment developed in the 1940s and 1950s in the belief that it might boost a patient's own immune system. Today we understand its potential harm to lupus patients in that it may increase the levels of antiwhite blood cells and antinuclear antibodies.

We dream of drugs of the future—instant cures, if you will. Many studies are being conducted with animals (primarily mice) with forms of lupus. Researchers are trying combinations of new immuno-suppressives (with hopefully fewer side effects); monoclonal antibodies that specifically kill cells that enhance antibody production; lymphokines that either enhance suppressor mechanisms (and therefore control antibody formation) or promote healing cells; diets rich in 3 omega lipids (fish oil) that influence leukotriene metabolism (see below); drugs that inhibit leukotrienes (substances similar to prostaglandins in both structure and function but not affected by aspirin and other currently available NSAIDs); sex hormones; etc. Drugs that look promising in animal studies are then tried in open trials on small groups of lupus patients, looking very carefully for both efficacy (greater than the 30 percent placebo effect common to *any* new drug) and toxicity. These trials all must have FDA approval. If a drug then looks both promising and safe, larger trials will be conducted and then double-blind crossover studies. In these studies two groups of patients are carefully matched, and half the patients are given the new drug, the other half a placebo. Neither the patients, their physicians, or the drug company know who is taking which. After a predetermined number of weeks, the groups are switched; those receiving placebo now receive the medication, and vice versa. The patients are unaware of the change because the pills resemble the placebo. After a few more weeks or months the trial ends, and the patients go back to their old medications. The code is broken then by the physician and the drug firm, and the results are analyzed. A drug is considered for manufacture when it is more effective and has fewer side effects than the placebo. The process to develop a new drug may take years and cost a pharmaceutical firm millions of dollars. If a medical urgency exists and the drug looks very promising in initial studies, the process may be hastened. Once a drug passes these stringent tests, it becomes available for marketing.

I have spent this chapter discussing medication. Only part of the therapy of the lupus patient, it is nevertheless a vital one. It is important to discuss medication with one's physician, as did Mrs.

Aladjem. Furthermore, as in her case, when a specific therapy (e.g., white-blood-cell injections) doesn't appear to cause any benefit, it should be discontinued. Treating a chronic disease often involves trial and error—searching for a better form or combination of medications in a sea of changing symptoms and organ involvements. But pills alone cannot substitute for the physician who provides support for the patient, helping him or her reach, find, and utilize inner strengths to deal with a chronic problem.

20. Hospital in Geneva
The Patient's Story

ON May 29, 1959, I entered one of the largest hospitals in Geneva, the same one that Jordan had stayed in thirty years before. The price per day was thirty-six Swiss francs, slightly under nine dollars. I was asked by the cashier to make a deposit of 650 francs, "for all eventualities." He seemed disturbed that I had no one in Switzerland to be notified in case of death and offered to notify a church of my choice. On the entry blank I had to write my maiden name, married name, number of children, their ages and sexes, my occupation, place of birth, date of birth, nationality, passport number, place of issue, and religion. I was given a number, 4673/11, and from then on I was referred to by this number. When I inquired about Jordan's doctor, I was told that the man was gravely ill and had hospitalized himself —an unfortunate situation, as he had been the reason for my trip.

A broad-bosomed nurse who spoke perfect English brought me into the cashier's office. She walked like a bird, hopping with incredible speed. I followed her as best I could to the elevator, up to the second floor, to a small private room with a high ceiling and two narrow windows showing a quiet street of gray stone houses.

The nurse told me to undress, showed me where to hang my clothes, and asked me to empty my bladder in a white enamel bedpan. She stuck a thermometer in my mouth and left the room. She returned almost immediately with a syringe and several glass tubes. She inserted the needle deftly, and I didn't feel a thing.

After a short while, a doctor, whom I shall call Professor de Malraux, walked in, accompanied by a young female assistant. Her eyes were in constant motion, like round black beets shaken in a jar. The professor spoke only French, but his assistant spoke English with a thick, nasal French accent. Another young doctor walked in. I noticed that when he bumped into the corner of my bed, he apologized in the most courteous way.

Professor de Malraux knew Jordan and Jordan's sister well, though he remembered only vaguely the details of Jordan's illness. He seemed astounded that I had come to consult doctors in Geneva when the United States—Boston in particular—was considered at the time the oustanding center of medicine in the world. When I explained my interest in the nicotinic acid, I was sure he knew what I was talking about, but he chose not to acknowledge it. Such simple medications were out of the question when more modern drugs like cortisone were available, he said, and that was that.

The spirit of this hospital proved very different from that of Peter Bent Brigham. The countenances were stern, especially those of the nurses—their starched expressions matched their crisp uniforms. In the presence of the doctors those women stood at attention like soldiers before their generals. At periodic intervals they took my blood pressure, pulse, and temperature, and I was fed at regular hours. There was a coldness in this hospital that separated the staff from the patients and one another. There was no friendliness.

Professor de Malraux moved in and out of my room, glowing in power like a celestial body. Not once did he tell me what tests were being taken. I didn't know from one moment to the next what to expect; everything kept me on edge.

On the second morning, a tall doctor with narrow stooped shoulders came to examine my eyes. He had a large head and a very dour expression. Whenever his droopy cheek came close to mine, I cringed. He spoke curtly, telling me in which direction to focus and nothing else. At the end of the examination, which lasted for over half an hour, he put several drops in each eye and left without a word. Later, when I opened my eyes, I was practically blind. The room, pitch black, moved in circles, spun by my exaggerated fear. Gradually, blurred vision reappeared. For the next few hours, I kept checking my eyes, anxiously trying to read my illustrated magazine. I was tense and fearful that the damage would be permanent. That night I couldn't fall asleep.

The next day, when a nurse wheeled me in for a cardiogram, the doctor, a stock, musuclar man, studied the strips of paper from the machine in perfect silence. When he was finished, I asked him if the EKG was all right.

He looked up in surprise and murmured a few incomprehensible words, and before I had a chance to say anything more, he stuck the strips of paper in his pocket, turned his back indifferently, and left the room.

The nurse who wheeled me back spoke only in a Romansh dialect that bore no resemblance to any other language I'd ever heard. I learned later that most of the nurses and attendants at this hospital had been recruited from the Romansh-speaking area of Switzerland.

Finally, the four days at the hospital mercifully came to an end. Professor de Malraux walked in with his young pale blond assistant. He declared that all the tests were concluded. No LE cell had been found—nothing suggestive of SLE. In his opinion, even the faded rash on my face was not a typical LE rash. He had seen such rashes before caused by drugs. When his young assistant pointed to the red V on my neck, Professor de Malraux impatiently muttered, "Yes, yes, drugs can cause the redness on the neck like hers. It can involve the cheeks, the nose, the brow." He made a motion with his hand over the bridge of his nose. Then he turned to me again. "If your rash grows redder again, apply some Ichthyol."

"Calamine lotion is close enough," murmured his assistant with a wisp of a polite smile.

"The persistent leukopenia could have been induced by drugs, too," Professor de Malraux addressed his assistant. I wondered what he meant by drugs. What kind of drugs? I remembered once having taken tetracycline* for an infected sore throat. The doctors in Boston had not been sure at the time that the drug had helped my throat but had rejoiced that at least I could tolerate an antibiotic. Two months later, when I contracted a bladder infection and the "cranberry juice" cure didn't work, I took tetracycline again. This time, after only three tablets, my temperature soared to 102 degrees, a rash erupted over my entire body, I had chills, and my eyes swelled up. I wished I could ask Professor de Malraux what he meant by "stay away from drugs," but he spoke much too fast. I could hardly understand what he was saying. I'm sure I had spoken better French before my admission to this hospital. Once inside, the language failed me, and I was sure the unfriendly atmosphere had something to do with the problem.

"Madame, you'll be all right." Professor de Malraux forced a smile, but his eyes remained as hard as marbles. "You must be careful not to become a chronic complainer."

A flash of indignation rushed blood to my cheeks. Here I was, lying in bed feeling like a deflated balloon, too weak to speak, and he was implying that my pains and aches were psychoneurotic. Was I turning into a hypochondriac?

Impervious to my emotions, Professor de Malraux said that he was intrigued by the white-blood-cell injections I had mentioned to him before. He had written already to Boston for more information. He said he would send the report of my visit to Dr. Gardner at Peter Bent Brigham Hospital. For the first time, he recalled having met Dr. George Thorn at a medical meeting in Belgium. His voice bordered on reverence when he pronounced Dr. Thorn's name.

While Professor de Malraux spoke, his assistant was eyeing the eruption on my arm caused by the smallpox inoculation. Cautiously, he expressed some concern over the inflammation, saying obliquely that perhaps I should not have been vaccinated. Both men bent down to examine the sore more closely, but neither said a word. Not be vaccinated? How could he expect me to return home without it?

---

*Tetracycline: an antibiotic effective against many of the bacteria that are not affected by penicillin.

Professor de Malraux wished me a good trip back to the States. His assistant remained in my room for another few moments. He handed me a tiny booklet that described the effects of the sun on the skin throughout the year and the intensity of the UV rays at different times of the day. He also gave me a prescription for Niconacid,* .05, to be taken morning, noon, and evening, and another prescription for a salve, called Homel creme, to rub on my face daily. He explained that the salve would shield me from the sun. He warned me that in my case the sun could be most troublesome.

Dangers, real or imaginary, crept deeper into my subconscious. I left the hospital in the worst possible mood. That night I spent tossing and turning, unable to sleep. I felt depressed and angry with myself for having taken this idiotic trip. But, then again, I reasoned, I could not go against my nature. I could not leave any stone unturned. Suppose the nicotinic acid was somewhat effective; suppose my trip had revealed more about the drug. I recalled again the story of the chloroquine, which, since 1941, had been used successfully in the treatment of lupus in Bulgaria and other parts of Europe but had not yet been used in the United States until much later. The same transatlantic route of acceptance might well be true of nicotinic acid. At least I hoped so.

When morning came, I was still awake. I wanted to be fresh and rested when my friends appeared the next evening, so that afternoon I asked the pharmacist in the apothecary next to the hotel for a mild sedative. I explained very clearly that I was sensitive to drugs, all drugs, and had never before taken a sleeping pill. The man behind the counter instantly handed me a tiny box. "*One* pill will put you to sleep, madame." He nodded amiably. "You'll sleep like a child."

After supper, while I packed my bags, I took two pills to ensure sleep. That's all I remember until I was awakened by the shrill ring of the telephone. I found myself fully dressed, shoes and all, sprawled on the bed. I could not imagine what had happened. Madeleine Landru was calling from the lobby. Sensing my confusion, she asked if I felt all right.

*Niconacid: Swiss-French trademark for a preparation of nicotinic acid.

"Yes, I'm fine, fine," I repeated. Groggily, I mentioned the sleeping pills I had taken at nine that night.

"Nine?" Madeleine repeated in a curious tone. "Then you've slept for twenty-two hours. It's seven-ten now!"

"Seven-ten?" I quickly glanced at the red traveling clock on my night table. "What day of the week is it?" I asked as I began to realize what must have happened. Next, I heard a pounding on my door.

"C'est moi. Tu m'écoutes?" I heard Madeleine's voice from afar. I had dozed off again, dreaming the most fantastic dream.

Madeleine helped me finish packing. "Some pills!" I remarked. I was frightened to think that I had lost an entire day.

"You must be terribly sensitive to drugs," Madeleine said.

I answered her with a drowsy yawn. An hour later we left Geneva, and I slept in the Landrus' car through the border inspection and all.

We spent the night in Voiron and set out for Chamonix the following morning. As Noel drove along the narrow, winding mountain roads, my short dream of two nights before returned vividly to my mind. Death in the abstract has always interested me in a philosophical way, and the end of life has filled me with curiosity. In my dream I had experienced the point of death. I had seen myself lying in bed at home, flat on my back, both arms stretched down by my side, my head tilted slightly to the left. My eyes were closed or possibly open just a slit. By my bedside my husband, son, and two daughters sat in contemplation. Their faces seemed sad and withdrawn, but did I actually see them or just imagine that I did? I was absolutely sure that these were my last moments. I had no power left over my body. The sensation reminded me of the time in Holland at the onset of my disease when I had awakened in the middle of the night with no sensation in my arms. But in the dream I felt no fear at all. I was not fighting death; I was at peace with myself. My consciousness was slipping away; already my brain functioned in a limited fashion. My world was shrinking to the row of chairs where my family sat; everything else was forgotten or didn't matter anymore. I felt their emotions keenly. In time I knew my husband would overcome his sorrow. My son, too, would manage somehow, and so would my oldest daughter. But Martha—she needed to be reassured that I felt at peace. In time of stress, we had a special signal between us; I used to smile at her a certain way to tell her not to worry. Just before my dream ended, a rush of warmth touched my lips, and I knew that Martha had gotten the message.

The dream cast a gloomy spell on me. I had tried to be as little of a worry to my family as possible, but how could they not be affected by my illness? Now that I was away, I could perceive more deeply their suppressed fears, their constant worry. I felt guilty and sorry for them. What could I do to lessen their burden? I still believed that someday I'd get well. As images from the dream kept reemerging, my thoughts returned to the act of dying and to death itself. I questioned if I had the strength to give up all the things I loved. "I'll miss the smell of freshly cut grass," I whispered to myself, "the feel of damp soil squeezed between my fingers; the spring, the summer, the fall, the winter . . . " I remembered a poem by Loren Eiseley I'd read some months before. Some of the lines resounded in my mind:

> I shall be part of all Octobers
> I shall be part of sleet and driving rain,
> I shall scurry with dead leaves on pavements,
> I shall be dust and rise from dust again.

I shuffled in my seat and Madeleine asked, *"Ça va?"*

"Yes, yes," I said reassuring her. But when I tried to stretch my legs, my knees felt locked; the pain was more than I could bear.

Noel drove fast, with the skill of a magician. Except for a brief stop for lunch, we drove for eight hours from Voiron through to Chamonix. In places, the narrow mountain roads clung to the edges of precipices that, from the car window, appeared dark and endless. I had the uncanny feeling of driving on a tightrope. By five in the afternoon, Noel had parked his Citroën in front of Hotel Mont Blanc in the center of Chamonix.

I stepped out with some difficulties. The aching and heaviness of my limbs had increased from having sat in the same position for so many hours. The crisp air made me shiver with cold. While Noel and Madeleine unloaded the car, I watched Mont Blanc. It looked like the Snow Queen bathed in the last rays of sunshine. Flowery bushes and trees covered the lower part of this giant beauty, which towers nearly 16,000 feet over Europe. The top, covered by ice and snow, sparkled like precious stones. I followed a large white cumulus that drifted across the sky toward the ridges and thought of the mountains back home in Sofia.

Noel had finished unloading the bags and was now standing by my side, viewing the mountains. I saw him as young, the way he used to look when I knew him in Bulgaria. He, my husband, and I used to go skiing or hiking on Vitosha Mountain before I was married. Noel used to tease me about going too fast for him.

"The mountains never change, Noel," I said.

He glanced at me and in a flash of optimism said, "You'll see; everything will be all right."

After a good night's sleep with the help of aspirins, I dressed and went for a walk around the lodge. Completely surrendering to the beauty around me, I fell into one of my old mountain moods, a retreat into childhood. I even tried to whistle again the way I used to in the mountains. No sound came. Whistling, I used to think, was just shaping my lips in a certain way and blowing. But now I was discovering that it was more than that. It was a strain on my larynx, my stomach, and my lungs. I had no strength to blow the air. My tired body could not keep up with my spirit. Since my arrival in Chamonix, I was aware that my voice had faded some. During the day I could hardly talk. I began wondering if someday my voice would disappear altogether.

All my life I had loved to whistle, and the loss added to my misery. As a child, this enthusiasm had often caused me trouble, for in Bulgaria girls were not supposed to whistle. But I always did. Whenever I came home from school, Mother would hear me whistling long before I reached the house, and she would reprimand me. "Girls don't whistle!" Minutes later, I would have forgotten and started a new tune. I used to tease the birds in our garden for hours, imitating their songs. That irked not just Mother but some of the birds, as well

To me, whistling was an expression of happy thoughts and happy feelings like laughing or singing, and I was surprised to learn that whistling was associated with bad luck and superstitions. I found that some believed whistling in the house was sure to call upon disease and misfortunes, while others thought that whistling on a ship would bring a storm and place the vessel in danger.

21. The Man Who Carried the Mountains in His Chest

The Patient's Story

TOWARD the end of our stay in Chamonix, I rose very early one morning and left the hotel before the sun grew too hot. I was anxious to see the new tunnel being built under Mont Blanc. The entrance to the place did not look very spectacular, just a dark hole. But I was excited. The tunnel was destined to open a direct motor route between Chamonix and Italy, thus shortening the distance by many miles. How unbelievable, I thought, that men should have cracked open the tallest mountain of Europe to build an ultramodern thoroughfare for thousands of cars. I searched around for someone to give me information about the project.

The small structure by the wire gate near the tunnel was deserted. Disappointed, I turned around to return to the hotel. And then I saw a man sitting on a large stone near me. His withered face and faded big blue eyes blended with the landscape. His arms were crossed over his chest the way I was forced, as a child, to sit in the French school in Bulgaria. The memory diverted me for a moment.

"Les mains croisées et la bouche fermé"—"Cross your arms and keep your mouth closed"—Sister Celeste would chant the moment

she entered the classroom. Both requests were torture for me. I could never sit still for more than a moment.

I saw that the man was ashen in the sunlight. He watched me, too. My long-sleeved blouse, wide-brimmed hat, and the huge flowery umbrella, a gift from Madeleine to protect me from the sun, must have intrigued him. I asked him how I might have a glimpse of the tunnel. He unfolded his arms with the air of a martyr. After he cleared his throat several times, he muttered that women were not allowed in the hellish place. Between wheezes and coughs, he added that even men could visit only on official business. "Why do you want to see the damn place?" he hissed unexpectedly.

"Just curious," I gave him a quick look and started to move away.

"*Attendez*," he called after me. "I can tell you all you want to know about the tunnel."

Something in his voice made me stop. "When will the tunnel be opened?" I asked, noticing his eyes again. They were blue and filled with sorrow.

He shook his head. "Who knows? It might take them another six months, maybe a year, but I won't live long enough to see this work of evil finished. I won't last through the fall." I looked at him aghast.

"It's a dump, madame, fit only for the devil to work in." He breathed with his mouth open. "For two and a half years I've swallowed dust and granite in that hole. My saliva mudballed in my mouth while I blasted the granite." A fit of coughing that seemed to tear his chest apart interrupted him.

"You are a pessimist, *monsieur*," I said, by now breathing as rapidly as he was. "People don't die just like that."

He glanced at the tunnel with hatred. His breathing sounded like nothing I had ever heard before. Then he relaxed some and explained that conditions on this project were much improved over what they used to be in other places. He was one of the few casualties on this job. "*Les pauvres chrétiens*," he muttered. "They used to die like flies from silicosis, just like me."

"I've never heard of silicosis."

"Tiens!" he uttered. "You've never heard of silicosis?"

"No, I've never heard of it." We were beginning to share a feeling of intimacy.

"It's a lung disease, madame." He tapped his chest with his thumb. "The doctor calls it an occupational sickness. It comes from blasting quartz; it's pure silica. I was told that the dust causes a fibrosis of the lung tissue. The disease spreads, madame; it spreads like fire. My lungs have decayed. . . . "

"What do you do for your silicosis?"

His lips twisted. "When the disease has spread like mine, one can do nothing. Perhaps if the blasted thing were discovered in time, one could survive. But how is one to know? Everyone down there coughs." With that he was swept by a new outburst of coughing. *"Tiens!"* he repeated, and gasped for air. "You've never heard of silicosis!"

"No, I've never heard of silicosis," I said, "but I know how you must feel. I have lupus. My condition is incurable, too." I guessed by his expression that he hadn't heard of lupus, either.

"Tiens." He shook his head a little. "I've never heard of—"

"Lupus, systemic lupus."

"Tiens," he repeated, then asked if I had any other questions about the tunnel.

"I've lost my interest in the *damn* place." The word "damn" made him laugh. Then he lapsed into a new coughing spell. I could almost hear the pieces of mountain rattling in his lungs. When his chest relaxed, I gave him my hand. I thought he kept it for a moment longer than is usual in his cold bony fingers. We looked at each other, he with his hopeless occupational disease and I with a disease that I suspected had been made worse by medical progress.

I walked toward the path that led downhill to Hotel Mont Blanc. The strange stillness of the valley grew stiller. Before I turned the last corner, I looked back at him once more. He appeared tiny now, almost a part of the stone.

The holiday in Chamonix helped me improve my spirit. The day before departure, I remembered the prescriptions given to me by Professor de Malraux's assistant in Geneva and stopped by a pharmacy to buy them. I asked the pharmacist what the pills were for and he said, "Nicotinamide helps pellagra and other photosensitive diseases. The other prescription, the cream, is also good. It will protect you from the sun." I could have kissed him. He almost made my trip to Geneva worthwhile.

The Landrus drove me back to Geneva. From there I was to take a plane to Paris. The long ride drained all my strength again. I was sure I was running a fever, but I refused to check it. I dreaded the thought of being hospitalized again away from home.

I felt exhausted when I arrived in Paris. My head ached, and I had chills. From the airport I went straight to the Hotel Louvois, where I had previously stayed several times. The staff never changed, and they were all charming people. When I entered the lobby, Jacques, the concierge, welcomed me warmly. Marie, the old chambermaid, was still there. I saw her polishing a rail of brass on the elevator and went to shake her hand. I told her that the last time I had seen her, two years ago, she had been polishing the same rail.

"You are probably right, madame." She nodded with amusement. Her narrow, shrewd eyes noticed immediately that I wasn't feeling well. She told me she would come to give me a hand with the unpacking.

I knew that at the Louvois, if worse came to worst, I would be taken care of better than at any hospital in Paris. The hotel provided a haven of quiet and peace. I had a nicely furnished room—it looked onto the Square Louvois, a small park with a few ancient trees that smelled of eternity, even from a distance. The benches beneath the trees were old and weather-beaten, the same color as the drab gray wall of La Bibliothèque Nationale, which I could see in the distance.

Since I had a fever and was confined to my room for a week, the Square Louvois became my world. The elderly people who came each day to sit in the park were always the same. A short, plump woman with thick white hair appeared each morning wrapped in a heavy black woolen shawl to feed the birds. She carried the bird feed in a motley quilted handbag. The woman settled herself comfortably on the bench and spoke intimately to the birds while they chirped and fluttered with all the animation of sophisticated Parisians. Why would anyone talk to birds? I wondered. Perhaps she was lonely, I speculated. Perhaps the birds did not intimidate her. I remembered a friend of mine in Cambridge with whom I used to work at Widener Library at Harvard University. She used to do the Sanscrit cataloging; I helped in the Slavic Department. After my friend retired from the library, occasionally I would see her walking around Harvard Square with a little bird perched on her shoulder. She never stuttered while speaking to her bird, though she did quite often when talking to one of her own species. "Perhaps the birds do not intimidate her," I told myself. I had never talked to myself before, but now I did. Watching the woman in the park, I recognized a likeness in us, however different we might be. I had been terribly lonely for the past week, and I, too, felt a need to communicate.

In the evenings before I went to sleep, I sat on the balcony. People came like shadows to the Park Louvois. These weather-beaten benches, I reflected, must know more stories of the human heart than all the books stocked on the shelves behind the gray wall of the Bibliotheque Nationale.

While I stayed at the Louvois, I could hardly eat any solid food. I was glad they cooked fresh *potage aux légumes* every day. It helped to settle my stomach, which was in a state of upheaval from taking an arsenal of drugs.

It was most embarrassing to open my suitcases for the customs officials. Usually I put my pills right on top of everything else to get them over with as quickly as possible. I'd tell the inspector, "These are my medicines." I dreaded the moment. By now I was taking cortisone, chloroquine, potassium chloride, Serpasil, atropine, the nicotinomide I bought in Chamonix, Pyribenzamine, and an array of vitamins—B_6, ascorbic acid, folic acid, riboflavin, and cod liver oil concentrate.

On my last night in Paris I phoned my husband in Wellesley and gave him my flight number from Paris to London and from London to Boston. I told the children they could expect me at Logan Airport the following day at twelve o'clock Boston time. I could hardly wait to reach home.

The week I spent at the Louvois had been free of household duties and cares, and the rest had helped me to restore some energy for my flight back home. The next morning, I felt well enough to get up and have a cup of hot chocolate with Jacques in the lobby. He drove me to Orly. He was afraid I wouldn't make it by myself. He had watched me all these days walk through the hotel lobby, resting from time to time for breath. We arrived at the airport with an hour and a quarter to spare. The weather was fine; the brand-new plane was moderately crowded. The seat next to mine was empty, and I looked forward to the luxury of a smooth flight and stretching out for an hour, just relaxing.

We taxied out. The twin-engine aircraft almost cleared the runway, but straining for lift-off, it skidded across a stretch of field. The plane rattled convulsively like a giant bird trying to fly with broken wings. The pilot's voice crackled over the loudspeaker: "Please remain calm." No one stirred, anyway. We were breathless. As the disturbance grew more violent, I smelled smoke and braced myself for an explosion. After some endless minutes, the plane was brought to a standstill, and a speedy evacuation was ordered. The police came right away. Sirens wailed as emergency equipment and Red Cross ambulances rushed to our assistance. Minibuses also converged to carry the passengers back to the terminal. Shaking, we praised the captain for averting a catastrophe, thankful to be safe after the near-tragedy.

Of course, I had missed my London connection. An Air France officer informed me, however, that I was being transferred to an Air France jet due to leave in ten minutes for New York. They were already singling out my luggage from the damaged plane. I told him that I had to cable home. But he said that my luggage might not be found in time and I could miss the new flight. Politely, he took my husband's name and address and promised that once I was safely on my way, he would send the cable himself. My luggage came, and as I boarded the plane, he reassured me about the cable and wished me bon voyage.

No cable reached home. When I didn't arrive at Logan, my husband and children were frantic. They told me later that they had called the Louvois and Jacques told my husband that he himself had seen me off at Orly. "It happens all the time, *monsieur*. Women are privileged to change their minds!" he added before he put down the receiver. But this light touch failed to abate my husband's anxiety. Next, he called London Airport, where he was told mistakenly that the plane from Orly had arrived on schedule but I was not among the passengers! At that point, my husband felt sure I must have collapsed at the airport in Paris. Sensing his distress, the Englishman volunteered to call him back after he had done some checking.

Upon arrival in New York, I called home from Kennedy Airport, but there was no answer. I suspected that Air France had not notified my family of my landing in New York instead of Boston. I paged my husband at Logan Airport and managed to find him before he had made a reservation to fly to Paris to look for me.

Finally, when my fruitless Geneva adventure was over and we were all fast asleep at home, the telephone jolted us awake at 3:00 A.M. London Airport was calling. Over my husband's shoulder, I heard the Englishman's voice. "We have been unsuccessful in locating your wife. So sorry, sir!"

"It's quite all right," My husband sleepily thanked him. "She's asleep next to me."

22. Back in Wellesley

The Patient's Story

AFTER I had been back in Wellesley for a week, Martha discovered one evening that I was getting bald.

"What do you mean, I'm getting bald?" I asked, knowing well that I was losing my hair by the handful.

"You have a round spot on the back of your head with almost no hair on it," she persisted with her usual frankness. My husband, reading the paper, quipped that up till then he'd been the only bald one around the house but now there would be two.

"It's not funny." Martha was indignant. "She's really getting bald." She asked her father to see for himself.

"Women don't get bald, silly," he said. "I have yet to see a bald woman or one who is as *bold* as you!"

But I was getting bald. When I held up a mirror to look at the back of my head, I saw that my hair was not just receding on top; as Martha had said, there was a round area that showed nothing but shiny pink skin. How incredible to lose my hair! I had always had such a thick mop of natural curls. In the ensuing weeks my thinning hair was very disturbing to me.

I was home only for a couple of days when my condition worsened. I was overcome by an alarming dizziness; I didn't trust myself to walk from one room to another, and to make matters worse, the twitching of my limbs recurred. It didn't help to stand, sit, or lie flat. In bed I had to roll from side to side, trying to find a position in which I could relax. The spot on my arm where I had been vaccinated a few weeks before pained me like an angry boil. When I phoned Dr. Gardner, he was mostly puzzled by the description of my sore. I mentioned to him the passing comment of the young doctor in Geneva that I should not have been vaccinated.

"He might be right," Dr. Gardner said. "I've thought of it myself. It's hard to know where to draw the line with you. In your case, anything can trigger a hypersensitive reaction."

He made an appointment for me to see him the next day. Before he hung up the receiver, he repeated his intention to start me on the nicotinamide by injection very soon. He had not heard from the Bulgarian doctors.

At my next appointment, the LE prep Dr. Gardner took was positive for the first time. Dr. Diamond also examined the cell. However, in the latter's opinion, the test result was still not definitive. This difference in opinion was enough to sustain my hope.

Dr. Gardner decided to withdraw the cortisone treatment slowly, and he stopped the white-cell injections. I was to continue with 250 mg of hydroxychloroquine, and he began to give me 1 cc of nicotinamide intravenously daily for the next month. This became known as the Bulgarian medicine in the lab. Dr. Gardner told me of another patient of his who had a serious blood disease, and was doing extremely well on herbs. The woman insisted on drinking tea made from violets.

I told him that Bulgarians were known for being fond of herbs. We had a story about an herb doctor who practiced folk medicine in a village. A peasant came to him complaining of a stomachache, and the herb doctor brewed some herbs for him. When the peasant returned to report that he was well, the herb doctor wrote in his notebook that the herb cures stomachaches. A few days later, a priest came to see him, likewise complaining of a stomachache, and the herb doctor brewed the same herbs for him. The priest died shortly after, and the herb doctor added in his notebook that the potion is not good for priests.

"I am sure that someday you'll tell me of some such herbs that are beneficial for lupus," Dr. Gardner said.

"I wouldn't be surprised." I smiled. Then I told him that Bulgaria has a long history of folk medicine. The five-centuries-old Ottoman dominion, which isolated the Bulgarian people from other civilizations, forced them to find their own ways of survival. Folklore was always intertwined with traditional medicine. Songs told of the magic of herbs that were gathered from one meadow or another, early in the morning when the cock was crowing or even earlier than that. I told Dr. Gardner that a Bulgarian doctor from Connecticut had reminisced with me about Bulgaria, saying that it was the largest rose-growing country in the world. He said that the country has some of the oldest rose distilleries where the finest attar of roses is produced. This attar is used in the most expensive French perfumes, and every ounce of it costs a small fortune. "When the rose bushes are in blossom," the doctor had told me, "the growers watch for a particular day when the roses are at their peak. They gather the petals before sunrise. It was common knowledge," he had said, "that if the sun touched the roses after their peak, the blossoms would lose some of their scent."

"The sun can do many things," I said. "It can even sap the strength out of the lupus patient." I told Dr. Gardner that I had read somewhere about the history of the aspirin and the willow bark; I found that it was first described nine centuries ago. I also read about hellebore (Helleborous odorous W.K.), a medicinal plant known to contain cardiotonic glycosides of the digitalis group. "If you were to speak with most Bulgarians, especially farmers," I said, "they would tell you that it was the human duty of every physician to learn about folk medicine."

Dr. Gardner smiled. "I'm sure they're right."

After two weeks of the new regimen of hydroxychloroquine and nicotinamide, I showed a marked improvement. The swelling of the glands on my neck regressed substantially, and the redness of my face faded. The nausea persisted, but I imagined that I felt somewhat stronger. The laboratory picture remained unchanged. Off and on, Dr. Gardner would ask casually if I had heard from the Bulgarian professor. I felt sure that Professor Popoff's answer had been delayed by "Red" red tape.

During one of my visits, I showed Dr. Gardner a photocopy of an article from a 1952 dermatology journal* that stated that the first use of mepacrine† in rheumatoid disease was credited to Professor L. Popoff (1941), Sofia. Dr. Gardner read the article carefully, but his response to it was noncommittal. I complained to him about the exhausting daily trips to the hospital. I had to travel for twenty-five miles, from Wellesley to Peter Bent Brigham and back, just for the nicotinamide injection. "I wish I could give my own injections," I said.

Dr. Gardner, who was just preparing the injection, looked at me challengingly. "Here"—he handed me the syringe—"do it yourself." He meant it. I took the syringe with uncertain hands, feeling as if I were going to commit hara-kiri, and followed his instructions. Since then, I have injected the nicotinamide myself, intramuscularly. I do not have the courage to do so in the vein.

At a later date, after seeing Dr. Gardner, my thoughts drifted to Flannery O'Connor, a writer I greatly admired. In the introduction to her book *Everything That Rises Must Converge*, Robert Fitzgerald wrote of her desperate illness. He emphasized that Flannery O'Connor did not have ordinary arthritis but a more serious illness called lupus, a related disease that had also killed her father.

Ever since I had read that introduction, I had been worried that lupus might be genetically transferable. At times, I would wake up and worry that my children would eventually be stricken with lupus. I made a mental note to ask Dr. Gardner about it when I saw him the next time. I should actually show him the book, I told myself.

Flannery O'Connor's condition seemed very close to mine. I could see her swollen face and hands; I could feel her pain and

*Pruitt, R. D. 1974. Death as an expression of functional disease. *Mayo Clin. Proc.* 49:627–35.

†Mepacrine: quinacrine, atabrine, the antimalarial drug that was taken by U.S. Armed Forces personnel during World War II.

helplessness. She, too, was losing her hair; she, too, could hardly walk up and down the stairs. Her doctor described her illness as dissem-inated lupus, an autoimmune disease in the general group of arthritis and rheumatic fever—primarily a blood-vessel disease that can affect any organ. It can affect the bones, too . . . and her body was forming antibodies to its own tissue. What a horrible thought.

When I showed Dr. Gardner Fitzgerald's introduction, he seemed to be interested in the medical part. I told him how worried I was about my children's getting lupus someday. He replied that he was not aware of large-scale genetic studies on this problem. If such familial incidence could be established, he thought that it would aid in understanding the SLE. He commented that several cases of siblings developing lupus had been reported in medical journals, but the reports were too sporadic to be conclusive. Nevertheless, relatives of lupus patients often had symptoms or positive laboratory tests for rheumatoid arthritis, a disease that is in some way related to LE.

Before I left his office, I complained again of my nausea. "Everything I eat makes me sick, but milk affects me the worst. Whenever I eat dairy products, I get diarrhea and abdominal cramps as well as nausea."

"Milk intolerance is uncommon," he said, "but some people cannot digest an important ingredient in milk called lactose." He reflected for a moment. "You might be able to have some cheeses which contain only a trace of lactose."

"Is there a test to prove sensitivity to milk?" I asked.

"Yes," he said, "they often do one at Children's Medical Center. It's time-consuming," he warned.

"May I have the test?"

"I don't see why not. You'll have to come to the hospital one morning before breakfast. The test takes a few hours. Come in at seven-thirty tomorrow morning. We'll determine once and for all if you are sensitive to milk."

The next day, Al, by then taller than I and on holiday from school, offered to give me a ride to the hospital. In the parking lot behind the hospital, we stopped to look at the trailer, Dr. Gardner's new acquisition. He had purchased it to expand the office space for the members of his research team who were crowded three and four to a room. This new gypsy-style addition was an innovation for the Harvard medical area. Fortunately, it was hidden within a courtyard of the hospital. Had it been perched more visibly, it would have detracted from the landmark surrounding it. I was told it had to be lowered into place by a derrick.

Al left the hospital, promising to pick me up at noon when the test would be over. As soon as I walked into Dr. Gardner's congested lab, he gave me a fair amount of lactose sugar to drink. Then a technician took blood from my right arm. She did this about five times at measured intervals. Toward 10:30 A.M., I began to have severe diarrhea. I was so nauseated that I had to rest my head in my lap. By 12:00, when the test was finished, my knees buckled, and I crumbled in a chair, bathed in cold sweat. One of Dr. Gardner's young assistants rushed for a stretcher, but by the time he returned, I felt somewhat better.

"You didn't have to go that far to prove your point," Dr. Gardner teased as I sipped some tea in his office.

The results of the tests showed that after taking the lactose sugar, I had no elevation of my blood glucose, the normal sugar of the blood. I tolerated a mixture of glucose and galactose* without any stress. Dr. Gardner admitted that I must have had a lifelong intolerance to lactose. Lactose could not be taken up directly by the intestine, he said. It had to be first broken down by an enzyme† called lactase into two simple sugars—glucose and galactose. These smaller molecules could be absorbed more easily.

In the past, Dr. Gardner had prescribed innumerable drugs to control nausea, but nothing had worked. I had already taken Sparine, codeine, Dimetapp, Serpasil, and atropine. "Try caffeine-free coffee," he said. "Forget your Turkish coffee for a while." He knew that I made coffee the way my father did in the old country and that I drank it constantly. "How do you cook that stuff, anyway?" he asked.

*Galactose: one of the sugars in milk, a part of the lactose molecule.
†Enzyme: a protein substance that catalyzes the reaction between two other chemicals.

I told him my father's recipe: a cup of water, a teaspoon of coffee, a teaspoon of sugar, and a teaspoon of love. Boil it three times over, and with some luck, it would come out just right, with lots of foam on top and sediment on the bottom.

Dr. Gardner was amused and said that he would have to try it.

One day, toward the end of the summer of 1959, three months after I had met Jordan, I received a reply from his sister, the physician, in Bulgaria. She confirmed her brother's diagnosis and his successful treatment with nicotinic acid. She also mentioned that Professor Popoff had written to us, as well, and she advised us to write to the Merck Company in Darmstadt, Germany (not associated with the Merck Company in America), for their prospectus (no longer available) on the treatment of lupus with nicotinamide. Her letter did not change Dr. Gardner's opinion of the drug. He was as skeptical as ever.

I wrote to the Merck Company and received a prompt reply. In a way, I was encouraged—it was the first time I saw the word "lupus" in print. I began to translate the almost forgotten German I had learned in school as a child. The words came back with magical speed. One of the articles stated that the tests showed, in a great number of cases, that a certain percentage of patients had good results when treated with nicotinamide. Sometimes the treatment produced complete remission. This was particularly true of cases that were precipitated by sunlight, even moderate exposure. This article also attempted to draw a comparison between light-sensitive LE and the nicotinamide vitamin-deficiency disease called pellagra.

A morbid thought occurred to me. Should I expose myself once again to the sun to prove my light sensitivity? The following weekend, when my husband and I drove to Maine to visit some friends, I held my bare arm out the window for over two hours, leaving it to the mercy of the sun and the wind. The following day, big angry welts erupted on my skin. The spots didn't fade for months. This experiment cost me permanent minor scarring of my arm. The redness always becomes intensified when I'm too cold or too hot.

After one of my visits with Dr. Gardner, while my arm was

still angry looking, a young student nurse noticed my sore and asked me what had happened. I told her it was a nasty sunburn. With big innocent eyes she bubbled that she had seen a patient with an obscure disease who had died in a matter of weeks after such a nasty sunburn. "I didn't believe the doctors when they said that the sun was the reason for the woman's death," she said. "I love the sun, don't you?"

23. Professor Dr. Liuben Popoff
The Patient's Story

"Healing," Papa would tell me, "is not a science but the
intuitive art of wooing Nature."
—W. H. Auden,
The Art of Healing

PROFESSOR Popoff's* letter arrived two weeks after the letter
from Jordan's sister. In the left upper corner of his stationery was
neatly printed in small black type:

PROF. DR. LIUBEN POPOFF
DIRECTEUR DE LA CLINIQUE DERMATOLOGIQUE
DE LA FACULTÉ
RUE MARIN DRINOV 9
SOFIA, BULGARIA

I looked at the French title and wondered about it for a
moment, then told myself that Dr. Popoff was probably trained in
France. Writing in Bulgarian and in longhand, he showed friendly
concern and eagerness to help me. What a joy after having waited
impatiently for three months. Professor Popoff wrote that he needed
the answers to a series of questions:

1. How are your stomach, liver, and kidneys functioning?

*Professor Popoff has died since I last saw him. The Bulgarian government
translated into Bulgarian the chapter about him and the material was read at an
international dermatological conference in Prague.

2. What do the blood tests show specifically with regard to the LE cells?
3. Do you have any local infections?
4. What is the condition of your heart and your endocrine system?
5. How are you affected by the seasons, solar rays, and other external factors?
6. What are the histopathological* findings so far?
7. What is the condition of your nervous system with respect to the vasomotor† functions? Are you restless, acrocyanotic?‡
8. What have the doctors done for you so far, and how have you been tolerating the treatments?

In reply to our inquiry about the nicotinamide and its therapeutic value in lupus, he said (in rough translation) that the cause and development of the disease had occupied him and his collaborators for many years. He saw an analogy between pellagra and some forms of lupus, which he described as pellagroid types. For more information, he referred us to some of his papers, which had appeared in various medical journals.

He further wrote that in 1944 he had introduced the treatment of LE with antimalarials. Finally, he said that the combined treatment of antimalarial drugs and the nicotinamide had been used in his clinic for many years. This treatment gave good results in some forms of lupus that are made worse by sunlight (the pellagroid types). In acute stages of the disease, which he called lupovisceritis, he recommended adrenal hormones, gamma globulins, perfusions of plasma, vitamin B_{12}, and nicotinamide. He also referred to his paper read at the Congress of Leningrad in 1960. He felt encouraged with the good results that Dr. Gardner and I had obtained so far with the new regimen of nicotinamide and hydroxychloroquine. He was pleased by our interest in his research. "Keep me posted," he urged, "on how you progress with the nicotinamide. I expect you to feel even better as time goes on." His words were tremendously reassuring to me.

*Histopathology: change in tissues and cells.
†Vasomotor: pertaining to control of the tone of the blood vessels. Contraction of blood vessels causes blanching, whereas relaxation causes blushing.
‡Acrocyanosis: mottled blue discoloration of the skin of the extremities.

As I read the letter to him, Dr. Gardner listened patiently but could not hide his skepticism. However, in the months that followed, his skepticism was replaced with curiosity as my illness changed its course. He even expressed a desire to read some of the lupus case histories that Professor Popoff must have accumulated over the years.

Each day I felt myself getting better, but the nausea persisted. Two weeks after I got Professor Popoff's letter, I wrote to him again and mentioned my nausea. He replied immediately, explaining that some lupus patients have digestive problems. He advised taking ten drops of hydrochloric acid and a teaspoon of Pepsencia* with breakfast each morning. He wrote that I probably lacked some digestive juices in my stomach and added that this was not uncommon with patients who had problems similar to mine. I translated this to Dr. Gardner, and he explained that after the food and water enter the stomach, they mix with gastric juices to start the digestive processes. The essential constituents of these juices are an acid (hydrochloric) and two or possibly three enzymes (digestive ferments) called pepsin, rennin, and lipase. The medicines containing those substances were old-fashioned patent remedies and could be bought without a prescription. He agreed with Professor Popoff that at some point I should have my digestive juices tested.

A few days after I took the Pepsencia, the nausea subsided. What bliss! In the morning, I used to lie in bed with my eyes closed, enjoying the sensation of feeling so much better. I was afraid to open them for fear I was dreaming. It took time for my family to get used to my coming into the kitchen before anyone else was up to prepare breakfast.

After about sixty nicotinamide injections, the clinical picture turned around. To the surprise of even the kidney specialist at Peter Bent Brigham, my kidneys were getting better, too.

Because Dr. Gardner constantly spoke to me using medical terminology, I developed a fair comprehension of what was going on. Thus, when he said, "Your BUN is eight milligrams percent and the

*Trade name for a medicine containing stomach digestive enzymes.

creatinine clearance is improving sharply," I knew that things were better. For only a few months previously, the BUN had been 50 mg percent, a level seen just before the last stages of Bright's disease, kidney failure. Furthermore, he added confidently, "The LE prep is now negative, and even the white-cell count is going up and has reached five thousand."

The sores healed. The red butterfly rash went away. The hair on my scalp grew back thicker than ever. I never had to wear the wig I had secretly bought from a department store in Boston. The color of my newly grown hair was slightly changed; it was a shade lighter and grayish at the temples. I had read somewhere that this could happen to people with blond hair after they have been on prolonged therapy with hydroxychloroquine. I certainly was glad it was my hair and not my eyes that were affected. Every time I swallowed the medicine, I had fears of becoming blind. I had had such bad luck with drugs.

One evening, when I played tennis for half an hour under the electric lights of the Wellesley public courts, my whole family came to watch. When I didn't drop dead at the end of the set, I knew that from then on my life would change for the better. The next day, my husband rushed out to buy me a new tennis racket.

The next four years brought good health. My ordeal seemed to be over. Once more I became interested in activities outside the house. I went back to Peter Bent Brigham to do volunteer work a few hours a week, and I joined the League of Women Voters in Wellesley. The newly formed Committee on the Development of Human Resources captured my imagination. My enthusiasm led me to become a member of the board, and I put all my heart into running the committee. However, the prolonged illness with all its uncertainties, had left me somewhat unsure of myself. I lacked confidence when I made an appointment; I was always afraid I wouldn't be able to keep it. It took some months, even years, before I outgrew those fears completely.

The clinical picture remained stable. My only therapy was taking the nicotinamide injections and the many vitamin pills. Dr. Gardner still came across an occasional "rare and atypical" LE cell, "an undernourished one," as he enjoyed saying, as if to denigrate its importance.

I kept in close correspondence with Professor Popoff, who continued to be extremely friendly and cooperative. It was late April when he wrote that he had been invited to an international dermatological congress in Lyon, France, in two weeks, and I became terribly tempted to go and meet him. I saw an opportunity to thank the man in person and also possibly to learn a little more about lupus. My husband began a tactical campaign to encourage the new venture. Dr. Gardner was also in favor of my taking the trip. He was still interested in getting some of Professor Popoff's case histories, teasing me about my "Bulgarian treatment" while persistently attributing my getting well to a spontaneous remission.*

The first week in May, I wrote to Professor Popoff that I was considering taking the trip to Lyon. I reasoned with myself that I should take this trip—I had to find out more about lupus. I vacillated until it was actually time for me to leave.

That same week my husband and I had supper with a couple who were old friends from Cambridge, and I mentioned that I was toying with the idea of meeting Professor Popoff in Lyon. Zelda, who had never been to Europe, said wistfully that if she were in my place, she wouldn't have to think twice about it. Her husband, a psychoanalyst at Harvard, suggested that Zelda and I travel to Lyon together. We all agreed in a sudden burst of enthusiasm.

The very next week, on May 15, Zelda and I boarded a Pan American plane at Logan Airport in Boston. The next morning, we landed in Paris and stayed at the Louvois for two days. I did more walking in those forty-eight hours than I had done in many years. I couldn't believe my own energy.

On the train to Lyon, most of the passengers were amputees. Every seat was occupied by a man lacking one limb or another. We watched them with an odd nervousness. The station in Lyon was a nightmare; in the bright sunlight, thousands of cripples seemed to haunt the platform. On the way to the hotel, our bewilderment grew

---

*A spontaneous remission describes a change in the course and severity of a disease that occurs without medical intervention.

into horror. The streets were crowded with men in wheelchairs, on crutches, lacking an arm or arms, or dragging artificial legs.

Zelda nudged me in the taxi. "I'm losing my wits." A little later, she whispered, "Whatever is happening here, it seems to strike only men." For the rest of the ride we didn't say a word. We should have had the sense to inquire what was going on, but we didn't. In our hotel room we saw a large wrapped box on the table. It was addressed to a guest, Marcel Le Rouge.

Zelda eyed the box suspiciously. "I'll bet it's an artificial arm or leg."

Just then there was a knock. When I opened the door, a man with only one arm asked if there was a package for him left by mistake in our room. He explained that there was much confusion in town with thousands of amputees, veterans of World War II, attending a congress. I placed the parcel under his arm, then watched him go down the corridor to the elevator. I was drawn to his tragedy in the same way as with the tunnel-construction man at Chamonix. Was he still alive? Somehow I felt the three of us shared a common bond—that of unnecessary man-made diseases, incurable afflictions. The lung damage from dust in the tunnel, the arm lost in battle, the disease made worse by drugs—all of these were avoidable problems in a life that had an abundance of the unavoidable to deal with.

When I slowly closed the door to our room, Zelda was frantically calling from the bathroom. She was examining the facilities and could not figure out how to operate the toilet. I explained to her that she was looking at the French bidet. The newly remodeled and strikingly redecorated modern bathroom, tiled in black and white, had everything except a toilet. We searched everywhere—I even poked the walls for a concealed door. Eventually, we did locate what we were searching for, outside our room near the elevator. It accommodated all the guests on our floor, ladies and gentlemen alike. Zelda and I agreed that one of us would stand watch by the door while the other was using the facilities.

Almost immediately after my arrival in Lyon, I got on the phone to locate Professor Popoff; I only knew the name of the congress. When, after a half hour of fruitless inquiry, I found no one who could identify such a congress, I became worried. I had already called the medical school, the chamber of commerce, and several newspapers. Nobody seemed to know what I was talking about. When I phoned the medical school for the third time, it was almost 5:00 P.M. This time, the switchboard operator had a vague idea about the meeting, which she thought was taking place somewhere outside Lyon. She advised me to call the following morning for more information. I knew from Professor Popoff's letters that he would be in Lyon for only three days: I had spent one in Paris, and now the second day was gone. This was incredible. I had the uneasy feeling that for the second time in two years I would have an unrewarding trip to Europe.

In the morning, struggling with another telephone operator at the medical school, my French faltered altogether. It always did when I was frustrated. Out of patience, I repeated my question loudly in English, and the response was instantaneous. The girl gave me all the information I needed in perfect English.

At 11:00 A.M., I went to meet Professor Popoff at his hotel. In the lobby, to my surprise, I found not only Professor Popoff but Mrs. Popoff, as well. They were equally delightful and equally surprised to see me looking so well—they couldn't quite believe that I was the patient from America. I looked much too healthy and energetic to fit the image they had created.

Mrs. Popoff was a large woman with a pleasant face and an almost shy smile. She wore a simple cotton dress and flat shoes. Her French was poor, but she managed to make herself understood. Professor Popoff, wearing a dark suit and a French beret tilted over his silvery hair, looked more like a Frenchman than a Bulgarian.

"My dear lady," he exclaimed in perfect French, "you look marvelous! Frankly, I expected to see . . ."

I gave him my hand and told him that I hadn't always looked as healthy as I did now.

Mrs. Popoff was the first to remember that we could all be speaking Bulgarian, our native tongue. I found it hard to address him as Mr. Professor Dr. Popoff, in the Bulgarian and European tradition, but he seemed to enjoy his titles even though he lacked the stiffness and hauteur of the Geneva doctors. It crossed my mind that he would not retain all those titles in Bulgaria, now that the Communists had taken over. He suggested we have lunch together and delay the medical consultation until that evening after the meetings. Lyon was his city—he had graduated from medical school there. Nostalgically, he enumerated a few of Lyon's choice restaurants, including the "four star" ones.

Over lunch, we spoke of trivial matters. I guessed his age to be close to sixty. Between courses, he told amusing stories of his student days in Lyon. We laughed. It was such fun.

"You laugh easily," Professor Popoff remarked. "What kept you going during your illness?"

"I don't know. My spirit never broke down. Maybe it's genetic. My mother had a will of iron."

"That may have helped more than you think. I like to see patients put up a strong fight. It helps the medical treatments to work. I'm sure of it. It also helps physicians. The physician's spirit is reinforced by a brave patient. Nature, when she turns against you, is a strong enemy. The doctor searches for allies. He first looks to the patient. Your Professor Gardner—he must have found strength in your spirit, and you must have trusted him and drawn strength from his optimism. Is that not so?"

"Yes, yes," I reflected out loud. Dr. Gardner and I had been allies, but with neither of us knowing just what to expect from day to day. This uncertainty had in a strange way helped me. The frustrating LE cells, the friendly disagreements among my physicians, the confusion in the literature, all held out the hope that I would fool everyone and get better.

It was a beautiful sunny day. Walking back to the hotel, we crossed a bridge over the Rhône. I could see in the distance the Seine River, too. The view was perfectly lovely. The city had an ancient look, with innumerable shimmering gold cathedral domes and ornamented bridges. I remembered some of my French history, and looking over the point of confluence where the bright sunlight was reflected in the ripples, I could almost feel Emperor Agrippa's spirit haunting the banks of the Rhône and the restless soul of Augustus following in his shadow. Professor Popoff remarked that the capital of the Celtic Gauls had changed very little since Napoleon had rebuilt it in the nineteenth century.

Professor Popoff saw me shielding the sunlight from my face and said that I should be wearing a wide-brimmed hat. "No need to ask for trouble," he cautioned.

I explained that I was covered with a protective film of sun cream and fumbled in my purse to show him the Doak Solar Cream I always carried.

He looked at the label and read, "Para-aminobenzoic acid, titanium dioxide, magnesium stearate. It looks all right. It must have some healing effect, as well," he said, and handed it back. As we walked along, he asked me if I had always been sensitive to the sun.

I responded by showing him the scarring on my arm and told him that I had done it on purpose to experiment and prove my photosensitivity to the sun.

"That was a dangerous thing to do," he said. "You shouldn't flirt with the sun."

I asked him if my photosensitivity was an aggravating feature or a basic factor in my disorder.

He looked at my arm from the corner of his eyes and said that in my case it might be both. He added, affirming the views of Dr. Gardner and Professor de Malraux's assistant, that a condition like mine could be acquired by a response to light of certain wavelengths. In his opinion, artificial UV rays were just as harmful. These rays, too, could produce systemic reactions and progression of the disease. Abnormal photosensitivity was one of medicine's most neglected areas, he said, and more research was needed to establish its connection with human diseases, particularly with LE. He also said that some clinicians seem to think that an abnormal reaction to light is only an aggravating and not a basic feature in LE. He shrugged and then added, "It will be very difficult to prove a relationship scientifically."

I commented that in my case sunlight and cold not only affected my skin but also mirrored how sick I felt after the exposure. My skin needed protection from heat, cold, wind, sunlight—anything that touched it. I related an episode when I had plunged into a swimming pool that wasn't heated. "I was almost in shock," I said. "My body turned navy blue, and I couldn't breathe normally for a while." In the winter I would never dream of going to bed without a hot-water bottle.

Professor Popoff explained that in some instances cold could cause an allergic reaction the same way lobster or strawberries affect some people. A cold sensitivity, or cryopathy, could conceivably precipitate lupus, he said. The rash that I got from the sun, or the blue blotches from the cold, indicated parallel changes in my system. The skin's reaction was more spectacular, whereas the reaction of the internal organs was more dangerous. "You must be a terribly allergic person," he concluded.

After some moments he added, "Climate has an effect on health. It takes only a small temperature change to alter the course of a respiratory infection. You know that. When you have a cold, you instinctively try to keep warm," he said. "Rest is important, too. You must take care and rest as much as possible. Rest is an old-fashioned remedy for healing lupus and other diseases, and being of the old school, I still believe in it. For that matter, emotional balance is just as important, and so is good nourishment."

He paused for a moment. "In sensitivities like yours, certain foods can cause trouble, and others should not be omitted. You probably know the foods that do not agree with you better than Professor Gardner or I do. But you must always keep in mind that a balanced diet is important in fighting all diseases. Do you eat enough fresh vegetables, or are you addicted to canned foods and those foolish crash diets? I hope that being a few pounds overweight does not trouble you. As long as you do not carry it to extremes, being a little plump is better than eating an abnormal diet."

I told him that we lived close to a farm where we could buy all the fresh vegetables we wanted. "They also sell fresh eggs and flowers there that smell like flowers," I said.

The Popoffs chuckled.

That evening, I visited Professor Popoff as a patient. Mrs. Popoff had gone out with some friends. The badly lighted hotel room was furnished with awkward old pieces of furniture. I noticed a pink-

and-red flowered porcelain basin and pitcher standing on a tall table
in the corner. The hotel was so old that I wondered if it had running
water. Externally, it had a pavilion style that had a vague structural
similarity to the Peter Bent Brigham Hospital. I half expected to see
a trailer on the side street housing the offices of the hotel officials.

"Make yourself comfortable." Professor Popoff pointed to a
sagging chair near a low table from which he had improvised a working
desk. His light tone of earlier in the day had changed to a medical
approach. The few letters he had received from Dr. Gardner and me
over the past few years were spread out in front of him. The room
was hot and stuffy despite the two open windows. His face, streaked
with perspiration, looked tired in the dim light, but his eyes were
alert. "How do you feel?" He asked the familiar question, then continued: "You look delightfully well. It's a pleasure to see someone
with such an abundance of zeal."

"Thank God I've been feeling well for some time now," I
said. "I've forgotten, or almost forgotten, how it used to be when I
couldn't lift my feet from the ground. I shudder when I remember
the bizarre feeling I had in my legs—they used to feel heavy, very
heavy. Now I wake up in the morning looking forward to the day!"

He looked down at the pile of letters and at notes he had
written to refresh his memory, then said, sounding like all the doctors
in Boston, "You were placed on salicylate therapy, vitamin therapy,
hormones, streptococcus vaccine, penicillin, and white-cell injections.
I've never heard of the white-cell treatment before." He speculated
that injecting blood might be a stressful situation, raising the patient's
own steroid level. After we'd covered some familiar ground, he questioned me with meticulous care. Halfway through the conversation,
he remarked that whatever ailed me must have started much earlier
than I or anyone else suspected. We reasoned that my problems flared
up when my resistance was low. "You must have strong genes, my
dear lady," he ventured. "That must be the secret of your recovery."

I started to laugh. "I take after my great-grandmother Henrietta, who lived in Munich over a hundred and seventy years ago.
She lived to be over ninety. I'm told that I have inherited not only
her name but also her looks, her stubbornness, and her determination.

I have a portrait of her back home. The likeness is truly remarkable, especially the gaze in her eyes. It's haunting! The woman must be living in my bones! Do you believe this possible?"

Professor Popoff grinned. "I don't see why not."

"Last week in Paris, a great-uncle sniffed my perfume and said, 'You like lilies of the valley, just like her.' It can get spooky sometimes."

"I can see that." Professor Popoff's grin widened.

Later in the evening, Mrs. Popoff came in, nodded a friendly greeting, and settled in an armchair by the window with a sigh of fatigue. Professor Popoff continued talking, undisturbed by her presence. "After ten years of multiple symptoms and minor clinical findings, you appear entirely well again, and you don't seem to have any visible scars to account for your experience. From the letters I've received from your Professor Gardner, I understand that at one point you had kidney involvement; it has cleared completely. One has to accept your case for what it is at the moment—simply that you feel well. The rest is really of academic interest." He wiped away the perspiration that had accumulated in the creases below his eyes and said, "Recovery from lupus does not mean the disease will not return. You will always have the predisposition for it." Parenthetically, he recommended a periodic chest X ray, which set me to thinking about tuberculosis. I recalled reading in a medical dictionary that lupus, at least in one of its forms, was a skin disorder caused by tuberculosis bacteria. This interested me at the time, because several uncles of mine had died of tuberculosis. I asked Professor Popoff to clear up my confusion.

He replied that tuberculosis was mistakenly believed to be a causative factor in SLE. However, he added that, more important, there was a type of lupus called lupus vulgaris, a form of tuberculosis of the skin. Tuberculosis infection often ran a serious course in patients with lupus, particularly those on cortisone.

I knew of such a case—a young woman from Australia who had come to Boston to consult with the hematology doctors at Peter Bent Brigham, only to learn that Dr. Gardner had gone to Europe. Ironically, I had had a similar experience when I had gone to Geneva, and now I was in Lyon, still trying to find out something more about the disease.

The Australian was from a part of New South Wales where the sun shone, unmercifully for a lupus patient, 360 days a year. Her family ran a sheep station, a ranch of five thousand acres.

One of Dr. Gardner's assistants had worked up her case and concluded that the disease was running a rapid course. Having compassion for the soft-spoken, trusting girl, he wondered whether a touch of the unsual—a visit with me, a "cured" lupus case—would give her hope. When he referred her to me, he suggested that we had wool interests as well as lupus in common and whimsically asked whether I would put her on nicotinamide. I responded to his phone call as members of Alcoholics Anonymous must respond to one another—by rushing in to Dr. Gardner's office to meet her and taking her to my house. She looked frail and could barely walk unattended.

In our living room, over a cup of tea, she told me that she'd been on large doses of prednisone for several years. She also indicated a squeamishness about giving herself nicotinic-acid shots, which would have been necessary because of the remoteness of her ranch from medical care. She was grateful to talk with me, though, and left for home with some hope.

After the young woman left our house, one of my teenage daughters commented that she had never realized that at one time I could have been as sick as this poor woman. My other daughter thought that the patient and I looked somewhat alike. She, too, admitted that she had not been aware of the seriousness of my illness except when I had to go to the hospital. She used to get frightened and reasoned with herself that there was nothing that she could do, but she had never been completely sure of that. She managed to laugh now. But I knew how difficult it must have been for the whole family.

After the Australian woman returned to Melbourne, we kept in touch. Her sickness grew progressively worse. My last letter was answered by her mother. I recalled her words: "Leslie received your letter before she passed away. She died of pulmonary tuberculosis."

Rising, Professor Popoff put on his glasses to examine my face. There was nothing abnormal to see. My skin was perfectly clear.

"The rash I used to have on my face was diagnosed as a typical LE rash," I said, and asked him if all lupus rashes were alike.

He said that the skin involvement in both the chronic discoid form and the acute type of SLE was just about the same and was easily confused with other types of skin conditions.

I made a point to tell him that the doctors in Boston were skeptical of the usefulness of the nicotinamide. "They don't understand why in the world it should work."

"Does anyone know why an aspirin relieves pain or why cortisone performs so well?"

In the course of our conversation, I reminded him that I had been feeling well now for over five years. "It's a miracle," I said.

"It's not a miracle," he countered. He reiterated very slowly as if to give emphasis that in his experience with the lupus disease he had found that certain patients who reacted strongly to sunlight acted similarly to those who had pellagra. He accepted that such patients were suffering from pellagroid lupus and that most of them responded favorably to nicotinamide, the way I did. He reflected for a moment. "On the other hand, your doctors in Boston have all the right in the world to be skeptical about attributing your remission to this simple medicine. One of the characteristic features of lupus is a high incidence of spontaneous remissions. Some of these remissions last indefinitely. I have records of patients who have been in remission for thirty years without any kind of therapy, so patients in America should not expect nicotinamide to make them all feel better or attribute recovery solely to this vitamin."

"How wonderful," I exclaimed. "Except for Jordan, I have not heard of long remissions. Just hearing about them is exciting."

He continued by saying that in my case it would be almost impossible to decide if my remission was spontaneous or induced. I had been on steroids, autogenous vaccines, antimalarials, penicillin, many vitamins, including nicotinic acid, and the white-cell injections. He also stressed that in my case I was lucky that I had help in the house and could afford medical care. "Rest is vital," he repeated. Then he paused and added, "Even though I am a nicotinamide enthusiast, I must admit that lupus is an unpredictable adversary."

I mentioned that a doctor at Peter Bent Brigham had told me once to get rid of my ovaries if I wanted to get well. He was not a lupus specialist, but he was impressed with the sex distribution of the disease and wondered if decreased hormone production would help. Dr. Gardner, too, at some point of my illness, had also wondered if female hormones could influence the lupus. But he never recommended either an operation or hormone therapy.

"The influence of female hormones has intrigued many investigators because so few men get the disease. And one obvious element of the difference is the sex hormones. But our understanding stops right there. It would be nice if someone could show how the female hormone is the troublemaker in lupus. There are ways of controlling the hormones. Anyway, I hope that lupus gets more attention in research. It seems to be a more common problem than when I started in medicine. That could be the result of better diagnosis, but somehow I feel that there are other factors bringing out the disease. Maybe it's the increased use of drugs." He shook his head a little. "The pharmaceutical industry has been very successful in producing new drugs in the past thirty years. And when drugs are around, doctors and patients will use them. Every drug will find a patient who reacts badly to it. Even so, any time I see a drug reaction, I think of lupus." He paused. "You didn't react too well to cortisone, did you?"

"No, I didn't. My rash and swollen glands didn't subside until I took the nicotinamide."

He went on in a professional manner, not looking at me directly, while pacing the floor with the exaggerated stride of the seasoned lecturer, his hands clasped and his fingers twitching nervously behind his back.

"Systemic lupus erythematosus and rheumatoid arthritis have so much in common. Even great clinicians with years of experience are fooled by one of the diseases masquerading as the other. It used to be said years ago that syphilis was the great imitator. It could mimic almost all other diseases. Now, if syphilis is treated early enough with penicillin, there are fewer late complications. Today the great imitators are connective-tissue diseases—rheumatoid arthritis, lupus, and other diseases like them. They can do anything. Believe me, they can affect any part of the body. They can even make you crazy without giving obvious trouble on the skin, in the kidneys, or anywhere else. Lupus is a very clever opponent for the clinician. That is why your Boston professors took so long to prove your diagnosis. This is not to criticize them. This is really to praise them for their stamina."

I reminded him that these uncertainties about my sickness had originally given me strength to fight for survival. "I clung to the doctors' lack of knowledge about lupus as a drowning man clings to a straw." I had to laugh.

He said that the fact that I was responding so well to the nicotinamide led him to believe that I might have a deficiency of nicotinamide. "I have the feeling that your system does not use nicotinamide efficiently. This would cause you to need more of it to do the same job that it does for most people. I came to this belief because of my experience with pellagra, which you may not know is common in some parts of the Balkans. Why, I don't know. There is so much good food there. The light sensitivity of pellagra goes away immediately with nicotinamide treatment.

"My reasoning was simple. If it helps one light-sensitive disease, it could help another. But the results have sometimes been remarkable. As in your case, I have seen many people helped by this simple vitamin." He handed me a slip of paper with a few more questions for Dr. Gardner to answer and told me that in my case the treatment should be limited to the use of skin preparations of cortisone, sunscreening creams, and the nicotinamide injections. He urged me to stay on those injections indefinitely, but on an intermittent basis. "Let's say you should take the injections for a month or two, then rest for a few weeks before starting up again. Eat good plain food and stay away from spicy, salty dishes. Salt is apt to retain fluids in your tissues. Even if you have a relapse someday, I feel that you will overcome it. I believe that many people have a quiet form of lupus and we bring out their disease by giving them too many medicines for innocent complaints. Then the medicine leads to new complaints, and we chase the problem with new medicine. We begin to believe that the patient is neurotic. The neurosis starts or finishes our chase. It is difficult to tell for sure in some patients."

He made me wonder if many women who were called neurotic really had a touch of lupus with no red butterfly rash to prove it. I knew only too well how one could be affected by the bizarre turns of the illness. I remembered the days when I would see double or wake up at night with the strange sensation that both my arms were gone. I remembered how, reaching for the telephone receiver, I wasn't sure that I could speak and the floating sensation I used to experience in West Newton when the radiators appeared distorted and I had dreaded focusing on them. I recalled the skin spots I used to get: red ones, pink ones, blue ones; the little bumps that came and vanished before I had a chance to reach the doctor's office. Thank God, those days were over!

Professor Popoff glanced at his watch. It was midnight. "You must be feeling tired," he said. "I know I am." Mrs. Popoff, who suddenly woke up, was surprised to see me standing next to her husband. She looked weary and disheveled.

"I should have gone long ago." I held out my hand to her. She took it warmly in both of hers and in a gesture of kindness invited me to visit them in Bulgaria the next time I came to Europe. Her husband repeated her words and said to forget about lupus— as much as possible.

"You can see that she has done that," Mrs. Popoff said, and squeezed my hands once more.

Professor Popoff promised me that as soon as he received more information from Dr. Gardner, he would go over my case once again and further search for clues to explain my remission. As he spoke, I mentioned that Dr. Gardner had asked to see some of Professor Popoff's lupus case histories. He made a note of my request. I thanked the Popoffs heartily, and we embraced in the French manner, which was most unusual for Bulgarians, who are not by nature a demonstrative people.

After I left the Popoffs, I walked slowly back to my hotel. The boulevard by the Rhône was brightly lit by the moon. The town seemed deserted, and the soft splashing of water made sounds of peaceful dreaming. The rhythm of my steps kept the strange magic alive. The tired feeling I had had in the past was now a memory. I felt nothing more than a healthy weariness.

Professor Popoff's words returned to my mind. Everything he told me sounded reassuring. I realized that the violence of my earlier emotional reaction to the disease had disappeared, and so I was no longer preoccupied with the thought of early death. Since my arrival in Lyon, the future looked brighter than ever. Back at the hotel, I tiptoed into my room, where Zelda was asleep with the lights on. Thinking it was morning, she opened her eyes and asked me eagerly what Professor Popoff had said.

As I undressed, I told her that everything about the disease was nebulous. Professor Popoff had even suggested that I had something like pellagra. He called it pellagroid lupus—lupus looking like pellagra. "I guess I'll live," I said. Then I added, "When I go back to the States, I'll tell my doctors to do more research on light waves of harmful strength in connection with photosensitivity." Then I mumbled, "Why do all doctors talk to me as though I could understand their *lingua medica?*"

"They always do that when they're at sea about an illness," Zelda replied with the authority of a doctor's wife. "They must hate the sound of lupus as much as you do."

I put out the lights and asked her how she had spent the day.

"You're taking your sickness with a lot more equanimity than I would have thought possible," she said between yawns. "I don't know what I would do if I had to cope with lupus."

"Be glad that you don't have to," I said.

The next morning, we packed hurriedly and drove for two hours to Voiron to see the Landrus. After spending two delightful days with them, Zelda and I continued on to Switzerland. This time Geneva appeared enchanting in contrast to the ghastly week I had spent there several years before.

At Orly Airport in Paris, Zelda and I boarded a plane crowded with a group of M.I.T. professors who had been studying the Common

Market while touring Western Europe. They seemed to have collected every funny story available in Europe's capitals, and the crescendos of their laughter interrupted our conversations across the entire Atlantic.

However, the happy atmosphere changed to apprehension when, nearing Logan Airport in Boston, word spread that I had not been inoculated for smallpox. Before I had left Boston, Dr. Gardner had decided not to give me the vaccine. Instead, he had written a letter for me to show the authorities in which he explained that in lupus patients such a vaccine could activate the disease. The passengers, feeding upon rumor, became jittery thinking that they might be quarantined at Logan. I was worried and self-conscious. Dr. Gardner had told me that he would be in Boston at the time of my return; I could call him from the airport if I ran into any difficulties. Waiting in line to pass the customs authorities, I could feel everyone looking in my direction.

After the inspector carefully read Dr. Gardner's letter, silently moving his lips to pronounce "lupus, lupus"—as if to say, "What the hell is that?"—he questioned me in regard to my whereabouts during the last three weeks of the trip. He then left hurriedly, instructing his colleagues to keep everyone on the premises. The M.I.T. group clustered in the background, viewing the proceedings with academic curiosity and whispering knowingly among themselves. He soon returned with a doctor in military uniform who immediately released the other passengers, then walked toward me, grinning. When the doctor came closer, he immediately told me that I, too, would be released but spoke so softly that no one responded. As I victoriously passed through the inspection area, a spontaneous cheer went up. France and Switzerland, he explained to willing ears, were the only two Western European countries that were absolutely free from smallpox. Reports of isolated cases had been coming in from several other countries, but there was nothing to be alarmed about.

"I shall let you go home, conditionally," he said as he handed me a piece of paper to sign. "This commits you to report to me if you develop any symptoms."

I signed the paper and gave him a smile. "With lupus, Doctor, one always has symptoms, and I would never know if I had smallpox or just an off day!"

"Lupus is a peculiar disease, isn't it?" he mused aloud. "I never saw a case of it in medical school or internship. Then my sister died of it in three months."

24. "Girls Don't Whistle!"

The Patient's Story

> Whistling girls and crowing hens
> never come to very good ends.
> Girls that whistle and hens that crow
> make their way wherever they go.
>   —Comments of a friend

It was early April 1966, thirteen years after the onset of lupus. The past seven or eight years had been wonderful for us. The children had grown up; two were in college, one in high school. We all loved our house on Temple Road. The garden I had envisioned when we bought the house was now a reality. The informal arrangements of flowers were splashes of color, the way gardens used to look in Bulgaria. I loved digging in the damp soil. One day, while planting some rose bushes, I became aware that I was whistling. I could not believe it! After all these years, I could enjoy once more this long-forgotten pleasure. Later, when I walked into the house, still whistling, Martha looked at me surprised and said, "Mothers don't whistle!"

"Your mother does!" I said. "She started way back in Bulgaria!"

Although I was feeling great, I still had to take precautions whenever the breath of spring tempted me toward my garden—I had to beware of the sun. I did not mind applying the Doak Solar Cream but hated spraying myself with insect repellent. Bugs loved me. In 1951 I had experienced something similar to lupus in Gorham, New Hampshire. It was during the month of June when the black flies were at their worst. The bites got infected and blistered, and I ran a fever of over 101 degrees. Luckily, I got over it quickly. In previous years, some doctors had suspected insect bites as a possible cause for the outbreak of my lupus—lupus has many ways of starting.

During the same afternoon that I had worked in the garden and discovered that I could whistle again, in the midst of arranging flowers in the dining room with my youngest daughter, a sudden pain gently squeezed the lower part of my chest. I grasped the edge of the table, afraid to move, but immediately felt a little better—the whole thing happened too quickly for my daughter to react. By nine o'clock in the evening, the pain had increased so badly that I had to call a doctor in Wellesley to come to the house. In the short time he took to come, the pain had grown unbearable. Wiping the perspiration from my face with a turkish towel, the doctor speculated that I was having a gallbladder attack. He jabbed a needle in my thigh, drew some blood from my arm, and said I'd fall asleep in a few minutes. He'd promised to return first thing in the morning.

Unsure of just what a gallbladder was, I fell asleep as soon as the doctor left the room. But not for very long! At two-thirty, I awoke in agony. I was rolling from side to side, moaning as if in labor, afraid that I would wake everyone in the house. By four o'clock, my husband called the doctor once more, and the good man arrived in a few minutes, wearing a light coat over his pajamas. After one quick look at me, he picked up the telephone and called an ambulance.

"You probably feel like crawling the walls," he said before he made a second telephone call to get a bed at Peter Bent Brigham. I was worried by the possibility that Brigham was full. My great hospital had only three hundred beds.

A few hours later, Brigham had me again, and Dr. Gardner was, as usual, by my bedside. He, too, took blood, and after I had a series of X rays, a diagnosis of cholecystitis was confirmed. I had a gallbladder full of stones. One of the stones had settled in the wrong place and caused an obstruction. Dr. Gardner stressed the need for an immediate operation. I knew that he was worried about my having major surgery. Anybody with a history like mine had to be shielded from stress, even from tooth extractions.

Four days after I entered the hospital, the operation was performed. On rounds the next day, the surgeon was pleased with his handiwork. As he looked at the gastric suction bottle, he said that he hadn't seen any signs of lupus. The spleen, liver, and kidneys "felt" normal, but no biopsies were taken. The gallbladder problem was as classic as it could be.

"A typical 4F's case," another doctor chortled at a medical student.

The student, who didn't know what he meant, had the *esprit du moment* to answer in the same low voice, "I'm sure it doesn't apply to her draft status."

I had to laugh even though it caused a lot of pain in the incision. My surgeon glanced at his watch and waved good-bye to me as if to spare me the need to push any words through my dry mouth and lips.

I later learned what they meant by their 4F joke: fair, fat, female, forty. One of the nurses told me, half apologetically. I told her not to worry—I had become used to Brigham. It was very much like a small town. Everyone spoke his mind—and nothing remained a secret.

The next day, Dr. Gardner was puzzled when my lips blossomed with blisters. He gradually eliminated many possibilities and narrowed suspicion down to the disinfectant solution in which the thermometer was kept. After that, the nurses washed the thermometer in soap and water, and the sores healed. But soon a rash appeared on all of my body. The drug list seemed harmless enough for a "postop" patient: Compazine, Demerol, Seconal, Meprospan. No antibiotics. None of the usual troublemakers. Nevertheless, they stopped all drugs, gave me nicotinic-acid injections, and happily the rash went away. The gallbladder attack had not been as difficult to handle as my tendency to react badly to many drugs. As the resident pointed out, I did illustrate the modern aphorism "This is the day of safe surgery and dangerous drugs."

Professor Popoff sent me a get-well cable. In his opinion, the gallbladder could have been a hidden source of chronic infection. He expected me to feel even better than before the surgery.

President Johnson had his gallbladder out the day after my surgery. I delighted in following his daily health bulletins. But as the days went on, I began to worry about him, since I was able to attend my household chores long before he returned to the White House.

25. Peter Bent Brigham Hospital, 1970

The Patient's Story

SEVENTEEN years after the onset of my disease, on May 28, 1970, I reentered Peter Bent Brigham Hospital for a routine checkup under the care of Dr. Chester Alper, who earlier had been a member of Dr. Gardner's group. In 1966, Dr. Gardner had taken a professorship in Philadelphia. He continued to direct my care from a distance, and once a year I went to Philadelphia for follow-up. Alper in Boston, Gardner in Philadelphia, Popoff in Bulgaria—wouldn't it have been nice if all of them could be in Boston together in the same hospital? No, that would eliminate my excuse for flying to see them, and I so very much loved to travel.

The main lobby of Peter Bent Brigham Hospital looked like a bus terminal—it was so crowded I could hardly move about. In the coffee shop behind the huge semicircular information desk, every chair and table was taken, and the gift shop was cluttered with books, candies, cards, gaily displayed as if to offset the struggle and sadness that must have spilled over from the sick beds less than a hundred yards away.

Many of the young doctors had beards and ear-length hair and wore pastel shirts; several nurses were in pants suits—a sharp change in style in only a few years.

In the admitting office, a heavyset man, submerged by mounds of paper, commented that the hospital nowadays was always bustling like this. Everyone had some sort of health insurance. Medicare, too, had brought more older people for treatment. "Yet the facilities stay the same; Brigham is not much bigger than it was in 1913, when it was built. It belongs to another age. Perhaps someday we'll have a modern building. Then we'll have the elevators to complain about. At least it's possible to climb to the top floor in this place—we have only three floors, you know."

Shortly I found myself back on the Coolidge Wing in a room next to the one where I had been twice before. Previously, I had been too ill to enjoy the pleasant, sunny room with large windows looking into a courtyard of fresh grass. Even though I was in perfect health now, I was getting quite fatigued from the history and physical examination by the student, the intern, and the resident, the traditional routine of the teaching hospital.

The next morning, the resident brought Dr. Thorn with him. The two entered my room at the head of a phalanx of white suits and lab coats. Dr. Thorn looked much the same, but now the group surrounding him appeared much younger. I noticed that his flaming red hair had been tamed by the added gray and that his many freckles had melted into his skin. His eyes were a little deeper set—perhaps a few more wrinkles around the edges—but they were just as keen as ever. His face expressed the same genial glow of friendliness.

"You look well," he said in his usual tone of voice—a blend of closeness and professional routine, which had become a part of him and effectively conveyed a feeling of welcome to his medical service. "How do you feel?" He gave me a quick, observing glance, knowing the answer.

"Wonderful," I said. "My lupus has declared a moratorium. I hope it's for good."

"Isn't it great to feel so well?" Dr. Thorn sounded very much pleased. He turned to his students and said, "You wouldn't think now that for many years she was very ill and utterly exhausted by lupus; and through all of it, she was fully aware of the gravity of her condition."

"I still tremble at the sound of lupus." I saw the many inquisitive eyes of the students looking down at me and said, "It wasn't all that bad. I tried to enjoy myself even during the worst times."

Dr. Thorn nodded and spoke to the group. "She has done quite a bit of research on lupus. She has a remarkable understanding of her illness."

An intense young man spoke up. "Perhaps the lady would give me some of her thoughts. I am interested in the psychological responses of patients to chronic diseases. Although I hadn't thought of it before, LE would be a good topic. It's like multiple sclerosis. Remissions and exacerbations keep the patient in a constant state of expectancy. Could I return to talk with you?" he asked.

"I'll be glad to oblige," I replied. "I've done it before." He looked so terribly young. He must have just been starting school when I had helped that other student nearly seventeen years ago.

Dr. Thorn held out his hand as if to congratulate me for the successful fight and at the same time to say good-bye again. I knew that he was going to retire in two years, and as I squeezed his hand, I sensed that it would probably be the last time that I would see him as chief. I did not like that feeling. It meant that both of us were getting older. Aging, as opposed to lupus, would have no remission, drugs or no drugs, vitamins or no vitamins.

As the group slowly filed out of my room, Dr. Thorn continued to philosophize about lupus. "Maybe the nicotinic acid really does reduce light sensitivity. It's always hard to prove what is going on in this disease. It's like a chameleon. Always changing. You'd have to set up a careful study to get worthwhile data. Can you imagine how hard that would be? It would take a lot of cases like this one to prove a point."

As in previous times when I stayed at the hospital, many young doctors and medical students came in to see me. Although I was well, they all believed I had lupus. Ironically, this recalled that when I had been sick they were skeptical of the LE cell, the peculiar rashes, the seemingly neurotic complaints. A bizarre turnabout, I thought. When you're sick, many believe you're not, and when you get better, your illness is spoken of as a fact. The word "remission" rolled off their tongues and mine enough times to give my case the authenticity that it never commanded during its darkest hours. The students, eagerly seeking a root cause of the problem, trying to reduce it to simple, workable terms, questioned me endlessly about the sulfa-drug story, having been told to read my case report in the *Journal of The American Medical Association*. I accepted the sulfa connection so completely—I had read the section in Meyler's book—I could not believe that anyone could look on it as pure coincidence. Yet some did. They offered other explanations and brought me up-to-date on new literature. They treated me almost as if I were a doctor. I understood all of the terms; I quoted this and that as though I were one of them and had fun doing so. I had returned from the gates of hell, and that gave me a lot to talk about.

"How does it feel to be well again?" a psychiatrist stopped to ask me. He was curious about the adjustments a person has to make in a complete remission like mine.

"It feels wonderful," I retorted. "Health has given me back my sense of reality. When the lupus was active, it was hard to function in a normal way. Sometimes the symptoms—pain, nausea, numbness—would dominate my thoughts. At other times, I would only be afraid of what was coming next. Lacking strength and lacking confidence, I withdrew from the outside world into the safety of family life."

"What do you mean by safety?" he asked.

"I have a good family. They did not blame me for my sickness; they did not blame themselves or God. They tried to help me, and they had complete faith in the doctors even when the doctors themselves did not know what was going on. I think my husband helped me to transfer worry and responsibility to the doctors' shoulders instead of carrying the burdens myself. That was very important. It gave all of us something to lean on. I became philosophical. I lived for the moment instead of the future. I spent more time with the children than I would have if I hadn't been sick." I shrugged. "I don't know if this was good or bad. Bulgarian parents tend to be overprotective. . . ." After a moment's silence, I said, "The family and the house became my universe for a while. Our social contacts decreased; the furniture, the flowers, books, and even food had deeper meaning. I constantly fought my illness. I never gave up. My family would not let me."

The doctor skillfully directed our talk. "You don't seem to feel the need to be ill any longer," he said. His elongated eyes, near slits, surrounded by puffed cheeks, reminded me of a Buddha carving I had admired once in a Japanese temple in Kyoto.

"No, I don't want to feel ill anymore. I never did. Why should anyone want to be sick?"

"Some do," he said. "But tell me, how does your husband feel about your recovery?"

"My husband? He seems pleased, of course. The remission makes his life easier. He, too, has been released from chains."

"Chains? Do you think he resented your illness? Do you think that your relationship was adversely affected by the duration of your trouble?"

"Adversely, no. But twenty years is a long time. Chronic sickness changes a house. It would have been easier if I had been well while the children were growing." I paused. "But in more than one way, life has been good to us. We have much to be grateful for."

"And the children?"

"They seem to have survived the ordeal, too. Ingrid is a third-grade teacher and likes working with handicapped children. She gives of herself. Our son is preparing to be a teacher, too, and Martha is a junior in college. The children seem to have a social conscience and want to relate to people. The trauma of having a chronically ill mother was not an albatross for them—at least I don't think it was. Perhaps it even helped in their development. It takes some suffering to bring out humanity. I believe that. But time will tell."

An immunologist also came to see me. Lean, intense, and very soft-spoken, he introduced himself as a research fellow who had done some work on LE and related diseases. Dr. Thorn suggested that he review my history. Perhaps here was a witch who would do for lupus what Withering's informant did for heart disease when, three and a half centuries ago, she recommended foxglove* for dropsy.†

He seemed unusually poised for one still in a white uniform. His approach was philosophical. He had come to swap tales about LE. He acted as if he would value my opinion in the same way as he would an LE expert on the boardwalk at the important Atlantic City meetings.

"When, in your opinion, did your disease start?" the young man asked in a friendly tone.

I had been asked that question many, many times. My answer had been rehearsed almost excessively, in French, English, and Bulgarian, at home and in the hospital, with students and professors. It brought forth the kind of response that an ancient Alsatian farmer might give to a traveler who asks about his experiences in the war. "Which war? Which experiences, *monsieur*? There were so many."

I began to reminisce, feeling that he would listen to the whole story and not judge me a fool if I rambled on and even theorized a little.

As I began, I realized that my story had been restructured by the events, the opinions, and the articles in the medical literature that contributed to the totality of my confrontation with lupus. I no longer had the advantage of ignorance. I had to consider all possibilities just like a scientist. And the litany of possibilities had grown too extensive for me to handle with ease. The scientist is able to give more weight to some things and less to others on the basis of experimental facts. My emphasis depended on subjectivity and was thus more fragile, more personal.

I told him of the sore on my leg after taking a miracle drug. "Was it a sulfonamide?" I mused aloud, not expecting him to answer.

"It probably was. How many miracle drugs were new in the thirties?"

"The sore did not heal for months. It was nature's warning to me. Years later, during one of my stays at Peter Bent Brigham, I

---

*Foxglove: a plant whose leaves resemble fingers (digits).
†Dropsy: the swelling of the limbs and abdomen that results from heart failure.

was given a strong sedative. Hours after I had taken it, a sore appeared on my arm that looked exactly like the one I had had in Bulgaria. The same thing happened after the smallpox inoculation, which was given to me before my first trip to Geneva in 1957. Still later, after taking tetracycline, I became covered with red blotches similar in shape and size and thickness to the sores I've just described. Luckily, the tetracycline was stopped immediately, and the blotches didn't ripen completely. These occurrences and a few others led me in retrospect to believe that I had the beginnings of lupus in Bulgaria."

Looking further into the past and letting my thoughts tumble, I wondered whether I had a genetic background that predisposed one to the disease. Yet I knew of no one in the family who had anything resembling LE. Many of the earlier signs had been misunderstood. In my adolescence, Mother used to attribute some of my afflictions to a delicate constitution: Constant strep throat, susceptibility to colds, recurring pneumonia, and the overreaction to mosquito bites were but a few of the problems. But Father contended that as the only daughter, I was spoiled by everyone in the family and may not have been so sick if I had not been so protected. He had a fundamentalist view of resistance to disease. He never thought of illness as something to spend time on.

The possibility of a genetic background for my disease stood out in my mind. I thought in simple terms: strong genes for this, weak genes for that. I fancied a series of stages in LE. Those with weak genes would put up a weak defense against LE at each stage of the disease. In this primitive theory, everyone could get the disease if the stimulus was strong enough.

Infections were the beginning—the first stage. I got too many of them, my defense was weak, and I needed drugs to help me over the trouble. The drugs were the second stage. Instead of helping, they caused new problems that were not interpreted correctly. The reactions should have been gratefully received as a warning signal from nature, not just for one drug but for all. Now I am even afraid of aspirin. Yet for nearly twenty years I swallowed new pills and took injections passively, without thinking twice. I should have learned from experience, but along with my doctors, I had had to be hit over the head with the allergic reactions many, many times before drawing the right conclusions.

"The next stage in my simple theory," I said, "has to do with stress in life. Fatigue, poor diet, too much worry—these things can erode the last defenses. They cannot push you over by themselves. But once you are exhausted or lose your appetite or have too many problems to solve, the weaknesses of your makeup make themselves known, particularly if you're a woman. The young housewife—losing sleep over her children's sicknesses, trying to balance the budget, having a cigarette and coffee for breakfast—who has a predisposition to lupus, takes the wrong drug, stays out in the sun too long, and gets an infection which is hard to throw off and the disease starts. Then the early symptoms, except for the butterfly, are so peculiar that they draw attention away from physical illness. The doctor thinks it's a neurosis. The patient goes one step further and thinks herself eccentric, inadequate, sometimes half crazy. There is no communication in this ignorance. The pills keep coming and are willingly taken. The barriers fall, the disease takes hold, and the diagnosis is easier to make. The doctor gets more sure of himself, while the patient gets more frightened. The unpronounceable name of the disease, the bad outlook, the unknown cause, the side effects of cortisone—all of it is so hard to understand. And the rash—you might as well have leprosy."

"I wonder how many women in the Middle Ages wore the Lazarus bell because of lupus," the young man interrupted. "Even today, skin troubles, because they are easily seen, bring out unreasonable fears in people. They think of contagion, of curses, of filth, of evil, of unworthiness. Lupus puts you in a lazaretto, a medical and a psychological one. The doctor does not know what to do with you. You do not know what to do for yourself."

I remained quiet for a few moments, then said, "What one needs with lupus is a doctor who will stick with you and give you courage. I was lucky—Dr. Gardner did that for me. He was always so full of energy and optimism. He was willing to try new things and to learn from his own mistakes. He stopped the white-cell injections when he thought they were not working and was quick to suspect that the Diamox might have given me problems. He never gave up, even when the kidneys became involved."

My listener never looked around the room nor at his watch; nor did he refill his pipe. I went on: "As sick as I was, Dr. Gardner didn't want me to live in a 'glass house,' as he would say and encouraged me to talk to and offer help to other lupus patients. He knew the value of sharing troubles. Who better to talk to than a fellow sufferer? And there were many—once we started to look. The fair Australian girl, a Wellesley College teacher, a black woman—Anne-Mae—from Roxbury, an artist from New Hampshire—all women, all desperately sick, sicker than I, crying out for understanding as much as for medical help.

"When I first talked of the nicotinamide, Dr. Gardner listened, not because he believed in it—he may not believe in it even now—but because he realized that it was therapeutic for me to seek ways to help myself.

"He asked me to gather the literature on the subject, cleverly referring to my 'valuable experience as a library worker,' and encouraged contacts with Professor Popoff. He revealed strength when he admitted medical ignorance of lupus. He was conventional in using prednisone and sun cream but unconventional in trying the Bulgarian remedy.

"Most importantly, Dr. Gardner was persistent . . . and he won. I should say we won. I was a good patient."

"Yes," the young doctor said absently. Perhaps he was thinking of the chemical reactions of nicotinic acid or the definitions of a good clinician or the role of inheritance in lupus or the preventive-medicine theme of the drug-reaction side of the story.

No single part of it was new to him, but the whole package, the interwoven tale of twenty years with LE, was entirely new. He groped for a simple explanation, a unifying concept, but failing that, accepted it as history, worth listening to even if its parts did not hang together and its narrator was excessively anecdotal for his scientific mind.

When I paused as if approaching the end of the story, he offered some fresh knowledge to keep me up-to-date. "Lately, people have found viruses which may have something to do with lupus. Just another in a long line of theories," he said. To my questioning look, he responded, "Viruses are very tiny and mysterious. They cause some diseases for sure—polio and measles. Other diseases with unknown causes are bound to be linked with viruses sooner or later, since viruses are everywhere." He suddenly stopped as if he had to turn a fresh page in a textbook, then took some matches from his trouser pocket and lit his pipe. Only after he inhaled deeply several times did he get up from his chair. On his way out, he paused by the door and said, "The nicotinic-acid magic—I will try that on some patients, I promise."

On my last day in the hospital, Dr. Alper summed up my status. All my tests were back and were remarkably normal. The LE cells had disappeared. The kidneys were perfect.

"If I had not known the history and seen you in your sicker days, I would not have suspected, much less made the diagnosis of, lupus. You must lead a pretty normal life now."

"I am a living example of one of Osler's aphorisms: If you want to live a long life, get a chronic disease and take care of it."

"What are you doing now to take care of it? Whatever it is, it's working and I wouldn't stop it."

"I don't really do very much about lupus anymore. I take my so-called placebo, the nicotinic acid. You have a skeptical smile. But I feel sure that the nicotinamide has helped me in some ways. It brought me some hope, something to hold on to. And who knows? Perhaps someday the doctors might find that it plays a role beyond the power of the placebo. Meanwhile, I'm not neglecting myself. I eat well, take my vitamins, and sleep eight to ten hours each night. Trying not to get overtired seems to be the main problem now. I want to do so many things. In the past few years I've rediscovered the pleasure of walking, and I start the mornings by exercising. I do a few push-ups to keep in shape—I call them push-ups, but everyone else in the family calls them 'half push-ups.' My days are filled with activities. I do lots of gardening. I still tend to the flowers in my bare feet. It must be something I've carried over from my ancestors in

Europe. Smelling and touching the damp soil has always been a weakness of mine."

"I hope you're careful of the sun."

"Don't worry, I am."

"And drugs, too," he was quick to remind me.

"I know. Even the newest 'miracle drugs' would not tempt me."

26. Paris, 1968

The Patient's Story

AT the end of April 1968, after many years of studying English and free-lancing, I met with Tom Winship, then the editor in chief of the *Boston Globe*, and asked him if I could get an assignment to write a few stories about the Vietnam peace talks in Paris. The conference was to open in a week, and I could fly over at any time.

Tom replied that the *Globe* was sending Darius Shabala and Bud Collins to cover the event. And then he said, "However, they won't be ready to leave this country for a few more days. If you could leave immediately, perhaps you could write something about the atmosphere in Paris before the peace talks get under way." He added, "I'll let you know by tonight or tomorrow morning."

"If I was willing!" I was bubbling with an inner excitement that was difficult to control. For so many years I had absorbed the world through books and the opinions of others. I had been remote from life for such a long time. And now I might be getting a chance to view the making of history firsthand, write about it, and perhaps report back about the end of the Vietnam War. I was fantasizing about this wonderful chance.

That same evening, I received a hand-delivered letter from

Tom. The conference was going to be heavily dominated by authorized diplomatic correspondents from papers from all over the world. It would be quite a mob scene. Tom had some reservations about my physical stamina and wanted me to give that some serious thought.

While I read Tom's letter, I felt a sudden panic. Suppose I went to Paris and my lupus returned? Suppose I landed in a hospital again and there was no one to help me? Suppose the old exhaustion and dizziness returned? I had not been in remission for very long, and I still shivered when I remembered what it was like to have an active disease. When I was last in Paris, I had felt lifeless. I could not move from one place to another without being helped. And I also remembered how relieved I had been when I returned to Boston and was close to Brigham and my doctors.

The children are young adults now, I thought to myself. My husband is busier than ever with his wool business and with his tennis. And I still had live-in help in the house—so why not go?

The next morning I called Tom and told him that I was ready to leave the same evening. Another letter followed, addressed to John O'Brien, Deputy Assistant Secretary of State for Public Affairs, U.S. Embassy, Paris, France. The letter read: "This is to introduce Mrs. A. of Boston. The *Boston Globe* has asked Mrs. A. to write some pieces for the paper on the Paris peace talks. I hope she can be issued the necessary credentials for this assignment." I read the few words, feeling more and more excited.

When I told my husband that I was going to Paris to write for the *Globe*, he was astonished. "You can't be serious," he said.

"I am serious and excited," I said.

"Remember what Dr. Gardner told you about your remission? It's not a permanent state. Your disease can flare up again. You can't exhaust yourself. You can't gamble with your health."

"I've been thinking about that," I said. "But it's all settled. I'm going," I said.

There was a deep silence, and then my husband turned his back on me and strode to the porch. He seemed amazed by my determination.

I stood for a moment, feeling the old submissiveness coming back. I also felt a deep sense of anger—something I had never felt before. "I have to do things like every other person," I snapped, suddenly furious. "I can't go on living in fear that the disease will come back. This is my life, and like everyone else, I want to feel that I'm free to make my own choices and direct my life toward a purpose. The children are practically young adults." I paused for breath, then continued, just as excited, "When I came to this country, I wanted to have a career, and I wanted to have a family. I worked for five years at the Widener Library, and I went to school. I wanted to have children—I wanted to have everything. That was my choice, just the way it was my choice to marry you and come to America."

My husband suddenly laughed. "I'm not so sure about that. . . . You could have still been in Bulgaria if I didn't marry you—and think where you'd be now. Aren't you grateful for everything you've got?"

I went after him on the porch and faced him. I didn't know how serious he was when he was saying these words, but my anger was mounting. I glanced at him and said, "Sure, I'm grateful for all I have in my life. I'm grateful for love, for the children, for music, for books, for my trees and the garden. I'm grateful for the comfort that I'm enjoying, but now that my life has been given back to me, I want to direct it toward other things. Every day after the children and you leave the house, I remain alone, encircled by these walls, and I feel useless and sometimes even lonely. Can't you see that I don't want to live any longer by letting things happen. If I want to take a chance and disturb this remission, it will be my choice to do so. If I want to live or die, this, too, should be my decision." After a moment I became a little calmer and said in a low voice, "I have to do something before I succumb to a creeping indifference all around. My wish to go to Paris is not just an eccentricity. I have to do something before this disease kills all my illusions about life. For all these years I've been busy just dying. I need some breathing space —I need some independence even if it's just for a very short period of time." I averted my face to hide the tears. He would never understand the depth of my despair and the need for my readjustment.

"Well," my husband said, "I had no idea that this trip meant so much to you. If you want to go—go! Nobody will stop you. But you must call Gardner and tell him about it."

"I'll think about that," I said, feeling a little better.

The following day was Saturday. My husband canceled his tennis game—something he had not done in many, many years. I found him lying on the living-room sofa, staring at the ceiling. Could he feel threatened about my wanting to be independent? Could he be jealous of my taking off all by myself? Would he tell me? I wished I knew what he felt at this moment, what his thoughts were.

For an instant I thought of my husband's office with the telephones, his endless late meetings. By Monday, he'll be lost in his business and I'll be back before he remembers that I was gone, I told myself. I was determined not to change my mind about this trip.

I dozed off on the plane. When I opened my eyes, I saw that the black air outside the window had softened. Purple rays crept in, followed by pink-and-blue ones, and suddenly there was a burst of red on the horizon and it was daylight. When I looked outside the window again, I could see the Seine winding around Paris like a silver necklace; Paris was perhaps the most beautiful city in the world.

In Paris, things were as hectic as Tom Winship had predicted. More than two thousand correspondents would attend the peace conference; two hundred or more were Americans. When I went to the Hotel Crillon, where the American correspondents had established their headquarters, and saw the lists of names from the United States, I started laughing. My name was listed right after Ellie Abel, followed by Walter Cronkite, Chet Huntley, and others. Looking around, I began recognizing the faces of famous TV persons and well-known correspondents. I had to refrain from staring at them. People stared at me, for I was the only woman in the room for the first few days. I recall having a glass of Perrier at the bar, sitting next to Walter Cronkite. I told him how Tom Winship gave me the assignment. He told me that he knew Tom well, and he was not surprised that Tom would do such a thing. He said that Tom's father had started his journalistic career after such an out-of-the-way assignment and later became the editor of the *Globe*. When I told Cronkite that I had sent a dispatch to the *Globe* that cost me $100, he laughed. "Good heavens, woman! What did you send, *War and Peace?* Have you used the teletype?"

I blushed when I said that I didn't know what a teletype was. I didn't know many things about the markings of a correspondent, but I managed to send back to the States some of the first stories about Paris and the opening of the peace conference—and they were all published.

During the first few days in Paris, I felt very tired. But I was quick to realize that the fatigue that I was experiencing now was caused by the excitement, the running around and the lack of sleep, which was quite different from fatigue experienced with lupus. This fatigue was a healthy fatigue—it diminished after a good night's sleep. It lacked the element of helplessness, of hopelessness. It didn't involve my whole being; my spirit and my feelings were not touched by the morbidity that's part of the lupus fatigue. If the physicians could only understand the difference between fatigue and fatigue before they denigrate the patients who complain of this symptom, so common in lupus.

I spent a month in Paris, stranded by the general strike and the student revolution at the Sorbonne. I kept a journal of the events that I might publish someday. In the meantime, I did a great deal of learning about the tensions of the world and about the tensions in myself. I became philosophical. Perhaps more profound, but what did the word mean? What were these people doing here around the conference table? I wondered. The talks were about war—weapons, killing, and human suffering—but not about solutions. All they had to do was order the troops to stop the shooting on both sides. To me, those things were simple . . . they should simply stop killing. Perhaps women should become more vocal about that? We teach the children not to hurt—not to inflict pains—and then they are shipped off to kill—and be killed. It was so futile.

When I try to remember that month I spent in Paris, I always think of the students at the Sorbonne. I felt a sense of time I had lost, and I had a sense that I wanted to make it up.

It took some courage for me to start on that trip, and I

knew it would take another sort of courage to pursue other projects when I returned home. My enthusiasm was boundless.

While in Paris, I took a trip to see the cathedral at Chartres. I drove for several hours through fields smelling of flowers and lily of the valley and by meadows that looked painted with bluish-green grass. Over an expanse of what seemed like unbroken fields was the upper bulk of the cathedral, alone against the horizon. The cathedral cast a spell over me. I felt its singularity and its dominance over the earth that surrounded it. I had read somewhere that nobody who started work on the cathedral saw it completed—not the workmen, stonecutters, or sculptors, not even the architect, who would never know if his dream had materialized.

When I returned from Chartres and was resting in my hotel room, a short vision of the cathedral came back to me. Does one need faith in order to surmount the challenges of life? I wondered, and then I thought, the paradox was that while the illness was destroying my body, something in me built awareness and determination that existed in me now. Perhaps one could only rely on faith, like the people of Chartres? The spirit of man has a magic resilience, I thought. It vibrates with excitement and soars to incredible heights. What mattered was to work hard today and begin again tomorrow. Did the life of the spirit influence the experiences of the body? What a strange thought!

When I returned to Wellesley from Paris, my garden was in full bloom. I looked at the trees and the flowers that I had planted through the years, and they seemed to be smiling. The rhododendrons were in bloom, and the dogwood trees by the kitchen windows were loaded with pink-and-white blossoms that shimmered in the sun like giant butterflies. The slope in front of the house was covered with lilies of the valley and a profusion of wild violets overtook the lawn.

In the back of the house, the branches of the lilac trees looked purple and green and fragrant. And farther down in the woods, under a brown blanket of leaves, hundreds of lady slippers were pushing up toward the light.

After the clamor in Paris, the quiet and beauty of my garden was like a small heaven. I was seized by a longing to lie in the grass and face the sun and the light. It was as if I did not have enough of the sky and its varying colors. At such moments, I felt happy to be alive. In the next few weeks I went back to digging in the soil, planting and watering the lawn, but I was still getting tired—extremely tired.

The month I spent in Paris had only intensified my feelings for some focus in my life. I was yearning to do something important, to be part of a larger human effort. This was my inner striving. I could not stop it. But where should I begin? In coping with lupus, I had learned to live entirely for the moment. Was Paris just such a moment? No, Paris was a beginning. I believed that.

Some years back I had written a manuscript that I had entitled "Twenty-Two Thousand Miles to America." The idea to send the story to a publisher had been on my mind for a long time, and I mailed it to Lippincott in Philadelphia. I did not know what to expect. A few weeks later, I was surprised and excited when one of the editors at Lippincott replied that the story was good but I had to resolve it and take it through two or three climaxes to finalize it. I had written to them that I was self-taught in the English language and would probably need lots of help with my grammar. I blushed with happiness when I read the editor's comment: "If you know 'little English,' then learn no more, stop where you are and go out and force the flowers to grow just as you wish them, which will be a very good way, indeed."

I went to work and took up the threads of the story once more. In my soul-searching mood I began creating fictitious characters for the first time, as if to restore my own youth and fill in the void of years I had lost when I was struggling with lupus.

Browsing through old magazines one day, my eye caught the word "Help!" The word appeared in large letters over a small picture of a woman's face that was covered with gauze. The caption below the picture read: "I suffer from an obscure human ailment—I have systemic lupus erythematosus. Can anyone, please, help me!"

I read the words several times. At first I thought it was an ad or some gimmick aimed at sensational effect. But I realized immediately that I was wrong. No one could exploit a sickness as painful as lupus. I understood only too well the woman's helplessness and felt compassion and sorrow. In the ensuing month, her plea haunted me.

It occurred to me that if I could write a detailed account of my own lupus story, perhaps that suffering woman and others might read it and benefit from my experiences. I convinced myself that if I wrote my story for all the people who have been smitten by this disease, perhaps I could go through with it.

I stopped writing "Twenty-Two Thousand Miles to America" and began delving into the painful memories of my illness, singling out the facts that had relevance to the case, anxious not to overdramatize the situation. It was difficult to dredge up memories. It was difficult to be accurate in attempting to describe the symptoms and indignities caused by this disease. Past pains and fears came back to life despite my having tried so hard to forget them. As I was writing, I recognized that I was telling not only my story but the story of all the patients who were suffering from lupus; I was writing the story I could not find at the medical libraries or anyplace else; I was writing of fears and pains, of human suffering and emotions that were the core of this disease.

It was a curious contrast to feel well and comfortable and yet conjure up those dreadful experiences with lupus and lure them into focus again. I wrote hour after hour, sometimes late into the night, afraid that I would never finish the story. Sometimes as I wrote, I came close to crying. There were those memories of evenings when I was too tired to undress to go to bed. And there were those memories of sitting at the mirror and looking at my moonlike face covered by rashes, the bald spots on my scalp, and the feverish, bulging eyes. Could this be me? This grotesque-looking person that was staring at me? I had wondered. I was thirty-four, and I had stopped dreaming. And now that my looks and my pride in my personal appearance had been restored and I was beginning to forget the unendurable, here I was crying for the others. It occurred to me that I was also transferring some of those tears to myself.

When I finished the manuscript, I took it to Herb Black, a medical writer at the *Boston Globe*. Herb was touched by the story and wrote the first article about lupus for the lay public to read. Otto

Zousmer, then the associate editor, syndicated the story, and lupus patients began writing from everywhere. All were anxious for information, and they all needed help. When Beacon published the story under the title *The Sun Is My Enemy*, my whole life changed. It also changed, perhaps, the lives of thousands of other patients.

The Sun Is My Enemy was reviewed from coast to coast, and I was interviewed by newspapers, radio, and television. I was invited to talk to small groups of patients and their families, schools of nursing, and medical students, and I spoke at seminars for physicians in their continual-education programs. I traveled from one place to another, and my life became filled with experiences of new cities and new faces. Lupus patients crowded my thoughts and my feelings. I felt particularly touched by the plight of the younger patients, who needed much hope and encouragement. So many were giving up hope. In dealing with the patients and in my desire to understand the essence of their feelings and problems, I was gaining a perspective on my own emotions and gaining a newfound maturity that would add more depth to my existence.

Then one day, after a radio interview with Maureen Reagan in Los Angeles, I had a call from Tom Bane, an assemblyman from Sacramento. Tom's fiancée, Marlene, had lupus. They both came to see me at my hotel. During lunch we talked about the need for a National Lupus Foundation; we talked about the need for public awareness of lupus, about self-help groups that would improve the quality of life of the patients, and Tom expressed concerns about the need for fund-raising and the promotion of medical research. This was in 1972. In 1974, I mailed a letter to around twenty independent lupus groups around the country and asked them to send representatives to Boston to start a lupus foundation. Tom Bane came to that meeting all the way from California. In 1977, with the help of many patients and several physicians, the Lupus Foundation of America was formed. Today it has a membership of over 30,000, with chapters in every state of the nation and affiliated groups throughout the world.

In May 1980, I received a thrilling invitation from Brigham and Women's Hospital, a Harvard University affiliate, to give the grand rounds before their medical community. (Brigham and Women's

Hospital is the new name for the merger between the old Peter Bent Brigham Hospital—where I have been treated for over 30 years—and the Robert Breck Brigham Hospital and Boston Hospital for Women.)

"Ordinarily, grand rounds provide an opportunity for the lecturer to show off a bit, to have the spotlight on his own intelligence," wrote Dr. Carl Pierce, an old friend of mine, in a book called *The Body Is the Hero*, by Ronald J. Glasser, M.D. Pierce wrote that "grand rounds" means just what it says. Unlike neurology rounds or hematology rounds during which only a few specialists are present, the whole department of medicine comes to grand rounds to listen to what they know will be a definitive discussion of the disease under consideration. The facts are usually presented in the monotone of the knowledgeable, self-assured expert totally in control of the facts. Sometimes a patient is present to further prove the expert's findings.

I remember trembling with emotion as I stood before some of the top medical scientists and clinicians in the world. I had to speak from introspection and personal experiences and conversations I had had with other lupus patients. I had no slides to give me a breather. I was the patient, with nothing to rely on except myself.

I could feel the absolute silence around me, and I could see some of the raised eyebrows in the audience. And I remember telling myself not to waver or panic, for this was a human experience not only for myself but also for these physicians, who were pursuing the practice of medicine. I was there to tell them what lupus really means to the patient and the price that one has to pay for it in human suffering. After I finished my talk, I walked back through the old parts of Brigham where Dr. Frank Gardner had had his laboratory. I sat on the same wooden bench by the door where I had awaited the results of my blood tests, and I reflected about then and now. In the past few decades there has been much progress in medical research and immunology, I thought to myself. But what have the doctors learned about the human condition and how lupus affects a human life? Not much. I questioned if they could properly treat the patient without knowing that. Our society is going through rapid technological and medical changes, but there is still a great need in medicine to be derived from the experiences and special needs of persons afflicted with chronic diseases such as lupus. Medications and technology can save lives, but a patient needs close human contact with his or her doctor; he needs to exchange thoughts and feelings. Such continued interaction is essential with lupus. The patient needs the comfortable feeling of being able to discuss emotional and psychosocial problems with the physician. The doctor has to be informed of all the possible changes with the disease so he can meet the unforeseen emergencies. Lupus is an unpredictable disease. Its problems transcend more ordinary medical activities. Scientific knowledge and statistics permit a broad spectrum of knowledge, but there still remain the individual's medical problems. The thoughts were rushing in my head. Today the doctors at Brigham had listened. It was a beginning.

Sitting on that bench, I thought of my illness when it was at its worst. During those days my life was directed toward a purpose—to stay alive and help the children grow up. For all those years I had been open to emotions and self-examination before I undertook a basic self-reeducation in order to survive the tribulations of the illness. I had to accept not only the disease but learn that this was life and one had to live it. After my kidneys collapsed, there were many nights when I couldn't sleep and asked myself what was my greatest fear? As I wrote in some other stories the answer was always the same—how would my children survive if I were to die? How could I leave them alone? And what could I do to help myself so I could help them?

In my moment of reflection, I felt like Lazarus, whose life was given back to him by divine forces. And in the silence of this remote corner of the hospital, I asked myself, what was the purpose of my life now? The answer was still the same—to be able to love in my own way and to be able to help others. The world doesn't always make sense, with the growing arsenal of nuclear weapons. But we must still go out and help one another, and we must still trust in the wisdom that nature has instilled in us.

In the car, on the way home, I reflected some more. What changed the course of my disease and brought this miraculous remission? Was it destiny? Strong genes? Love of life? Discipline? Good medical care? A good doctor-patient relationship? Family support? Having help in the house? Perhaps it was all of these—one will never know.

In early March 1985, I received a letter from the Volunteer National Center in Washington, congratulating me on being chosen as one of the recipients of the President's Volunteer Action Awards for health.

At the White House, waiting in line to receive the award from President Reagan, I had to take deep breaths not to show my emotions. There was something especially touching about receiving an award from the president of the United States. My thoughts flickered back to another time in my life when I was standing in a different line waiting to pass the immigration inspection, feeling as if the ground were rocking like the Pacific Ocean. It was a beautiful spring day in 1941. I remembered the San Francisco pier, jammed with cargo and flocks of sea gulls. I had left Bulgaria three days after the German occupation with nothing more than an inner hope and a strong will to meet a tremendous challenge. I had traveled twenty-two thousand miles from my native country. How far from anything I could have imagined on that day was this unforgettable morning at the White House, which marked, in a way, the culmination of a far longer and more difficult journey—my struggle with lupus. When I took President Reagan's hand, I felt its warmth spread to my heart. To me, it expressed the warmth that has been extended to me by all the Americans I've met since 1941.

Filled with many emotions, I stole a glance at my nine-year-old granddaughter Ani, who accompanied me to the White House. She was sitting, poised and proud and smiling, surrounded by her illustrious luncheon companions, and at that moment I was just as proud of Ani as I was of the beautiful medallion given to me by President Ronald Reagan.

27. Emotional Healing
The Physician's Point of View

NEUROLOGICAL involvement. Psychiatric problems. These phrases touch primal fear in patients and their families. Being helpless and unable to control one's body, spirit, and destiny are truly overwhelming thoughts. One conjures up fearful images of Bedlam, insane asylums, and psychiatric hospitals. Physicians thus have an enormous responsibility regarding such fears to reassure the patient calmly and repeatedly that the neurological and psychological components of lupus are manageable.

The neurological system consists of the brain, the spinal cord, and the nerves that spread out from the brain and spinal cord to the peripheral parts of the body. Physicians refer to neurological involvement as organic disease of the brain, that is, an alteration of brain function detectable by pathological examination of the brain or tests of brain function. Lupus can affect the neurological system by causing inflammation in any one of its parts. Seizures, paralysis, loss of sensation, vision, headaches, migraines, psychosis, sleep disturbances, mood swings, and related symptoms may result. The inflammation can usually be effectively treated with anti-inflammatory drugs, thereby eliminating the symptoms. However, as in many inflammatory situations, instead of tissues healing completely, scarring may occur. Scars in the brain, spinal cord, and peripheral nerves may cause neurological dysfunction and permanency of the various symptoms mentioned above. These symptoms do not require anti-inflammatory drugs, for the problem is not one of swelling, but of scarring, but often respond to medications that modify neurological function (viz., antiseizure drugs).

In contrast to the organic, neurological aspects of lupus that physicians and patients must consider are the psychological aspects of the disease, that is, those behavior patterns that have no apparent organic, biochemical, physiological, or immune cause but represent an abnormality of the function of a person's psyche. True, these phenomena are seen in many physically healthy individuals, but they are often aggravated by organic disease (especially of a chronic nature) and by the myriad stresses a chronically ill patient must endure. Learning to recognize and deal with the psychological issues of illness is critical for physician, patient, family, friends, work associates, and others.

Do lupus patients experience psychological problems? Indeed they do! Patients may experience anger and frustration, depression, fatigue, insomnia, headaches, decreased ability to concentrate, memory loss, anxiety (nervousness), hallucinations, disorientation (confusion), hysteria, weakness (loss of vigor), loss of sensation (numbness), "funny sensations," tingling, difficulty breathing, tension, and crying spells.

Compounding the neurological and psychological problems are the hormonal problems that women with lupus often face. Many women have hormonally induced mood swings that coincide with their menstrual cycles. Before the onset of a period, some women become tense, anxious, nervous, weepy, and moody. These fluctuations are associated with salt and water retention (an effect of the change in hormone levels accompanying the menstrual cycle), which results in weight gain, dissatisfaction with one's appearance, and general feelings of discomfort.

The most significant medication that can affect the personality of the lupus patient is prednisone. While it can make one feel good and high, it can cause nervousness and make sleeping difficult, depending on the dosage. It can also cause depression. Other medications are less likely to affect the personality. However, every time a personality changes, the institution of a new medication as a possible cause should be considered.

Recognition of which behavioral symptoms represent organic versus nonorganic causes is critical, for their treatment is very different. How does one distinguish between the four causes (neurological, psychological, hormonal, and drug induced) of personality changes? The hormonal effect is perhaps easiest to recognize. It only occurs in women while they are having menses and is cyclical. A good medical history will usually reveal this pattern. Treatment is directed toward recognition of the problem, reduction of salt intake, perhaps a diuretic, or hormonal regulation of the menstrual cycle.

The physician usually treats a drug-induced psychosis by withdrawing that drug. However, when a particular medication is critical and no substitute is available, one must (temporarily) accept its side effect. The physician should consider adding other medications to counteract the psychological effect of a particular medication (e.g., an antipsychotic to counter the psychosis that may be induced by prednisone).

Differentiation between the organic and nonorganic causes of a change in the psyche is more difficult. Sometimes a history and physical examination will provide the clue. Often, however, tests may differentiate the two. These tests include a spinal tap with examination of the spinal fluid (for cells, excessive amounts of protein, or infectious agents), an EEG (electroencephalogram or brain wave—looking for abnormal patterns or waves), a CT (computerized tomography) scan of the brain (looking for masses, atrophy), PET (positron emission), MRI (magnetic resonance imaging—looking for masses or atrophy), and psychological tests. The tests are mainly performed to detect organic disease. If the tests are normal, by exclusion it is presumed that the symptoms are psychological. Most patients would rather have an abnormal test, an organic cause of their symptoms, than to find none and be told, "It's all in your head." "You're imagining these things." "There's nothing physically wrong with you." "Go see a psychiatrist." These familiar lines are inexcusable from a physician, even when he knows the disorder is functional and nonorganic. However, even though no organic cause of the symptoms may be found, the symptoms are real for the patient, and if the physician is to treat the patient, these symptoms need to be recognized and treated with patience and understanding.

Anger and frustration are commonly experienced by the newly diagnosed lupus patient. Being sick, sensing an irrevocable change, feeling that leading a normal life is an unlikely proposition, the lupus patient is crestfallen. Why me? Why now? Change of any kind is difficult. Loss of health is a cross to bear for the rest of one's life, requiring adaptation and patience. Up to one hundred years ago disease was considered a consequence of psychic or spiritual imbalance. Today we accept illness as just plain bad luck.

Lupus patients feel angry about their loss of independence. When we are young, we feel immortal. We want to travel, try new fashions, form relationships. We escape the bondage of home and adolescence and make our way excitedly into a world that we plan to change for the better. How frustrating to have that enthusiasm come crashing up against the specter of a chronic illness such as lupus. No wonder young lupus patients become depressed. Who wants to be dependent on physicians, medications, or a family member?

Lupus patients are often reluctant to discuss their stressful family life. Family members may put real or imagined pressure on the patient to perform many household chores (dressing, cleaning, shopping, cooking, driving, taking care of children, parents). The chronic fatigue that they often feel may be misbelieved or misinterpreted when they are told, "But you look okay—the doctor said your tests are okay." Spouses may be impatient when the house gets dirty, dinner isn't ready on time, or the children aren't cared for. Patients may want to participate in normal family activities but don't possess the energy. The patient may often be told to stay out of the sun and has to miss out on family activities outdoors.

Low self-esteem is no stranger to dependency, and lupus patients, coping with a markedly changed appearance, indeed are challenged to maintain feelings of self-worth and attractiveness. An obvious facial rash, weight gain, a "moon" face, acne, stretch marks, all chip away at inner confidence. People ask, What's wrong with you? Try to explain in twenty-five words or less what lupus is! It becomes tempting to just stay at home rather than risk the embarrassing stares and questions.

Lupus patients often worry about the future. They have read old medical textbooks that define lupus as "a fatal disease of young women." They worry about imminent death. They know that they have a 90 percent probability of surviving ten years if they have no kidney or brain disease; a 75 percent chance if they do. These medical statistics simply mean after ten years 75 or 90 percent of a large group (hundreds) of lupus patients will be alive—and if one extrapolates from that data, after twenty years most will still be alive! These statistics are considerably more hopeful than twenty years ago, when only 50 percent of patients were expected to live only four years, and after ten years, 90 percent were dead! Nevertheless, patients have a fear of sudden relapse and "dying young." It is vital to remember that as physicians learn more and more about lupus, its treatment improves, and the chances of a normal life expectancy increase. Be positive in your outlook. Tell your friends how happy you are (even though you are not convinced yourself). Dress well. Wear attractive jewelry, stylish clothing. People notice an overall attractiveness rather than a particular defect. If you feel positive about your appearance, people will respond accordingly. Take heart—medications exist that can clear up rashes, and makeup can disguise scars. Happily, fewer patients are experiencing side effects from prednisone to the extent they did years ago. Physicians now recognize those side effects and either adjust dosages to prevent them or employ other medications.

Lupus patients often need special diets, and preparing several dishes at one meal may be necessary. Expensive medications, household help, doctors' visits, costly hospitalizations, all may strain the family budget. The patient's desire for sex may decrease, even while his or her desire for tender loving care, affection, warmth, intimacy, and understanding increases. Having sex may be painful. Desire to please the spouse may conflict with the discomfort it creates. Discuss your sexual relationship with your partner. Feel free to demur, to set limits, to suggest a change in place, time, and position, all requisites for an intimate, pleasurable sexual experience. Do not fear to initiate a sexual relationship by describing what pleases you. Explore. Find ways that can afford both you and your partner sexual satisfaction and pleasure. Some lupus patients may be advised not to have children. This special situation requires in-depth discussion with your spouse and physician.

How understandable, then, is the patient's sense of defeat, and how vital is the family's acceptance, encouragement, support, participation, and love! Recognition of all the factors that can cause stress and discussing them with the physician, a friend, a counselor, or in a support group can redirect psychic energies toward acceptance of how things are and how they can be improved. Focusing on the positive aspects of your life rather than on its stressful components is an essential part of treatment!

The consensus of patients and doctors alike seems to encourage a positive outlook on life, relationships, and self. Maintaining a sense of humor, exchanging ideas with other lupus patients, finding time to pursue hobbies, and sustaining one's religious faith and practices are but a few constructive suggestions. How about posting your own list on your refrigerator door? Needless to say, the physician and the patient's family all play a vital role in supporting and reinforcing that attitude.

28. A Dialogue
Between the Patient and the Physician

H.A.: Dr. Schur, I was diagnosed as having lupus in 1956. Do you think that lupus has changed in thirty years?

P.H.S.: Not really. Lupus hasn't changed, but our knowledge and understanding regarding it has changed considerably. Physicians have been better trained in medical schools and in postgraduate courses to recognize lupus in its early stages and treat it more effectively. Sensitive tests have been developed to aid in the diagnosis of lupus in its earlier and milder forms. Improved tests have also been developed to monitor patient therapy and fine-tune the doses of medications. A better understanding of the mechanisms whereby organs become injured and the development of many new medications and therapies have dramatically improved the prognosis for lupus patients.

H.A.: If the disease hasn't changed, have the physicians who treat it?

P.H.S.: Yes. Improved methods of treatment have helped physicians improve the outlook of the lupus patient from the medical point of view. However, physicians are busier than ever. They have more administrative obligations and must attend many hospital committee meetings. As a result, they often have less time to spend with a patient, and house calls are a thing of the past. Today it is unrealistic and logistically impossible to expect a physician to be all things to all patients!

P.H.S.: What do you personally consider to be potential problems in a patient-physician relationship?

H.A.: First and foremost, a patient needs a physician who inspires confidence and optimism. If there is uncertainty in either the diagnosis or the suggested therapy, a patient will tend to look elsewhere. If a physician is consistently unavailable, the process of disengagement will accelerate. The patient's confidence is eroded if a physician exhibits poor personal habits (e.g., smokes in the offices and is obese and sloppy). By extension, an office that is dirty, cluttered, and disorganized exacerbates the problem. On a personal level, patients are skeptical of a physician who does not examine them for a specific complaint, instead ordering tests and conducting a perfunctory workup. Poor communication is another red flag. Physicians who do not listen, do not give adequate explanations, or are patronizing in attitude or terminology do no service to the relationship.

H.A.: What do *you* personally consider to be potential problems in a physician-patient relationship?

P.H.S.: Hospitalization is often an area of confusion and conflict. Some patients actually want to be hospitalized, "to be taken care of," and think that definitive diagnosis can only be achieved in a hospital. They may feel, correctly, that insurance coverage is often more comprehensive for hospitalizations than for office visits. But most people are unaware that admission often requires approval from an administrator. Many others are reluctant to be hospitalized, and to accept how sick they are, are afraid of dying alone, and are unwilling to leave the warmth of home and family, fearing that spouse and/or children cannot manage without them. All of these concerns need to be addressed. An additional potential problem occurs when a patient does not follow the recommendations of the physician regarding treatment, requesting unwarranted medications (viz, antibiotics for a viral cold, narcotics, tranquilizers, sleeping pills), refusing to diet, exercise, or stop smoking, and persisting in demanding more and more detailed information (yet complaining that medical textbooks are too technical). A related problem arises when the patient actually does know more about a subject than the physician. An honest physician will listen, accepting and appreciating the patient's insights. However, when the patient *thinks* he or she knows more about a particular subject than the physician but really doesn't, conflict can easily result.

Not the least of a physician's problems is the hypochondriac, someone for whom illness is a way of life, a person with a Ferris wheel of complaints, who physician-hops, obsessed with the notion that all the tests and physicians have missed the "real" disease. These individuals are so preoccupied with their health that they develop the illusion of controlling the uncontrollable with vitamins, jogging, dieting, etc. The chronic complainer loses credibility (the "cry wolf" phenomenon) as false alarms eventually fall on the deaf ears of family, friends, and physicians, who grow uneasy at the notion of missing a real illness. Difficult as it may be, the physician's role is to convince these individuals that an annual checkup usually suffices in pinpointing major diseases.

H.A.: What do you think characterizes the ideal physician?

P.H.S.: The perfect physician should be patient, supportive, and understanding of his patient's anxiety. He should have a solution for every problem, a treatment for every complaint. He is an excellent clinician, with a pleasant bedside manner, available day and night, and willing to give his home telephone number to his patients. Many older physicians fit this description well, having gained successful diagnostic and clinical experience over many years.

H.A.: What do you think characterizes the ideal patient?

P.H.S.: The ideal patient comes to the office with an accurate, concise, prioritized written list of symptoms, allocating a reasonable number of problems for each scheduled visit. Patients ideally should be cooperative, that is, be able to express their anxiety, anger, frustrations, and depression, discuss their concerns regarding family, sex, friends, school, job, etc., and adhere to the physician's recommendations. The perfect patient is willing to endure tests and procedures, is accepting of a period of uncertainty until a diagnosis is established, and is willing to suffer the often unpleasant side effects of medication.

H.A.: Assuming that neither physician nor patients fit these ideal descriptions, what do you think are the factors that contribute to a realistic patient-physician relationship?

P.H.S.: Both patient and physician should enjoy a mutual respect, set explicit goals, and share responsibility for achieving those goals. To that end, the physician should instruct the patient to monitor accurately the course of the disease. Patient and physician should view the illness in a similar vein, and recognize that their relationship will alter as other individuals (family members and/or consultants) become involved and as the nature of the illness itself changes, shifting priorities and requiring flexibility on everyone's part.

29. Questions Asked by Lupus Patients
The Physician's Point of View

1. *How can I lose weight?*

Keep a daily log of all that you eat and the number of calories each item contains. Gradually reduce your average daily calorie intake so that you lose one to two pounds per week. Avoid foods with high contents of sugar, fat, oil, and alcohol. Substitute fresh fruit for fattening desserts. Eat three meals per day. Eat slowly. Exercise.

2. *My doctor says I need to be on a low salt diet, but the food tastes so bland. What can I use to make my food taste more interesting?*

Use herbs, spices, lemon juice, herb vinegar, and exotic fruits and vegetables now available in supermarkets.

3. *I often get constipated. I hesitate to use laxatives. What foods offer relief?*

A high-fiber diet will help. Foods rich in fiber include fresh or dried fruit, raw vegetables, and bran (one tablespoon of bran has a fiber content equivalent to one head of lettuce!); prunes and prune juice (high in calories) will also help.

4. *Milk and dairy products make me feel bloated and cause diarrhea; but I was told to take dairy products for their calcium content. What can I use instead?*

You may have lactose intolerance. You can get your calcium needs from yogurt, lactose-reduced milk, hard cheeses, collard and turnip greens, tofu, salmon, and sardines.

5. *I've been told repeatedly by my doctor to exercise. How do I determine what is the best kind of exercise for me?*

In my experiences with lupus patients, aerobics, swimming, jogging, walking, and bicycling may all be good forms of exercise. The best choice is one you like to do. To be of cardiovascular benefit, you must do it three to four times a week for about 20 to 30 minutes. You should try to increase your pulse by about 50 percent and work up a sweat. If you are unaccustomed to exercising, start by doing just a very small amount (say, for just a minute) and then gradually, but steadily, increase what you do.

6. *I was told that people with lupus are very likely to get cancer. Is this true?*

It is definitely not. People with lupus are no more likely to get cancer than anyone else.

7. *I frequently get pain in my chest. Could it be in my heart?*

There are many causes of chest pain. The most common cause is a pulled or sore muscle or tendon in the chest wall. Chest pain can also come from the pleura (the tissue that lines the outer portions of the lungs) or from a pinched nerve from your spine. Muscle pain is usually related to movement and stretching and position and may last minutes or days. Heart pain is not related to motion, usually lasts a few minutes, or longer, may radiate up the neck and/ or down the left arm, and may be accompanied by feelings of nausea and/or weakness. When in doubt, consult your physician.

8. *What can I do to relieve premenstrual cramps, irritability, and weight gain?*

A low-salt diet, diuretics, exercise, nonsteroidal anti-inflammatory drugs (viz. ibuprofen) all seem to help. Stress reduction prior to a period helps control mood swings.

9. *I often get a urinary-tract infection (cystitis) after intercourse. What can I do to help prevent that?*

Urinate after intercourse. To help relieve dysuria, avoid alcohol, coffee, and spicy foods.

10. ***Are people with lupus generally more allergic than other people?***

Lupus patients have no more allergies than the rest of us. A true allergic reaction is one charactreized by a specific immune response (the development of IgE antibodies) and symptoms of either hives, angioedema (a specific swelling of the throat), wheezing, sneezing (but not all sneezes), runny eyes (but not all), and itchy skin (due to local contact dermatitis—not the typical dry, itchy skin). True food allergy (causing hives, anaphylactic shock, explosive diarrhea) is rare, but many patients are intolerant of different foods (keeping a good, accurate journal can pinpoint these). However, lupus patients *are* prone to allergic reactions to drugs and should avoid as many as possible. Many patients with lupus get hives, but not necessarily as part of an allergic reaction.

11. ***If I have severe headaches, does that mean I have migraine headaches?***

A migraine headache is a specific form of so-called vascular headaches caused first by a spasm of blood vessels in or on your head, followed by blood-vessel dilation and local edema. It is only in the later phase that you get a headache. During the spasm phase there may be symptoms of visual, auditory, or sensory disturbances. A severe headache is not necessarily a migraine headache. The most common cause of headaches is tension in the muscles as a response to stress. Other causes of headaches include sinusitis, cervical disc disease, dental problems, and arthritis in the jaw.

12. ***Can large (mega) doses of vitamins harm me?***

Yes! Large doses of vitamin A can cause liver damage, excess vitamin D can cause bone and kidney problems, and too much vitamin B_6 (pyridoxine) can result in nerve damage.

13. ***Will large doses of vitamin C prevent colds?***

Not according to current data.

14. ***I find that I often forget things. Am I losing my mind?***

Probably not. As we get older, we become forgetful. Medication and lupus brain involvement may aggravate this condition. However, most people are not "losing their minds."

15. ***I get a lot of heartburn after many medications. What can I do to relieve it?***

Avoid smoking, chocolate, peppermints, fatty foods, alcohol. Drink milk. Take antacids. If the heartburn persists, consult your physician.

16. *How can I prevent osteoporosis, which I understand is aggravated by taking prednisone?*

Get a minimum of 800 mg of calcium per day (1500 mg if you are a postmenopausal woman). Exercise and avoid smoking and alcohol. Your physician may also prescribe estrogen.

17. *I often hear noises inside my head. Is this a symptom of a brain tumor or a sign of lupus?*

It could represent either a psychological or a neurological problem. Consult your physician for a definitive diagnosis.

18. *I have trouble sleeping at night. What can I do?*

Insomnia has many causes. The most common cause is associated with waking up in the middle of the night and having difficulty falling back to sleep. This form of insomnia is usually caused by anxiety and/or depression. Seek help from a psychiatrist or psychologist. Difficulty in initially falling asleep is another form of insomnia. Heavy meals, coffee, smoking, and alcohol may be the culprits. Light exercise a few hours before retiring, drinking a warm glass of milk, taking a warm bath, and reading a boring book have all been reported to successfully lull one to sleep.

19. *My back often hurts when I bend down or lift groceries. Am I getting a disc problem?*

The most common form of low back pain is weak-muscle strain. The symptoms typically come on after (over) exertion, and there is local pain, usually on one side of your back. Radiation down the leg (sciatica) is rare. A disc may cause foot weakness, lack of sensation in your foot, and bladder, or anal problems. When in doubt, consult a physician. In either case, bed rest should help. You can prevent lumbar strain by regularly doing exercises to strengthen your back. Losing weight so your back has less to carry will obviously help.

20. *Will antibiotics help a cold go away faster?*

Most colds are due to viruses and will not be affected by treatment with antibiotics. In fact, many colds treated with antibiotics may last longer due to complications from taking antibiotics.

21. ***I often wake up in the morning in winter with a headache and a bloody nose. What is this due to?***

You probably have a very dry house. Get a humidifier, use it regularly, and keep it very clean. A humidifier will also help clear up colds and coughs.

22. ***I'm afraid of taking a flu shot for fear of catching the flu. Is this true?***

A flu shot represents a vaccine of killed H. influenza virus. It will not cause the flu (because the viruses are dead), but it will not protect you against the hundred or so other viruses that can cause a cold, upper-respiratory-tract infections, or intestinal flu. However, the vaccine will protect you against the worst virus.

23. ***What is the best way to prevent catching a cold?***

Catching a cold is unavoidable unless one stays completely away from all other people!

24. ***Is there any relationship between lupus and AIDS?***

No! Although they are both immune disorders, the nature of the immune abnormalities is very different.

25. ***Can I catch lupus from someone else?***

No. Lupus is not contagious.

26. ***Can I use a medication after its expiration date?***

No.

27. ***How can I relieve the stress in my life?***

Learn a relaxation technique (viz., meditation). Take a quiet lunch break every day—don't use that hour to do errands. Prioritize your tasks—stick to the list! Take a half day off each week and enjoy a hobby, etc. Learn your limitations, accept them, and live within them. Allow enough time to accomplish each task satisfactorily. Learn to say no—and don't feel guilty about it.

28. ***If I have many of the symptoms of SLE but my tests are negative, what are the chances I really have it or will develop it?***

The chances of having it are considerably less than 1 percent. On the other hand, you may be developing it. It pays, therefore, to have tests repeated periodically (about one to two times per year). If the tests remain negative, it is highly unlikely that you have or will develop SLE.

29. *What is the benefit of plasmaphoresis for the treatment of lupus?*

Plasmaphoresis was advocated as a treatment for all aspects of lupus until recently. Two studies, one done at the National Institutes of Health (NIH) and the other supported by the NIH, have failed to show benefit for lupus patients with either moderate disease or with kidney involvement. Thus, the benefit of this form of treatment is at present somewhat dubious.

30. *Can lupus patients give blood or serve as organ donors?*

No.

31. *Do yeast infections cause lupus?*

Everybody carries yeast organisms in their bodies. In certain situations (viz., certain diseases, including lupus) or by taking prednisone (or immunosuppressives), a yeast infection will develop. However, the presence of yeast organisms in the body neither causes lupus nor immune or allergic disorders.

32. *I lost a lot of hair when my lupus was active. Will my hair grow back?*

Hair loss is common to all of us. Many men—and some women—lose a lot of hair for genetic reasons. Generalized hair loss is often associated with activity of lupus. When the disease quiets down, the hair usually grows back. The patient may also have patches of considerable hair loss, even small areas of baldness (called alopecia areata). If associated with an acute rash (the usual case) and if treated promptly, there is a good likelihood that the hair will grow back. However, if the rash evolves into a scar or the scalp becomes very shiny, chances are that the hair will not grow back in that area. High doses of prednisone can also cause increased generalized hair loss in some people. Fortunately, as the dosage is decreased, hair grows back.

33. *It is possible to adopt children if one has lupus?*

Yes, but there are many factors that must be considered. Are you physically able, emotionally willing, and thoroughly committed to raising children? If your illness is periodically severe or incapacitating, who will care for and help raise the children? Social-service agencies, concerned with properly placing a child for adoption, will question you very carefully regarding these issues. Discuss the pros and cons with your family and your physician before contemplating adoption.

34. *Should I test my children for lupus?*

I recommend against this unless the children have symptoms or signs that would make one suspect lupus. About 10 percent of children of lupus patients will have positive ANA tests or other abnormal immune tests without having or developing lupus. Abnormal tests would only cause a lot of worry. Lupus in children is quite rare.

35. *Can I do anything to prevent lupus in my children?*

No—but hopefully when research finds the cause and a cure, one will be able to prevent transmitting it to offspring.

36. *Are there any laboratory, blood, and/or genetic tests that predict who will develop lupus?*

There are none as yet, but a number of researchers, including myself, are actively pursuing this approach.

37. *What are the chances that I will become handicapped from having lupus?*

If by "handicapped" you mean that you cannot perform a job because of a physicial disability (e.g., paralysis, a deformity to a limb, severe arthritis of a joint), the chances are rare. Most deformities that limit activity can be corrected by surgery. Heavy work must be curtailed, but light work is acceptable. Many employers will help you adapt. Many states have rehabilitation programs to retrain you for the kind of employment best suited to your disability.

38. *Will my rash go away?*

Most lupus rashes will fade. The sooner they are treated, the sooner they will disappear. Rashes that evolve into scars, however, seldom disappear.

39. *If I have lupus, can I get medical and/or life insurance?*

Yes, but it may be difficult. The best, easiest, and cheapest way to obtain insurance is to get a group policy through your (or your spouse's) place of employment or through an organization to which you belong. It may pay to join an organization simply for its lower rates and the lack of a waiting policy or noninsurance status for preexisting conditions. If you are eligible for either, you will still be able to get insurance but may have to pay much higher premiums.

40. *I'm not sure that my physician is doing everything he can for me. When do I seek another medical opinion?*

Often another physician will confirm your doctor's treatment. However, he may provide a new insight that will be useful to you and the management of your lupus. A good physician will not mind a second opinion and will cooperate by giving the consulted physician copies of his records.

41. *Are there any dangers of surgery for a lupus patient?*

The physicial stress of surgery may cause a relapse of lupus. Your physician (not just the surgeon) should monitor you carefully both preoperatively and postoperatively, especially in the week or two following surgery, for signs of a relapse. If you are on prednisone or have recently been on prednisone, your adrenal glands may not adequately respond to the stress of surgery. Consequently, your physician may administer supplemental prednisone (often intravenously) for a few days.

42. *Why do doctors often put lupus patients on Valium?*

Valium is the trade name for the generic drug diazepam. It is often useful for the short-term treatment of anxiety or muscle spasm. It is of no use for depression. Valium can be a habit-forming drug for some susceptible individuals and should therefore be used judiciously.

43. *If I have SLE, do I have to be on prednisone for the rest of my life?*

Not all patients with SLE are treated with prednisone, although many are. Prednisone is given to control the inflammations often accompanying SLE. The dosage varies depending on the organ(s) involved and the severity of the involvement. As the inflammation subsides, the dosage is decreased. As one lowers the dosage, low-grade inflammation often ensues, requiring the continuation of prednisone. Periodically, one should try to eliminate all prednisone. A problem of prednisone therapy is that it suppresses the function of the adrenal gland, which produces cortisone. As the prednisone dosage is gradually reduced (below 5–10 mg/day), the adrenal gland usually starts functioning again. However, depending on age and how long one has been on prednisone, the adrenal gland may not start functioning again properly—in some cases it may never do so. Therefore, as one decreases the dosage of prednisone below 5–10 mg/day one looks for signs of hypoadrenalism (Addison's disease), which include fatigue, low blood pressure, and generalized aches and pains—(sounds like lupus!). To help differentiate the symptoms of lupus and hypoadrenalism, one assesses both adrenal function and lupus activity. If the adrenal function is normal, the lupus is treated (but not necessarily with prednisone). If the adrenal gland is not functioning adequately, one can continue the low-dose prednisone (as a replacement for an inadequately functioning adrenal) and attempt to reduce the dosage, at a future time, once again hoping for natural adrenal function.

44. *Can a lupus patient be a source of infections to others?*

It's unlikely.

45. *What kind of a physician should a lupus patient seek?*

This question usually means: Can a family physician or internist treat lupus, or does one need a specialist? It basically depends on which organs are affected, how severe, the competence of the physician, and the degree of confidence the patient has in the physician. Many patients with mild lupus can be adequately treated by their family physician or internists with periodic visits to a lupus specialist. Patients with a more complicated case should be followed by an internist—and also be seen periodically by a lupus specialist. If the overriding problem is skin related, one should seek a dermatologist; for blood problems, one should see a hematologist; for kidney problems, a nephrologist; for heart problems, a cardiologist; for neurological problems, a neurologist; for psychiatric problems, a psychiatrist; for arthritis, a rheumatologist (whose multiple training in internal medicine and rheumatology qualify him as an expert in lupus diagnosis and treatment).

46. *Can cold weather aggravate my lupus?*

Many lupus patients are sensitive to cold, both indoors and outside. Cold causes painful constriction of susceptible blood vessels, which may manifest as Raynaud's phenomenon of the fingers or toes (characterized by blanching, then patches that are often blue, occasionally purple, and occasionally red in color—it may be painful at any of these stages). Gangrene (blackness of the fingers or toes due to *irreversible* loss of the blood supply) is rare. Capillaries may also be affected by the cold, presenting as livedo reticularis of the arms and/ or legs, and rarely causes serious problems.

47. Can drugs cause lupus?

Certain medications can cause a disease that mimics SLE, which physicians call "drug-induced lupus." It is similar in many respects to SLE but differs significantly in that it tends to affect older individuals, rarely causes renal or CNS manifestations, and does not result in antibodies to DNA or low complement levels. A complete history, thorough physical examination, and laboratory tests can distinguish SLE from drug-induced LE. More importantly, in contrast to SLE, when the drug is stopped, the disease eventually goes away, usually within a few weeks or months. If the symptoms are severe, prednisone may be prescribed. It is very, very rare to go from drug-induced lupus to SLE. Two drugs have been strongly implicatd in drug-induced lupus. About 75 percent of individuals taking procainamide (for heart problems) develop a positive ANA test, and of these about 25 percent develop drug-induced lupus. Therefore, a positive ANA test does not mean you have lupus; it just means you are at increased risk of developing it—therefore, the drug does not have to be stopped if you do not have lupus symptoms. The other drug is hydralazine (used for treatment of hypertension). About 14 percent of such individuals develop drug-induced lupus. About 15 percent of individuals taking isoniazid for the treatment of tuberculosis develop a positive ANA test; none has developed lupus. Other drugs have been suspected of being associated with drug-induced lupus, but this has not been proved.

Can you take these drugs if you have SLE? Yes.

48. Are there any drugs that will make SLE worse?

Penicillin (not synthetic penicillins) and some sulfonamides have been suspected, so it is prudent to avoid their use, if possible.

49. Why do more blacks develop SLE?

We don't know. Interestingly, SLE is more common in American blacks than in African blacks or American Caucasians. These observations suggest that some environmental, social, economic, genetic, or combination of these factors may make American blacks more suseptible.

50. *Does SLE affect Orientals?*

Yes. SLE is relatively common in China, Japan, Malaysia, and Thailand.

51. *What is the treatment of osteoporosis?*

Osteoporosis means thin, fragile bones. The best treatment is prevention, that is, maintaining a good calcium intake (minimum of 800 mg/day) and an exercise program. If one is postmenopausal, one may consider the use of estrogen. Prednisone often produces osteoporosis. Your physician may therefore recommend calcium and vitamin D.

52. *How can I treat diarrhea?*

It is important to know the cause of the diarrhea. It could be due to an infection, food intolerance or allergy, too much roughage, medications, malignancy, lupus. Decreasing the roughage in one's diet and using Kaopectate and/or Alka-Seltzer will help temporarily. If diarrhea persists, notify your physician.

53. *Can stress cause hypertension?*

Yes, but usually only temporarily.

54. *Are there warning signals before having a seizure?*

Some patients will have a warning before a seizure. Symptoms may include abnormal taste, smell, hearing, or sight or sudden changes in mood. Most people who have these symptoms do not develop seizures, but some patients who do experience seizures report having these symptoms shortly before the actual seizure develops.

55. *If one has seizures, should one drive?*

Generally, no. If one has blackout seizures (loss of consciousness), it is not wise to drive. If one is on medication that controls the severity and frequency of the seizures, a neurologist can be consulted who may write a letter to the state bureau of motor vehicles indicating his assessment and approval.

56. *What causes double vision?*

Diplopia (double vision) has many causes, including isolated muscle weakness of a particular ocular muscle (as in severe muscle strain), severe headaches, migraines, seizures, or local eye diseases. When it persists, or occurs often, see your physician.

57. *What causes numbness in the fingers?*

People often confuse numbness (absence of feeling) with tingling (dysesthesia), or a "funny feeling." These sensations result from pressure on the nerves or blood vessels of the arm, wrist, or hand while sleeping or resting. We say that an arm "falls asleep." A few minutes of movement will usually eliminate the feelings. If they persist, it may mean constant pressure on a nerve in the arm, wrist, or hand and may require immediate medical attention.

58. *Is renal disease (nephritis) reversible?*

If the kidneys are inflamed, causing nephritis, loss of protein in the urine with resultant edema, high blood pressure, or uremia may occur. If the inflammation is acute (sudden) and not very severe, prednisone (and occasionally added immunosuppresive drugs such as azathioprine, cyclophosphamide and chlorambucil) will often reverse the inflammation and restore normal kidney function. Control of hypertension is critical in restoring kidney function to 50–100 percent of normal. Obviously, the longer the kidney is inflamed and the less it responds to treatment, the more likely kidney function will remain abnormal. It is important to note that spilling a few grams of protein in the urine does not necessarily indicate active disease, and people can survive forever on 30 percent of normal kidney function. Persistent mild hypertension will not cause problems per se but does increase the risk of heart attack, stroke, and/or decreased kidney function.

59. *How can one differentiate the pain of arthritis from pain due to osteoporosis?*

Arthritis (inflammation of a joint) usually involves painfully swollen joints. Pain in muscles, tendons, and connective tissues does not represent arthritis and usually has other causes. Osteoporosis does not cause any pain, because it simply means "thinning of the bones." Conditions secondary to osteoporosis, for example, a vertebral collapse, may cause severe pain in the back as the collapsed vertebra puts pressure on local nerves. A physician's assessment of what causes pain is needed prior to any course of painkilling treatment.

60. *Why do some skins and/or rashes itch? What can you do about it?*

     Rashes often itch because of a release of histamine and other mediators as part of the local inflammatory response. Treating the inflammation with topical local anti-inflammatory medications (e.g., some form of corticosteroid) will often bring relief. Using an agent that blocks the action of histamine (e.g., an antihistamine) and other mediators may also help. Dry skin (no matter what the cause) will also itch, and taking baths using Alpha-Keri bath oil or its equivalent will afford not only soothing comfort but relief from the itch/scratch cycle. Using a moisturizer or anything with vaseline in it will help if applied often enough. Remember that both heat and air conditioning will dehydrate you and your skin. Humidifiers help counteract dryness.

61. *Should physicians interfere in a family situation?*

     I prefer the word "intervene" rather than "interfere" and feel that a physican can do so if the patient and/or family requests it.

62. *How can a physician help the spouse of a lupus patient?*

     A concerned physician should meet and talk with both the patient and his/her spouse, together and/or separately. Referral of patient and/or spouse to a (lupus) support group is often helpful. Suggested reading material that can be shared and discussed by patients, family members, friends, and physician may also be beneficial.

63. *How can a physician help lupus patients who are in school?*

     The physician should communicate with teachers and school administrators regarding the special needs and possible limitations of the patient, stressing (in this era of AIDS hysteria) that *lupus is not contagious.*

64. *I understand that some mice, dogs, and monkeys can develop lupus. Can one catch lupus from these animals?*

     There is no evidence that lupus can be contracted from these animals.

65. *Can lupus patients have pets?*

     Yes, indeed! A purring cat, a tuneful bird, or a friendly dog can brighten up the home. Owning a pet assuredly means work, but it has its positive reward in a devoted animal and happy children.

The only medical reason for not owning a pet is if the animal has a transmittable disease such as worms, psittacosis, etc.

66. *Why are some of the characteristics of lupus named for animals?*

The association between animals and lupus is ancient as well as modern. Historically, physicians often named diseases after observations in nature. Since some wolves have red faces and wolf bites resemble butterflies, lupus was named for the wolf (*lupus*, in Latin). Butterflies (a more gentle image, to be sure) are commonly associated with lupus because of the configuration of the typical lupus rash across the nose and cheeks. I prefer the symbol of the butterfly because it also represents freedom and beauty, a goal to which lupus sufferers aspire. Today, a meeker animal is associated with lupus. The mouse, whose similar immune defects, similar genetics, and ability to develop lupus within months, is an effective model for testing new therapies.

Glossary

ACROCYANOSIS: Mottled blue discoloration of the skin of the extremities.

ALBUMIN: Protein of human blood serum that may be found in diseases of the kidney.

ANERGY: A condition in which there is no response to an injected antigen.

ANTIBODY: Serum protein made in response to an antigen.

ANTICONVULSANTS: Drugs used to reduce frequency of convulsions.

ANTIGEN: Protein that stimulates formation of antibodies.

ANTINUCLEAR ANTIBODY (ANA) TEST: Blood test to detect antibodies to nuclei.

ARTHRALGIA: Aches and pains in one or many joints.

ARTHRITIS: Inflammation in a joint with heat, swelling, pain, and redness.

ASEPTIC MENINGITIS: Inflammation of the meninges (lining of the brain) that is not due to any (apparent) infectious agent.

ASPIRIN: In 1763, researchers discovered that an extract of the willow bark was effective in relieving the pains of rheumatism. Willow extract owes its therapeutic efficacy to a substance called salicyclic acid, from the Latin name for willow, *salix*. A chemically modified form, acetylsalicylic acid, is marketed under the name of aspirin. Aspirin helps relieve pain and reduce inflammation.

AUTOANTIBODY: Antibody directed against the body's own tissue.

AUTOGENOUS VACCINES: Vaccines made from the patient's own bacteria, as opposed to vaccines made from standard bacterial cultures.

AUTOIMMUNE: Sensitive to one's self; a person's body makes antibodies against some of its own cells.

BASAL METABOLISM TEST: Determines whether the body's metabolism is overactive or underactive.

BASOPHIL: One of the granulated white blood cells.

BIOPSY: Sample of tissue taken for microscopic study.

BLOOD CELL: Three main kinds are recognized: Red blood cells (erythrocytes) carry oxygen and carbon dioxide; white blood cells (leukocytes) help fight infection; platelets (thrombocytes) help prevent bleeding.

B LYMPHOCYTE (B CELL): Lymphocyte that makes antibodies.

BRONCHI: The tubes formed by the division of the windpipe, which convey air to the lung cells.

BUN: Blood urea nitrogen; when the kidneys fail, the BUN rises, as does the uric acid.

BUTTERFLY RASH: Form of double-wing-shaped skin rash around the nose and cheeks highly suggestive of lupus.

CAPILLARIES: Smallest of the blood vessels that connect arteries and veins.

CELL BIOLOGIST: One who studies cell architecture and function.

CELLULAR IMMUNITY: Immunity to an antigen in which the role of cells is predominant.

CHROMOSOME: Rod-shaped bodies in nucleus of cell containing the genes. Their number is constant in each species.

CHRONIC: Lasting for a long period of time.

CNS: Central nervous system.

COLLAGEN DISEASE: Group of diseases characterized by inflammation of the tissues of the musculoskeletal system—rheumatoid arthritis, SLE, scleroderma, Sjögren's syndrome, juvenile rheumatoid arthritis—also usually synonymous with rheumatic disease.

COMPLEMENT PROTEIN: Regulatory molecule of the immune response.

CONNECTIVE TISSUE: Substance that binds the body together, like a body glue. Connective tissue is the most widespread and abundant tissue in the body.

CORTICOSTEROID: Product of adrenal cortex.

CORTISONE: Potent hormone of the adrenal glands, now synthesized as a pure chemical.

COVALENT: Chemical bond formed by the sharing of electrons.

CRYOGLOBULIN: Serum protein(s) that precipitate(s) in the cold.

CUTANEOUS LESIONS: Visible changes in skin that are abnormal; rashes, sores, or scars.

CYTOPLASM: Part of the cell that surrounds its nucleus.

D AND C: Abbreviation for dilatation of the cervix and curettement of the uterus.

DEOXYRIBONUCLEIC ACID (DNA): Basic constituent of genes. Deoxyribonucleic acid is a large, complex molecule composed of sugars and nucleic acids.

DERMATOMYOSITIS: A chronic inflammatory disease of the skin and muscles.

DIPLOPIA: Double vision.

DISCOID LUPUS: Lupus confined to the skin.

DIURETIC: A drug that helps to make more urine.

DROPSY: Swelling of the legs and abdomen that is most often caused by heart failure but can be due to kidney or liver disease.

EKG (OR ECG): Electrocardiogram, a recording of electrical forces from the heart.

ENDOCRINOLOGY: Study of the glands of internal secretion.

ENDOCARDITIS: Inflammation of the inner lining of the heart.

ENZYME: Protein substance that catalyzes a biologic or chemical reaction.

ERYSIPELAS: Contagious, infectious disease of skin and subcutaneous tissue, marked by redness and swelling of affected areas and with constitutional symptoms.

ERYTHEMA NODOSUM: Painful red bumps on the skin; a skin manifestation of several diseases but rarely of lupus.

ERYTHROCYTES: Normal nonnucleated red cells of the circulating blood; the red blood corpuscles.

ESTROGEN: Female hormone produced by the ovaries; it is responsible for secondary sexual characteristics in females and for the preparation of the uterus for implantation of the fertilized egg.

EXACERBATION: Recurrence of symptoms; another word for flare-up.

FALSE-POSITIVE SYPHILIS TEST: There are a number of tests for syphilis, including the Wasserman, RPR, Hinton, and VDRL tests. Some people, including lupus patients, can make antibodies to a lipidlike (fatlike) substance structurally similar to the syphilis organism and consequently develop a false-positive test for syphilis. Therefore they will have a positive test for syphilis without having the disease. This is called a false-positive test for syphilis.

FOXGLOVE: A plant whose leaves resemble fingers.

GALACTOSE: One of the sugars in milk; made of one molecule of lactose and one of glucose.

GASTRIC: Belonging to the stomach.

GASTRIC PARIETAL CELLS: Acid-producing cells of the stomach.

GENE: The biologic unit of heredity located on a particular chromosome.

GENETIC: Pertaining to the genes; the word genetic refers to the property of transmission of parental characteristics to offspring. See DEOXYRIBONUCLEIC ACID

GI SERIES: Gastrointestinal series; an X-ray examination of the esophagus, stomach, and small intestine.

GLOMERULONEPHRITIS: Type of kidney inflammation characterized by involvement of the glomerulus of the kidney.

GM: Genetic markers on human immunoglobulins.

HAPTEN: Chemical that will induce an immune response when coupled to a protein.

HEMATOLOGIST: Specialist in the study of blood.

HEMATURIA: Red blood cells in the urine.

HEMIPARESIS: Paralysis or weakness of one side of the body.

HEMOLYTIC ANEMIA: Condition characterized by a reduction in circulating red blood cells due to increased destruction of the cells by the body.

HEPATITIS: Inflammation of the liver.

HEPATOSPLENOMEGALY: Enlargement of both liver and spleen.

HISTIOCYTE: Tissue macrophage scavenger of cell debris, viruses, and bacteria.

HISTOCOMPATIBILITY ANTIGEN (HLA): Cell-surface protein involved in transplant rejection; HLA proteins are controlled by genes on the sixth chromosome.

HISTOLOGY: Examination of tissue under a microscope as opposed to the gross clinical examination.

HISTOPATHOLOGY: Pathological change in tissues and cells as seen under a microscope.

HORMONE: From the Greek "to excite"; hormones are chemical messengers that excite a response in other tissue.

HYBRIDOMA: Fusion of an antibody-producing cell and a myeloma (tumor) cell that makes a great deal of monoclonal antibody.

HYDANTOIN: An antiseizure medication (Dilantin).

HYDRALAZINE: An antihypertension medication (Apresoline).

HYDROXYCHLOROQUINE (Plaquenil): Antimalarial drug that has also been used as a treatment for lupus.

HYPERSENSITIVITY: Form of allergy generally mediated by antibodies.

HYPOCHONDRIAC: One who has morbid anxiety about health.

IMMUNE COMPLEXES: Specific combination of antibodies with their corresponding antigens.

IMMUNE MEDIATED: Produced by the immune system, that is, antibodies and lymphocytes.

IMMUNE RESPONSE: Response of the body's immune system to antigens.

IMMUNITY: Power to resist infection.

IMMUNOFLUORESCENCE: Special technique of histology using a fluorescent dye to mark antibody or immune process taking place at a given site in the tissue.

IMMUNOGEN: Any substance capable of eliciting immunity.

IMMUNOLOGIC TOLERANCE: Specific suppression of immunity to antigens. Normally, we do not make antibodies to our own antigens, such as our own cells, tissue proteins, or DNA.

INFECTIOUS MONONUCLEOSIS: A self-limited, infectious disease that presents, with fever, upper respiratory symptoms and swelling of the lymph nodes due to the Epstein-Barr virus.

INTERSTITIAL PNEUMONITIS: Atypical pneumonia either due to a virus or unknown factors.

ITP: Idiopathic thrombocytopenic purpura. A condition of various causes, including SLE, characterized by very low platelet counts.

IVP: Intravenous pyelogram, an X-ray examination of the kidneys.

LE CELL TEST: The LE cell is a white blood cell that has swallowed (phagocytosed) the nucleus of another white blood cell; the latter appears as a blue-staining spot inside the first cell.

LEUKOPENIA: Low white-cell count.

LIVEDO RETICULARIS: Reddish blue netlike mottling of skin of extremities due to spasm of capillaries and/or small arteries.

LUPUS PROFUNDUS: Panniculitis; inflammation of subcutaneous fat.

LYMPHOKINE: Proteins made by monocytes and lymphocytes that affect other lymphocytes.

LYMPHS (LYMPHOCYTES): White blood cells.

LYSE: To produce disintegration of cells, causing them to release their contents.

MACROPHAGES: Tissue cells that eat antigens, complexes, bacteria, and viruses.

MAJOR HISTOCOMPATIBILITY MARKER: See HISTOCOMPATIBILITY ANTIGEN.

MEPACRINE (quinacrine, Atabrine): Antimalarial drug also used in the treatment of lupus.

METABOLISM: Series of chemical processes in the living body by which life is maintained.

METHYLPREDNISOLONE: Synthetic form of corticosteroid.

MIXED CONNECTIVE TISSUE DISEASE: Consisting of two or more of the connective tissue diseases, for example, lupus, polymyositis, scleroderma.

MOTOR APHASIA: Loss of speech due to a brain defect affecting the muscles of speech.

MUCOSAL IMMUNITY: Immunity of the gastrointestinal, genitourinary, or bronchial tracts.

MYASTHENIA GRAVIS: Disease in which antibodies block nerve impulses being properly transmitted to the muscle cells; as a result, muscles all over the body become weak.

MYOCARDITIS: Inflammation of the heart.

NAPROXEN (Naprosyn): One of several nonsteroidal anti-inflammatory drugs (NSAIDs).

NATURAL KILLER CELL: Cell that kills (lyses) other cells.

NEPHRITIS: Inflammation of the kidney.

NEUROSIS: A disorder of the mental constitution.

NEUTROPHIL: Granulated white blood cell.

NICONACID: Swiss-French trademark for preparation of nicotinic acid.

NICOTINAMIDE (NIACINAMIDE): Amide of 3-Pyridinecarboxylic acid (niacin); its chemical formula is $C_6H_6N_2O$). A form of niacin.

NOXIOUS STIMULUS: Unpleasant or damaging substance or influence.

NUCLEIC ACID: Pertaining to DNA and/or RNA.

NUCLEOSIDE: One of the four types of building blocks of DNA.

NUCLEUS: That part of a cell containing DNA.

PANTOTHENIC ACID: Constituent of the vitamin B complex.

PATHOGENIC: Producing disease or undesirable symptoms.

PATHOLOGIST: Expert in pathology.

PATHOLOGY: Branch of medicine that deals with changes in tissues or organs of the body caused by or causing disease.

PELLAGRA: Deficiency of niacin (one of the B vitamins) that causes diarrhea, dermatitis, and dementia (loss of intellectual function).

PENICILLIN: An antibiotic.

PERIARTERITIS NODOSA: Form of vasculitis (inflammation of blood vessels) affecting small and medium-sized blood vessels; may be caused by hepatitis.

PERIPHERAL NEUROPATHY: Malfunction of nerves of the arms and legs.

PERITONITIS: Inflammation of the lining of the abdomen.

PERNICIOUS ANEMIA: Condition caused by vitamin B_{12} deficiency and characterized by anemia and spinal-cord abnormalities.

PHAGOCYTE: Cell (macrophage, monocyte) that ingests other cells or debris.

PHAGOCYTOSED NUCLEAR MATERIAL: White cells that have ingested nuclei from other cells.

PHAGOCYTOSIS: Ingestion by phagocytes of foreign or other particles or of cells harmful to the body.

PHLEBITIS: Inflammation of a vein.

PHOTOSENSITIVITY: Sensitivity to light energy.

PLACEBO: Inactive substance given to a patient either for its pleasing effect or as a control in experiments with an active drug.

PLASMA: Fluid portion of the blood in which the blood cells float.

PLASMA CELL: Tissue cell that makes antibodies.

PLEURISY (PLEURITIS): Inflammation of the membrane between the chest wall and the lung.

POLYARTERITIS: Same as periarteritis nodosa.

POLYARTHRITIS: Inflammation of several joints at the same time.

POLYMORPHONUCLEAR LEUKOCYTE: Same as neutrophil.

PREDNISONE: Chemical name for a synthetic steroid hormone.

PROCAINAMIDE: A medication used to treat arrhythmias of the heart (Pronestyl).

PROGESTERONE: Female hormone produced during pregnancy that is primarily responsible for maintaining pregnancy and developing the mammary glands.

PROPERDIN: One of the complement proteins.

PROSTAGLANDIN: The prostaglandins are a large family of pharmacologically active lipids (fats) widely distributed in mammalian tissue.

PROTEINS: Building blocks of the body; regulators of cell function.

PROTEINURIA: Protein in the urine.

PSYCHOSOMATIC: Relationship of the body to the mind; having bodily symptoms from mental rather than physical disorder.

PTOSIS: Drooping of an eyelid.

PULMONARY: Pertaining to the lungs.

PUPILLARY REACTION: Constriction or dilation of the pupil of the eye in response to light.

PURPURA: Rupture of blood vessels with leakage of blood into the tissues.

RAYNAUD'S PHENOMENON: Spasm of arteries to fingers and toes causing them to turn white and later blue and/or red. Pain may accompany these skin-color changes. Gangrene rarely ensues.

RENAL: Pertaining to the kidneys.

RHEUMATOID ARTHRITIS: Chronic inflammatory disease of the joints.

RHEUMATOID FACTORS: Antibodies to gamma globulin found in most patients with rheumatoid arthritis; may also be found in the serum of patients with any chronic inflammatory condition, including lupus.

RNA: Ribonucleic acid is a large, complex molecule composed of sugars (which differ from the sugars of DNA) and nucleic acid. Functions to translate DNA messages into making proteins, etc.

SCLERODERMA: "Hard skin," a chronic connective tissue disease characterized by leathery thickening of the skin; the internal organs may also be involved.

SEDIMENTATION RATE (ESR): The rate at which red blood cells settle to the bottom of a test tube. Levels correlate with the degree of inflammation.

SEROSITIS: Inflammation of lining tissue—usually either pleurisy, pericarditis, or peritonitis.

SERUM: Blood from which cells and fibrin have been removed.

SERUM CREATININE LEVELS: Creatinine is a substance normally found in blood in low concentration, since it is eliminated from the serum by the kidneys; high serum creatinine levels indicate malfunction of the kidneys.

SERUM PROTEIN: Any protein in the serum.

SIDE EFFECT: Adverse effect produced by a drug.

SJÖGREN'S SYNDROME: Autoimmune disease characterized by dryness of the mouth, eyes, and skin.

SPONTANEOUS REMISSION: Marked improvement in a disease that occurs without medical intervention.

STREPTOCOCCUS: Bacterium that may cause sore throats (strep throat), skin infections (erysipelas, scarlet fever)—that may result in nephritis or rheumatic fever (inflammation of the heart and joints).

SUBACUTE CUTANEOUS LUPUS ERYTHEMATOSUS: Lupus with characteristic skin lesions.

SULFADIAZINE: Anti-infective drug; one of the sulfonamides.

TELANGIECTASIA: Dilated capillaries and small arteries, often appearing on the face in normals but frequently individuals with lupus, hypertension, trauma, and other conditions. They represent a scar, not an inflamed lesion.

TESTIS: Synonym for testicle, the male reproductive organ responsible for production of sperm cells.

TETRACYCLINE: An antibiotic.

THERAPEUTICS: Study of the action of drugs and their application to the treatment of disease.

THERMAL BURNS: Injury to tissue cased by heat.

THROMBOCYTOPENIA: Reduction of circulating platelets.

THYROID GLAND: Gland located in the neck that produces thyroxine.

THYROIDITIS: Inflammation of the thyroid gland.

THYROXINE: Substance that affects the body's metabolic rate.

TITER: Highest dilution of a serum that gives a reaction with a substance.

T LYMPHOCYTE (T CELL): Lymphocyte involved in cellular immunity.

TOLERANCE TO NUCLEIC ACID ANTIGENS: Unresponsiveness to nucleic acids.

ULTRAVIOLET (UV) RADIATION: Radiation of energy of wavelengths 200–290 nm (UVC); 290–320 nm (UVB); 320–400 nm (UVA).

UV-ALTERED DNA: DNA molecules disrupted by UV energy, causing them to become antigenic.

UREMIA: Marked kidney insufficiency characterized by nausea, vomiting, and even coma or convulsions, and a urine odor to the breath.

VASCULITIS: Inflammation of the blood vessels.

VASOMOTOR: Pertaining to control of the tone of the blood vessels; contraction of blood vessels causes blanching, whereas relaxation causes blushing.

VIRAL ETIOLOGY: Caused by a virus.

VIRAL PROTEIN: One of several constituents that make up a virus particle.

References
General Medical

Aladjem, H. 1985. *Understanding lupus: What it is, how to treat it, how to cope with it.* New York: Charles Scribner's Sons.

Bergstresser, P. R. 1986. Ultraviolet B radiation induces "local immunosuppression." *Curr. Probl. Dermatol.* 15:205–18.

Cohen, P., and Gardner, F. H. 1966. Sulfonamide reactions in SLE. *JAMA* 197:817–19.

Crichton, M. 1970. *Five patients: The hospital explained.* New York: Alfred A. Knopf, p. 162.

Daynes, R. A., Samlowski, W. E., Burnham, D. K., Gahring, L. C., and Roberts, L. K. 1986. Immunobiological consequences of acute and chronic UV exposure. *Curr. Probl. Dermatol.* 15:176–94.

Dubois, E. L. 1978. *Lupus erythematosus.* Los Angeles: University of Southern California Press.

Kripke, M. L. 1986. Photoimmunology: The first decade. *Curr. Probl. Dermatol.* 15:164–75.

Lahita, R. G., ed. 1986. *Systemic lupus erythematosus.* New York: John Wiley and Sons.

Lee, S. L., and Siegal, M. 1968. Drug-induced lupus erythematosus. In *Drug-induced diseases,* eds. L. Meyler and H. M. Peck. Amsterdam: Excerpta Medica Foundation, pp. 239–48.

Lewy, A. J., et al. 1985. Supersensitivity to light: Possible trait marker for manic-depressive illness. *Am. J. Psychol.* 142:725–27.

Popoff, L., Popchristoff, M., and Batchvaroff, B. 1939. Lupus erythemateux et troubles de la secretion gastrique. *Bull. Soc. Franc. Dermatol. Syph.* 46:1038–41.

Rogers, M. 1985. Is sunlight good for depression? *Lupus News* 5:1–4.

Ropes, M. W. 1976. *Systemic lupus erythematosus.* Cambridge, Mass.: Harvard University Press.

Rothfield, N. F. 1975. Systemic lupus erythematosus. *Clin. Rheum. Dis.* 1: December.

Schur, Peter H., ed. 1983. *Clinical management of systemic lupus erythematosus.* New York: Grune & Stratton.

————. 1986. Systemic lupus erythematosus. In *Rheumatology and immunology.* 2nd ed. A. S. Cohen and J. C. Bennet, eds. Orlando, Florida: Grune & Stratton, pp. 247–56.

Ti nei ching su won, Huang. 1966. *The yellow emperor's classic of internal medicine.* Chapters 1–34 translated from the Chinese with an introductory study of Ilza Veith. Berkeley: University of California Press, p. 184.

Tuffanelli, D. 1986. *Photosensitivity and lupus erythematosus.* San Francisco: Bay Area Lupus Foundation.

Winchester, R. J., guest ed. 1978. New directions for research in systemic lupus erythematosus. *Arthritis Rheum.* 21:51–524.

Wurtman, R. J., Baum, M. J., and Potts, J. T., Jr., eds. 1985. The medical and biological effects of light. *Ann. NY. Acad. Sci.* 453:1–408.

PSYCHOLOGICAL ASPECTS

Allen, T. W., and Glicksman, M. 1986. Psychologic involvement in systemic lupus erythematosus: A psychometric approach. *Clin. Rheum.* 4:64–74.

Atkinson, H. 1982. *Women and fatigue.* New York: Putnam.

Benson, H. 1986. The relaxation response. How to lower blood pressure, cope with pain, and reduce anxiety in 20 minutes a day. *Harvard Med. Alumni Bull.* 60:33–35.

Besedovsky, H. O., del Rey, A. E., and Sorkin, E. 1983. What do the immune system and the brain know about each other? *Immunol. Today* 4:342–46.

Bradley, L. A. 1985. Psychological aspects of arthritis. *Bull. Rheum. Dis.* 35:1–12.

Hall, N. R., and Goldstein, A. L. 1986. Thinking well. The chemical links between emotions and health. *The Sciences*.26:34–40.

Kinash, R. G. 1985. Needs and relationships of patients with systemic lupus erythematosus. *Clin. Rheum.* 3:227–31.

Liang, M. H. et al. 1983. The psychosocial impact of systemic lupus erythematosus and rheumatoid arthritis. *Arthritis Rheum.* 27:13–19.

Markowitz, R. 1986. Your self image and how lupus impacts on your sexuality. *Minn. News and Notes.* 56:1–6.

Pitzele, S. F. 1985. *We are not alone. Learning to live with chronic illness.* Minneapolis: Thompson and Company.

Rogers, M. 1985. Could Lupus affect the brain? Could this be happening to me? *Lupus News* 5:10.

DOCTOR-PATIENT RELATIONSHIP

Auden, W. H. 1969. "The art of healing (in memoriam Davis Protetch, M.D., 1923–1969)." *New Yorker,* September 27, p. 38.

Carson, Rachel. 1962. *Silent spring.* Greenwich, Conn.: Fawcett, p. 170.

Cousins, N. 1985. How patients appraise physicians. *N. Engl. J. Med.* 313:1422–24.

Doctors and patients—are they really communicating? 1986. *The Internist.* August. (The whole issue is devoted to this subject.)

Dubos, R. 1965. *Man adapting.* New Haven, Conn.: Yale University Press.

————. 1971. *Mirage of Health.* New York: Harper and Row, p. 167.

Kroenke, K. 1986. Ambulatory care: Practice imperfect. *Am. J. Med.* 80:339–43.

Lanier, B. G., and Lewis, K. 1986. *The physician-patient relationship.* Atlanta: Lupus Horizons.

Leslie, A. 1954. *Am. J. Med.* 16:854–62.

McCord, D. 1963. *The fabrick of man, fifty years of the Peter Bent Brigham.* Boston: Published for the hospital by the Fiftieth Anniversary Celebration Committee, p. 3.

O'Connor, F. 1967. *Everything that rises must converge.* Introduction by Robert Fitzgerald. New York: Farrar, Straus and Giroux.

Peabody, F. W. 1930. *Doctor and patient.* New York: Macmillan.

Potts, M., Weinberger, M., and Brandt, K. D. 1984. Views of patients and providers regarding the importance of various aspects of an arthritis treatment program. *J. Rheum.* 11:71–75.

Uncertainty in medical care: Are we coping? 1986. *The Internist* 27:Jan. (The whole issue is devoted to this subject.)

MISCELLANEOUS

Many publications of the Lupus Foundation of America and their chapters, the Arthritis foundation, and the National Institutes of Health.

Lupus Foundation of America, Inc.

CONSTITUENT CHAPTERS

Alabama

LFA, Birmingham Chapter
924-A 26th Street
Birmingham, AL 35205
Ms. Earlene Hall
(205) 252-3068

Montgomery Chapter, LFA
P.O. Box 11507
Montgomery, AL 36111
Ms. Ainsley Norris, RN
(205) 288-3032

Alaska

LFA, Alaska Chapter
P.O. Box 211336
Anchorage, AK 99521-1336
Ms. Marilyn Davidson
(907) 338-6332

Arizona

LFA, Greater Arizona Chapter
6010 W. Northern Ave., Suite 304
Glendale, AZ 85301
Ms. May Markley
(602) 842-4994

Arkansas

Fort Smith Chapter
P.O. Box 3863
Fort Smith, AR 72913
Ms. Mary Crawford
(501) 452-3349

California

Bay Area L.E. Foundation, LFA
265 Meridian Avenue
Suite 5A
San Jose, CA 95126
Ms. Jo Dewhirst
(408) 280-7616

Greater Los Angeles Chapter
1101 South Robertson Blvd.
Los Angeles, CA 90035
Ms. Nancy Horn
(213) 278-5878 (home)
(213) 278-9530

LFA, Greater San Gabriel Valley
    Chapter
P.O. Box 251
West Covina, CA 91793
Mr. John Nelson
(800) 544-9779

Colorado

Lupus Foundation of Colorado, LFA
P.O. Box 22621
Denver, CO 80222
Mr. Robert G. Bangert, President
(303) 758-0538 or 670-1972

Connecticut

LFA, Connecticut Chapter
P.O. Box 7-T
West Hartford, CT 06107
Mr. Al Palmero
(203) 521-9151

Florida

Dade/Broward Lupus Foundation,
  LFA
P.O. Box 4131
Miami, FL 33169-4131
Ms. Iris Olivia, President
(305) 458-5700 or (Ms. Rawitz 441-
  1144)

LFA, Florida Big Bend Chapter
4909 Easy Street
Tallahassee, FL 32303
Ms. Eleanor Turner
(904) 562-5569

LFA, Palm Beach County Chapter
P.O. Box 948
West Palm Beach, FL 33402
Ms. Kate Schneider (305) 968-8827

Lupus Foundation of Florida
12392 Coriander Drive
Orlando, FL 32821
Ms. Sandy Swift

LFA, Pensacola Chapter
P. O. Box 17841
Pensacola, FL 32522-7841
Mrs. Barbara Ward (904) 478-0163
(904) 434-4551

North Florida Chapter, LFA
P.O. Box 10486
Jacksonville, FL 32207
Mr. Bill Luke
(904) 396-5164
(904) 389-4581 (home)

Suncoast Chapter, LFA
P.O. Box 1994
Largo, FL 33540
Ms. Laurie Colburn
(813) 536-8524

LFA, Inter-Coastal Chapter
Star Route 1, Box 2
Bunnell, FL 32017
Ms. Monica Stua, President (904)
  439-3898
Mr. John McNeeley (904) 437-3505

LFA, Tampa Chapter
305 South Hyde Park Avenue
Tampa, FL 33606
Mrs. Lisa Jorda
(813) 253-0620
(813) 877-3628

Georgia

LFA, Augusta Chapter
P.O. Box 5125
Augusta, GA 30906
Ms. Georgia Alsbrook
(404) 790-5605

LFA, Columbus Chapter
3911 Steam Mill Road, #J-11
Columbus, GA 31907
Ms. Autherine Lee
(404) 689-5795

LFA, Greater Atlanta Chapter
2814 New Spring Road, Suite 215
Atlanta, GA 30339
Ms. Bea Brandenstein, Director

Ms. Carla Roby, President (404) 432-9675
(Office Hours: 9:00 A.M—3:00 P.M.)

LFA, Savannah Chapter
Route 1, Box 228, Lot 1
Bloomingdale, GA 31302
Ms. Patsy Hutcheson
(912) 748-5892

Illinois

LFA, Illinois Chapter
P.O. Box 812
Chicago, IL 60642
Ms. Nancy Walsh
(312) 779-3181

LFA, Danville Chapter
322 East 13th Street
Danville, IL 61832
Ms. Alice M. Peck
(217) 446-7672

Indiana

Indiana Lupus Foundation, LFA
2701 E. Southport Rd.
Indianapolis, IN 46227
Ms. Betty Lauterbach
(317) 783-6033

LFA, Northeast Indiana Chapter
P.O. Box 12736
54011 Keystone Drive, Suite 205
Fort Wayne, IN 46853
Mr. Jerry Young
(219) 482-8205

Northwest Indiana Lupus Chapter,
  LFA
3819 West 40th Ave.
Gary, IN 46408
Ms. Phyllis Simko
(219) 980-4826

Iowa

LFA, Iowa Chapter
P.O. Box 1723
Ames, IA 50010
Ms. Cindy Kruckenberg
(515) 232-3083

Kansas

LFA, Wichita Chapter
P.O. Box 16094
Wichita, KS 67216
Ms. Delwin Dorsey
(316) 524-4973

Kentucky

Lupus Foundation of Kentuckiana
2210 Goldsmith Lane, #209
Louisville, KY 40218
Mr. Gary Hayden
(502) 459-6554

Louisiana

LFA, Cenla Chapter
P.O. Box 12565
Alexandria, LA 71315-2565
Ms. Barbara Terry
(318) 473-0125

Louisiana Lupus Foundation, LFA
7732 Goodwood Blvd., #B
Baton Rouge, LA 70806
Ms. Pat Picard
(504) 927-8052

LFA, Shreveport Chapter
1961 Bayou Drive
Shreveport, LA 71105
Ms. Rosemary Cole
(318) 861-2838

LFA, Northeast Louisiana Chapter
P.O. Box 7693
Monroe, LA 71201

Mrs. Ben Davis
(318) 388-3731

Maine

Lupus Group of Maine, LFA
P.O. Box 8168
Portland, ME 04104
Mr. Richard Sevigny
(207) 774-9219
(207) 871-9014

Maryland

Maryland Lupus Chapter, LFA
12 West 25th Street
Baltimore, MD 21218
Mr. Raymond J. Baginski
(301) 366-7272

Massachusetts

LFA, Massachusetts Chapter
215 California Street
Newton, MA 02158
Dr. Tamara Bethel, Executive
   Director
Ms. Henrietta Aladjem, President
(617) 523-8266

Michigan (All Areas)

Michigan Foundation, LFA (State
   Chapter)
19001 East Eight Mile Road
East Detroit, MI 48021
(313) 775-8310

Minnesota

LFA, Minnesota Chapter
640 11th Avenue South
Hopkins, MN 55343
Ms. Corrine Muller, Office Manager
(612) 933-4137

Mississippi

LFA, Central Mississippi Chapter
600 South Pear Rd., Apt. 161
Ridgeland, MS 39157
Ms. Kathleen Thornton
(601) 865-9297

Missouri

LFA, Kansas City Chapter
10804 Fremont
Kansas City, MO 64134
Ms. Myrtie Gourley
(816) 454-1303 (Hotline)
(816) 761-2674 (Home)

Missouri Chapter, LFA
8420 Delmar Blvd., #LL1
St. Louis, MO 63124
Ms. Suzanne C. Pfeffer
(314) 432-0008

Ozark Lupus Chapter, LFA
1814 West Katelle
Springfield, MO 65897
Mrs. Ruth Johnson
(417) 887-1560

Montana

LFA, Montana Chapter
3308 Lower River Road #40
Great Falls, MT 59405
Ms. Ruby Peterson
(406) 454-1116

Nebraska

LFA, Omaha Chapter
P.O. Box 14036
Omaha, NE 68124
Mr. William A. Lorenz
(402) 333-9128

LFA, Western Nebraska Chapter
R. R. 2
No. Platte, NE 69101
Ms. Janet Johnson, President
(308) 532-7249

Nevada

LFA, Las Vegas Chapter
2217 Santa Rosa Drive
Las Vegas, NV 89104
Ms. Patricia Mahoney, President
(702) 369-0474

LFA, Northern Nevada Chapter
480 Galletti Way, #14
Sparks, NV 89431
Ms. Fran Schilingheyde, President
(702) 323-2444

New Hampshire

New Hampshire Lupus Fdn., LFA
P.O. Box 658
Durham, NH 03824
Mr. Thomas Mullin
(603) 868-1274 (home)
(603) 424-5668

New Jersey

LFA, South Jersey Chapter
P.O. Box 2101
Cherry Hill, NJ 08034
Ms. Peggy Ziegler
(609) 354-1234

Lupus Foundation of New Jersey,
  LFA
P.O. Box 320
287 Market Street
Elmwood Park, NJ 07407
Ms. Marilyn Calderaro
(201) 791-7868
Note: Contact this chapter for North
  Jersey groups.

New York

LFA, Brooklyn Chapter
Note: Temporarily contact Long
  Island/Queens chapter.

LFA, Central New York Chapter
P.O. Box 176
Liverpool, NY 13088
Ms. Pam Nybo, President
(315) 451-3305

LFA, Genessee Valley Chapter
P.O. Box 251
West Henrietta, NY 14586
Ms. Caroline Turner
(716) 334-3230

LFA, Long Island/Queens Chapter
1602 North Bellmore Avenue
Bellmore, NY 11710
Ms. Doris Shaer
(516) 783-3370

LFA, Marguerite Curri Chapter
P.O. Box 853
Utica, NY 13503
Mrs. Angela LoConti
(315) 732-4291

LFA, Northeastern New York
  Chapter
126 State Street
Albany, NY 12207
Ms. Penny Dykeman-Apple
(518) 465-3603

LFA, Rockland/Orange County
  Chapter
14 Kingston Drive
Spring Valley, NY 10977
Ms. Martha MacRobbie, President
(914) 354-0372

LFA, Westchester County Chapter
26 Vineyard Avenue

Yonkers, NY 10703
Ms. Patricia Guidice

LFA, Western New York Chapter
205 Yorkshire Road
Tonawanda, NY 14150
Ms. Honi Kurzeja
(716) 835-7161

New York Southern Tier Chapter
410 Press Building
19 Chenango Street
Binghamton, NY 13901
Ms. Judith L. Jones
(607) 772-6522

SLE Foundation, LFA
95 Madison Avenue
Suite 1402
New York, NY 10016
Ms. Susan Golick
(212) 685-4118

North Carolina

Blue Ridge Chapter, LFA
29 Kingswood Estates
Lenoir, NC 28645
Mr. Tim Story
(704) 758-5870

LFA, Charlotte Chapter
2401 Thornridge Road
Charlotte, NC 28226
Ms. Cheryl Heard, President
Ms. Susie Morrison
(704) 399-3761

LFA, Raleigh Chapter
P.O. Box 10171
Raleigh, NC 27605
Mr. Billy Burch
(919) 782-4112

LFA, Western North Carolina
   Chapter

90 Westgate Shopping Center
Asheville, NC 28806
Ms. Joan R. Perez
   home:
   Rt. 3, Box 305
   Candler, NC 28715
   (704) 665-2282
(704) 254-4112

LFA, Winston Triad Chapter, NCLF
   Chapter
2841 Foxwood Lane
Winston Salem, NC 27103
Ms. Ruth Banbury
(919) 768-1493

Ohio

LFA, Akron Area Chapter
501 Market Street
Akron, OH 44303
Ms. Dorothy Arbogast
(216) 535-3761

LFA, Columbus, Marcy Zitron
   Chapter
5180 East Main
Columbus, OH 43213
Mrs. Gail Brunson
(614) 267-0811

LFA, Dayton Chapter
5181 Pundt Road
Lewisburg, OH 45338
Ms. Rose Bower
(513) 962-2887

LFA, Greater Cleveland Chapter
P.O. Box 22319
Cleveland, OH 44122-0319
Mrs. George Sagaris
(216) 531-6563

Northwest Ohio Lupus Chapter
1615 Washington Avenue

Findley, OH 45840
Ms. Rosemary Cook
(419) 422-9180

LFA, Stark County Chapter
P.O. Box 1038
Massillon, OH 44648
Ms. Lucille Elbert
(216) 833-4811

LFA, Youngstown Chapter
4196 Adeer Drive
Canfield, OH 44406
Ms. Mary Gentile (216) 779-1853
   (home)
(216) 743-5877

Oklahoma

Oklahoma Lupus Association, LFA
6521 NW 30th Terrace
Bethany, OK 73008
Mrs. Jane Bozarth, Director
(405) 495-8787

Tulsa Chapter, Oklahoma Lupus
   Association, LFA
P.O. Box 55174
Tulsa, OK 74155
Ms. Coral Waters
(918) 835-5483

Pennsylvania

Lupus Alert, LFA
P.O. Box 8
Folsom, PA 19033
Mr. Ron Guy
(215) 532-6771

LFA, Delaware Valley Chapter
248 Kalos Street
Philadelphia, PA 19128
Ms. Ruth Zeit
(215) 483-5445

Lupus Foundation of Philadelphia,
   LFA
5415 Claridge Street
Philadelphia, PA 19124
Ms. Goldie Simon
(215) 743-7171

LFA, Western Pennsylvania Chapter
3380 Boulevard of the Allies
Pittsburgh, PA 15213
Ms. Gretchen Klindworth
(412) 647-3676

LFA, Northwestern Pennsylvania
   Chapter
P.O. Box 10814
Erie, PA 16514-0814
Ms. Gladys Smith
(814) 899-6263

Pennsylvania Lupus Foundation, LFA
P.O. Box 264
Wayne, PA 19087-0264
Mr. Richard Thomson
(215) 477-7020

LFA, Northeast Pennsylvania Chapter
433 Madison Avenue
Jermyn, PA 18433
Ms. Mary Jones
(717) 876-4897

Rhode Island

LFA, Rhode Island Chapter
#8 Fallon Avenue
Providence, RI 02908
Ms. Barbara Arditte, President
Ms. Jackie Kemble, Executive
   Director
(401) 421-7227

South Carolina

LFA, South Carolina Chapter
P.O. Box 7511
Columbia, SC 29202
Ms. Barbara Bradshaw, Dir.
(803) 794-1000

Tennessee

LFA, East Tennessee Chapter
5612 Kingston Pike, #5
Knoxville, TN 37919
Mr. Don Kidd
(615) 584-5215

LFA, Memphis Area Chapter
5117 Scrivener Dr.
Memphis, TN 38134
(901) 377-2555
Ms. Dorothy Fincher (901) 388-2090
   (home)

Mountain Empire Chapter, LFA
3132 Memorial Blvd.
Kingsport, TN 37664
Doug & Shirley Newton
(615) 246-5178 (chapter)
(615) 247-8881 (office)

Texas

El Paso Lupus Foundation, LFA
9348 Dyer Street, #F
North Park Mall
El Paso, TX 79924
Ms. Sandi Yerby
(915) 755-8374 or 755-9585

LFA, Dallas Chapter
P.O. Box 740005
Dallas, TX 75374-0005
Ms. Sandra Niell
(214) 289-2344

LFA, Houston Chapter
3100 Timmons Lane, #100

Houston, TX 77027
Ms. Catherine Thomas
(713) 965-0034

San Antonio Lupus Foundation, LFA
McCullough Medical Center
4118 McCullough Avenue, #19
San Antonio, TX 78212-1905
Ms. Betty Hickey
(512) 824-1344

Utah

LFA, Northern Utah Chapter
385 24th Street, #800
Ogden, UT 84401
Ms. Eve C. Baird
(801) 621-3748

Vermont

LFA, Vermont Chapter
P.O. Box 209
South Barre, VT 05670
(802) 479-2854 (home)
Mr. David Stefaniak
(802) 479-2326

Virginia

LFA, Central Virginia Chapter
P.O. Box 14507
Richmond, VA 23221-0507
Ms. Dela Hunter
(804) 262-9622

LFA, Eastern Virginia Chapter
7404 Oceanfront
Virginia Beach, VA 23451
(804) 422-2862
Ms. Jan Dort, President
(804) 498-3721

Peninsula Lupus Chapter, LFA
P.O. Box 9341
Hampton, VA 23670
Ms. Bonnie Bocrie

(804) 596-7000
(804) 596-6858

West Virginia

LFA, Kanawha Valley Chapter
P.O. Box 8274
South Charleston, WV 25303
(304) 340-3517

Lupus Foundation of West Virginia,
  LFA
4 Flemming Street
Shinnston, WV 26431
Ms. Mary Louise Menrodez
(304) 592-0015

Washington, D.C.

Lupus Foundation of Greater
  Washington, LFA
7297-D Lee Highway
Falls Church, VA 22042
Ms. Betty Duncan
(703) 533-9852

Wisconsin

Lupus Society of Wisconsin, LFA
P.O. Box 13856
Milwaukee, WI 53213
(414) 781-1111

Lupus Foundation of America, Inc.

INTERNATIONAL ASSOCIATES

Australia

Ms. Pam Flanagan
Lupus/Scleroderma Group
Arthritis Foundation of Australia—
  SA
99 Anzac Highway
Ashford, South Australia 5035

The Lupus Group of Western
  Australia
P.O. Box 420
Claremont, Western Australia 6010

Coleen Hook
The Lupus Association
P.O. Box 271
Cammeray
New South Wales, Australia 2062

Loma Nahrung
Queensland Lupus Group
Gundiah, m/s 221
Mayborough
Queensland, Australia 4650

Lupus Association of Tasmania, Inc.
P.O. Box 404
Rosny Park
Tasmania, Australia 7019

Trevor Guy, President
P.O. Box 639

Launceton
Tasmania, Australia 7250

Roslyn Stellmach, Occupational
  Therapist
Arthritis Foundation of America—
  Queensland
P.O. Box 901
Toowong, Australia 4066

Ann C. Monger, Secretary
Victorian Lupus Association
Box 811 F, G.P.O.
Melbourne
Victoria, Australia 3001

Brazil

Dr. Cristiano A. Zerbini
Rheumatologia—Clinica Medica
R. Pedroso Alvarenga. 1203
CEP 0453
São Paulo S.P., Brazil

Canada

Alberta

Patricia O'Connell, President
L.E. Society of Alberta
Box 8154, Station F
Calgary

253

Alberta, Canada T2J 2V3
(403) 278-2349

British Columbia

Elizabeth J. Murray, President
British Columbia Lupus Association
895 West 10th Avenue
Vancouver
British Columbia, Canada V5Z 1L7
(604) 879-7511

    Other support groups located in:
    Nanaimo
    Penticton
    Prince George
    Victoria

Manitoba

Arthritis Self-Help Group, Inc., &
    Lupus Group
c/o Rheumatology Department
Rehabilitation Centre
800 Sherbrook Street
Winnipeg
Manitoba, Canada R3A 1M4
    Zella Vermeulen, President
    (204) 786-3486

New Brunswick

Ms. Bonnie Smith, President
New Brunswick Lupus Association
65 Brunswick Street
Fredericton
New Brunswick, Canada E3B 1G5
(506) 454-6114

Nova Scotia

Anu Joshil
15 Arbor Drive
Antigonish
Nova Scotia, Canada B2G 1S5

Mrs. Lynda Cavanaugh
L. E. Society of Nova Scotia
71 Penhorn Drive
Dartmouth
Nova Scotia, Canada B2W 7KB
(902) 435-0320

Ontario

Mrs. Karen Thompson
Oshawa/Whitby (Durham) Branch—
    O.L.A.
35 Rosalynne Avenue
Bowmanville
Ontario, Canada L1C 3X7
(416) 623-2765

Mrs. Susan Klop
York/Simcoe Regions Branch—
    O.L.A.
R.R. #2
Branford
Ontario, Canada L3Z 2A5

Lupus Society of Hamilton
236 King Street, W.
Hamilton
Ontario, Canada L8P 1A9
(416) 527-2252

    Ms. Joan McKee (liaison)
    180 West 31st Street
    Hamilton
    Ontario, Canada L9C 5E9
    (416) 388-3925

Mrs. Rhoda Mangus, Chairman
Lupus Foundation of Ontario
P.O. Box 687
289 Ridge Road N.
Ridgeway
Ontario, Canada LOS 1N0
(416) 894-4611

Mrs. Frances Gotkin, President
The Ontario Lupus Association
250 Bloor Street E., Ste 401
Toronto
Ontario, Canada M4W 3P2
(416) 967-1414

Quebec

Lupus Society of Quebec
Att.: Sally Drummond
    Monique Martineau
P.O. Box 486, Station H
1970 Ste. Catherine Street, W.
Montreal
Quebec, Canada HG3 2L5
(514) 731-1273

Saskatchewan

Mrs. Polly Ann Sereda, President
L.E.S.S. Alberta Chapter
48 - 22nd Street, East
Prince Albert
Saskatchewan, Canada S6V 1M9
(306) 922-8515

Mrs. Cindy Bates
L.E.S.S. Regina Chapter
Box 3881
Regina
Saskatchewan, Canada S4P 3R8
(306) 545-9629

Ms. Pat Leece, President
L.E. Society of Saskatchewan
Box 88, University Hospital
Saskatoon
Saskatchewan, Canada S7N 0W0
(306) 477-2523

Future Groups

Newfoundland
Prince Edward Island

England

Cheryl N. Marcus
British SLE Aid Group
25 Linden Crescent
Woodford Green
Essex, England 1G8 0DG
01-504-9488

France

Mireille Naitaoudia, Présidente
Association Française des Lupiques
15 rue Jean-Baptíste Say
69001 Lyon, France
78-27-17-16

India

Dr. A. N. Malaviya, M.D., F.C.A.I.
Professor of Medicine in Charge of
    Clinical Immunology
All India Institute of Medical
    Sciences
Ansari Nagar
New Delhi, India 110029

Ireland

Mrs. Maire de Baroid, Honorary
    Secretary Cork Branch
3 Ard na Greine
Evergreen Road
Cork 4, Ireland

Mrs. Catherine Delaney, Honorary
    Secretary
Irish Lupus Support Group
40 Kellester Park
Dublin 5, Ireland

Israel

Yael Isaacs
Israeli Lupus Association
P.O. Box 4160
Jerusalem, Israel
(02) 630240

Italy

Vena Gino Antonio, Associate
 Professor
Clinica Dermatologica Università
Policlinico
Piazza Giulio Cesare
70100 Bari, Italy

Professor Albert Marmont
Direttore Divisione di Ematologica e
 di Immunologica Clinica
Viale Benedetto XV, 10
Ospedale S. Martino—XIII U.S.L.
16132 Genova, Italy
010-54841

Japan

Susumu Sugai, M.D.
Department of Internal Medicine
Kanazawa Medical University
Uchinada-machi, Kahoku-kun
Ishikawa, 920-02 Japan

Malaysia

Florence Wang, Associate Professor
Department of Medicine
Universiti Malaya
Lembah, Pantai
Kuala Lumpur 22-11, Malaysia

Mexico

Dr. J. Humberto Orozco-Medina,
 Co.
Club de Lupus Centro
Medico de Occidente

Pedro Buzeta 870-B
44660 Guadalajara
Jalisco, Mexico
41-43-05 or 16-01-32

The Netherlands

Riek en Wim Viejou
National Association of L.E. Patients
Postbus 40
1180 AA Amstelveen
Amsterdam, The Netherlands

New Zealand

Lupus Foundation of New Zealand
c/o Arthritis & Rheumatism
 Foundation
P.O. Box 10-020
Wellington, New Zealand

Philippines

Tito P. Torralba, M.D., Chairman
Arthritis Foundation of the
 Philippines, Inc.
Santo Tomás University Hospital
c/o Room 216B, España Street
Manial, Philippines

Singapore

Dr. P. H. Feng, Vice-President
Lupus Group of the National
 Arthritis Foundation of Singapore
c/o Department of Medicine IV
Tan Tock Seng Hospital
Moulmein Road
Singapore 1130

Sweden

Svenska SLE-Gruppen
c/o Yvonne Enman
Vegagatan 31
172 34 Sundbyberg, Sweden

Index